George W. Smalley

George W. Smalley

FORTY YEARS A FOREIGN CORRESPONDENT

by Joseph J. Mathews

G. SMALLEY.

The University of
North Carolina Press
Chapel Hill

Copyright © *1973 by*
The University of North Carolina Press
All rights reserved

Manufactured in the United States of America
Printed by Rose Printing Company, Tallahassee, Florida
Library of Congress Catalog Card Number 72–87496
ISBN 0–8078–1205–6

Library of Congress Cataloging in Publication Data

Mathews, Joseph James, 1908–
   George W. Smalley, forty years a foreign correspondent.

   1. Smalley, George Washburn, 1833–1916.
I. Title.
PN4874.S52M3   070.4'092'4   72–87496
ISBN 0–8078–1205–6

Illustration by Harry Furniss from
his book, My Bohemian Days
(London: Hurst & Blackett Ltd., 1919).

Contents

Acknowledgments

I am particularly indebted for aid in the preparation of this book to the staffs of the Emory University Library, the Manuscripts Division of the Library of Congress, and the British Museum. The Cornell University Library kindly sent me microfilms of Smalley's correspondence with Andrew D. White, Bayard Taylor, and Moses Coit Tyler, and Smalley's letters to Sydney Howard Gay were made available to me on film by the Columbia University Library. I am grateful to the Houghton Library of Harvard University for permission to use the Charles Sumner Papers, to the Manuscript Division of the New York Public Library for access to the R. R. Bowker journals, to Cambridge University for the use of the papers of Sir Charles Hardinge, and to the University of Birmingham for certain papers of Joseph Chamberlain. Lord Salisbury, who asked that he be consulted about the use of the Salisbury Papers at Christ Church, Oxford, read without objection an earlier article of mine that cited the papers used in the present study. John F. A. Mason of Christ Church was helpful in making these Salisbury Papers available to me before they were completely catalogued.

Stanley Morison, author of the official history of the *Times*, obtained permission for me to use the archives of the paper, and John Maywood located the materials and found working space for me. Sir Bruce Richmond, Sir Arthur Willert, and Wickham Steed all told me what they knew of Smalley's work for the *Times*.

Joseph O. Baylen of Georgia State University has been the

most helpful of my professional colleagues in locating Smalley material. In this respect I owe thanks also to Thomas E. Mullen of Wake Forest University and David Donald of Johns Hopkins University.

The *New England Quarterly* has kindly allowed me to use material from my article, "The First Harvard–Oxford Boat Race" (1960) and the *Mississippi Valley Historical Review* (now the *Journal of American History*) has given me permission to use portions of my article, "Informal Diplomacy in the Venezuelan Crisis of 1896" (1963).

I am grateful to Mrs. Winifred Scherer for typing the final draft of the manuscript and to Mrs. Jocelyn Shaw, secretary of the Emory University Department of History, for typing and other assistance. The Emory University Research Committee awarded me two grants to support the project.

My greatest debt, as is true in all my publications, is to Marcia Mayfield Mathews for her research assistance, criticism, and encouragement.

George W. Smalley

1. The Career of a Foreign Correspondent

For a half century many newspaper readers in the United States and Great Britain could identify instantly the initials "GWS" as those of George Washburn Smalley. Most of them reacted strongly, some even violently, to the sight of the initials, for Smalley was a controversialist who provoked both vigorous favorable and unfavorable response. "My admiration for Smalley is boundless," Henry James declared. Theodore Roosevelt called him a "copper-riveted idiot" and referred to his views as "contemptible beyond words." Yet when the assassination of McKinley brought Roosevelt to the presidency, he at once wrote Smalley, then London *Times* correspondent in the United States, suggesting a visit from the journalist and a frank discussion of their differences. The president's invitation was a tribute to the position and influence of the journalist as well as an illustration of Roosevelt's appreciation of the power of the press. Smalley's slightly pompous reply, characteristic of the man, assumed equality between the position of the president and the journalist. "I shall, of course, be delighted to come to Washington for the talk you suggest," he wrote. "I shall come with an open mind and, you will not doubt, with the heartiest wish to find myself mistaken in any opinions which divide us."

In 1901, the year of this exchange of letters, Smalley was a sixty-eight-year-old newspaper veteran. From 1867 to 1895 he was the *New York Tribune* representative in London; from

1895 to 1906 he was the London *Times* correspondent in the United States. Smalley's long service set a record for his time. There were "special correspondents" who made a career of flitting from place to place, or from war to war, but the men who reported the news from a fixed position seldom tarried long. It was a difficult and ever-changing assignment. When Smalley went to London, the transatlantic cable was a year old, still too costly to be used for anything more than brief news items of great interest. Like other European correspondents of American papers, Smalley cabled the spot news and sent letters, usually two or three each week, by sea mail. Gradually the cable revolutionized both the timing and character of the news and Smalley was one of the revolution's early leaders. In 1866, before he had taken up residence in London, he sent one of the Atlantic cable's first lengthy news messages concerning the end of the Austro-Prussian War. During the Franco-Prussian War he organized the *Tribune's* war coverage so effectively from London, using the cable and telegraph freely, that the paper could claim with some justice the best reporting of the event by any newspaper on either side of the Atlantic.

The telegraph also encouraged the growth of press associations and in time they relieved the correspondent for the individual newspaper of his responsibility for urgent news and completeness of coverage. To Smalley, whose great forte was interpretation, this was a blessing though the transition was not complete at the end of the century. In the latter decades of the nineteenth century foreign correspondents enjoyed greater freedom of choice both in what they wrote and how they wrote about it than did their twentieth-century successors.

When Smalley went to London, he bore already, and proudly, the stamp of *"Tribune* man." After graduating from Yale in 1853, he studied law at Harvard, was admitted to the Massachusetts bar, and for a brief time practiced law in Boston. There he fell under the spell of Wendell Phillips, whose adopted daughter he married and for whom he acted as a bodyguard when the abolitionist's outspoken lectures endangered his life. It was Phillips who obtained employment for Smalley on Greeley's *Tribune* for which he worked, first with distinction as a war correspondent, and later in editorial capacities. He was a "Radical Republican" in full measure, taking with him this somewhat peculiar brand of liberalism to London in 1867. A "bloody shirt" was also in the baggage Smalley carried to London. For several years he engaged ardently in Rebel witch-hunting. He judged Englishmen by the attitude they had taken toward the American Civil War. Americans in Britain who bore any taint of association with the Confederacy he denounced, and demanded their dismissal if they had official employment. His friends and associates were political liberals and writers. His admiration of John Bright was unrestrained and for years he was a devoted follower of Gladstone. His criticism of Disraeli included the charge of drunkenness on the floor of the Commons and he sometimes belittled the royal family. All of this was welcome grist for the Greeley mill.

Smalley's later conservatism, which made him a favorite target for critics on both sides of the Atlantic and won for him such labels as "snob," "squire," and "Tory," in itself created no great problems with the *Tribune*. Under Whitelaw Reid's management the paper gradually abandoned Greeley's zeal for causes and in most respects could itself be considered conservative. Although Reid occasionally twitted Smalley about his social life, he was proud of a correspondent whose letters in the eighties were often written from Britain's greatest and most aristocratic country houses where he was a frequent guest, or on the stationery of exclusive London clubs of which he was a member.

For a news reporter, more especially for a foreigner who had established a reputation for belligerence and harsh criticisms, Smalley had traveled a long and difficult social path. Benjamin Moran, First Secretary of the American legation in London, was shocked in 1866 to learn that Thomas Hughes, then a member of Parliament, had agreed to write letters for the *Tribune*. To some extent the attitude toward men of the press changed—Moran himself became a close friend of several journalists including Smalley—but Smalley's social triumph, if triumph is the right word, was the success story of an individual. He took great personal pride in it but with him it was also a professional necessity. In the prehandout days of the Old Diplomacy, information that gave a correspondent the advantage of his competitors, or often any worthwhile news at all, came almost solely through personal contacts and confidences. To a man, Smalley's American competitors in London recognized this basic fact: they simply failed where he succeeded. Smalley had an unusual talent for making himself persona grata with men and women of prominence and could be counted on to be discreet with confidences to the point that even his friends joked about it.

The Crimean historian, A. W. Kinglake, once declared that Smalley had done more for the cause of bettering Anglo-American relations, had been a more successful ambassador to Great Britain than any of the official representatives of the United States. While the accolade must be taken with reservations, it suggests a function of the foreign correspondent that goes beyond the usual concept of his work. No correspondent ever took more seriously his role in international relations than Smalley, and it was a many-faceted role. From the first he considered it within his province to sit in judgment on U.S. ministers and consuls abroad. He was especially critical of U.S. ministers Reverdy Johnson and General Robert C. Schenck; he even urged in his newsletters the recall of the former. With some ministers, James Russell Lowell especially, he was on terms of intimate friendship. For many years the Smalley home in Hyde Park Square was a meeting place for visiting Americans with English friends and acquaintances of the Smalleys. He made a specialty of obtaining introductions and invitations for American visitors to Europe and English visitors to America.

There were occasions, too, when he took a direct part in diplomatic negotiations. The most important of these occurred in 1896 during the Venezuelan crisis that brought the United States and Great Britain to the verge of war with each other. At the peak of the crisis Smalley played a dual role of publicly voicing in his letters to the London *Times* the views of Secretary of State Richard Olney, while secretly serving as a private channel of communication, through *Times* editor G. E. Buckle, between Olney and Lord Salisbury, British prime minister and foreign secretary. During his last eight years with the *Times* he enjoyed the friendship and confidence of U.S. Secretary of State John Hay for whom he was often a spokesman.

Even though Smalley had considerable freedom of choice, the freedom was not complete. Much of his private correspondence both with his *Tribune* and *Times* employers is enlivened by quarrels over his selection and slanting of the news. The managers of both papers pleaded with him, edited some letters and discarded others, and sometimes denounced him editorially. He won some of the battles and he lost others. His great, running quarrel with the *Tribune* was over the Irish question. It was an old and bitter issue between him and the *Tribune* when he followed the Whigs who defected from Gladstone over Home Rule, and he would not curb his anti-Irish pen. The *Tribune* was concerned about Irish votes in New York, especially after Reid developed political ambitions, and Smalley was ordered to take a vacation for several months while Sir Henry Lucy, who was friendly toward the Irish, substituted for him. The *Times* forbade him on one occasion to write about Anglo-American relations, certainly the most natural and obvious of all subjects for the American correspondent of a British paper. In a sense Smalley's continued employment is proof that he won the campaigns, for he seldom modified his views or softened his arguments in response to the remonstrances of his employers. But this is an oversimplification of a question that has many angles and intricacies.

Early foreign correspondents have not been studied in detail. There are few biographies of them. One reason for this is that the records that provide answers to many basic questions have seldom been preserved. It is usually possible to identify the writings of a correspondent even when, as in the case of the London *Times*, contributions were anonymous. But for whom did the writer speak? Where did he get his information? Which of the views expressed were his own, his paper's or his informant's? Neither questions involving the influence of the correspondent nor the basic character of the news are answerable without first determining the influences that shaped the news. Information on the background of Smalley's writings is far more available than is usual with correspondents. For most of the period that he represented the *Tribune* in London, Whitelaw Reid was editor of the paper. Reid kept every scrap of correspondence he received and in his later life preserved copies of his own letters. Also, some of Smalley's private letters to his London *Times* editor, G. E. Buckle, and manager C. F. Moberly Bell, were preserved at Printing House Square. Unfortunately most of the letters Smalley received do not appear to have been preserved. But he was an indefatigable private correspondent and many of his letters have turned up in the papers of scores of prominent people of his time. His proud boast was that he knew "everybody worth knowing on both sides of the Atlantic" and he seems to have corresponded with most of them. One of his books, though not as revealing as the biographer would like, contains valuable information on his life.

George W. Smalley is rightly regarded as America's foremost foreign correspondent in the early years of the profession. In England he was the only member of this group to be ranked with Henri de Blowitz, Paris correspondent of the London *Times* from 1870 to 1902, and was generally accepted as the leader of the profession. Among other things Smalley was a master of journalistic writing and a perceptive judge of men. In innumerable biographies he appears in a footnote, the author of a telling phrase about the central character. But the chief value of the present study is its contribution to the history of international news. Smalley's singular long service, his association both with an American and an English paper, and his role in the rapidly changing character of the news provide the basic framework. His views, his personality, his relations with his employers and with the important figures of his time give special coloring to a role that is highly individualistic yet illustrative of the times.

2. Early Years

George Washburn Smalley was born in Franklin, Norfolk County, Massachusetts, on 2 June 1833. "I am on my mother's side of Plymouth Colony and on both sides of Puritan ancestry for as many generations back as I know anything about," he wrote.[1] Before her marriage his mother was Louise Jane Washburn. His father, the Reverend Mr. Elam Smalley, D.D., was at the time of his son's birth associate pastor of the Congregational Church in Franklin. A graduate of Brown University, D.D., 1827, and Phi Beta Kappa, 1830, he published a number of sermons and a history of the churches of Worcester, Massachusetts.[2] When George was five years old the family moved to Worcester where his father became pastor of the new Second Congregational Church.

Worcester in those days was "a charming example of the thriving New England village which had grown to be a town with pleasant, quiet streets—even Main Street, its chief thoroughfare, was quiet—and pleasant houses of colonial and later styles standing in pleasant grounds."[3] There was a simplicity and dignity of life in the Heart of the Commonwealth, as the natives called their town, that Smalley later remembered with nostalgia. No one in Worcester doubted that the eminence of Massa-

1. Smalley to the Duchess of Sutherland, 28 December 1897, George Washburn Smalley Papers, Library of Congress, Washington, D.C.
2. Elam Smalley, *The Worcester Pulpit: With Notices Historical and Biographical* (Boston, 1851).
3. George W. Smalley, *Anglo-American Memories* (New York, 1911), p. 2. Chapters 2 and 3 contain information on Smalley's boyhood and college days.

chusetts in all good things was equalled by no other state. Smalley never quite got over his youthful acceptance of this conviction. The great hero of his early years was Daniel Webster whom he heard speak during the presidential campaign of 1848. "We boys in Massachusetts were all brought up to worship Webster, and worship him we did."

The hard grip of Calvinism made a lasting impression on the young man, one he was reluctant to admit in later, more sophisticated years, but one that helps account for his lifelong dislike of the Irish and suspicion of Roman Catholics. It was not to his father, "whose mind ran strongly toward liberalism," but to his father's deacons that Smalley attributed the Puritanical strictness of his upbringing. "They constituted themselves the guardians of the morals of the flock, the pastor and his family included. . . . They would have made absence from divine service a statutory offense, as the earlier Puritans did." The Smalley children—George had one sister—were regular and punctual in their attendance at two services on Sunday, with Sunday School in between, and prayer meeting on Wednesday evenings. When the time came for George to go to college he wanted to be sent to Harvard, "as every Massachusetts boy naturally would." But the deacons would have none of a Unitarian college where the professors did not believe in a Trinitarian God. For the good of his immortal soul young George was sent to Yale where there was no danger of "laxity or heresy," where the "strictest Presbyterianism was taught," and where there were "some eighteen separate compulsory attendances at religious exercises each week." Smalley felt later that he had earned at Yale the right to some relaxation in church attendance.

At Yale Smalley was a member of the celebrated "class of '53." One of his closest friends was Andrew D. White, scholar, U.S. minister to Germany and to Russia, and president of Cornell University. Another classmate and lifelong friend was Edmund C. Stedman, poet and journalist. Still another was Wayne MacVeagh, ambassador to Rome and U.S. attorney general. Then there were Mr. Justice Shiras, Supreme Court justice, Randal Gibson, Confederate general and U.S. senator from

Louisiana, Isaac K. Bromley, editorial writer for the *New York Tribune*, Charlton T. Lewis, Fred Davies, James M. Whiton, Benjamin K. Phelps, and Theodore Bacon. Among these Smalley was most strongly attached to Stedman, Davies (who became an Episcopal minister), and White. To White he wrote: "I look back, Andrew, to our intercourse of Senior Year, and more especially its last two terms, with more pleasure than any other part of my college life. None of my friends, not even those who had stood by me in the dark days of Lang Syne had gained for himself so large a place in my heart, as you."[4] One of Smalley's classmates said that he was the "best Latin scholar in the class."[5] Another said: "Though somewhat indifferent to honors, it was plain that such as he cared for were within his reach. He was a born classicist, and one of his division men says that to hear him read and construct Greek was like listening to a trout brook."[6] In acknowledging his debt to Yale, Smalley himself said it would have been "heavier had I been more industrious." His honors also might have been greater had he been less independent and more observant of discipline. One of his Latin tutors regarded Cicero's *De Senectute* as pages on which to hang Sumpt's rules for the subjective mood. Tiring of this, George announced to his friends, "with a very round expletive," that he would answer no more such foolish questions and proceeded thereafter to respond to all questions on the subjective that he was unprepared. The result was that he received no place on the program at the Junior Exhibition.[7] On another occasion he escaped suspension from the college for an infraction of the rules only through the intervention of one of his teachers who promised to answer for the culprit's future behavior.

"We learnt Greek, so far as we learnt it, in the same unquestioning spirit as we read the Bible, so far as we read it," Smalley wrote. But it was his classics teachers he later remembered most

4. Smalley to White, 20 December 1853, Andrew D. White Papers, Cornell University Library, Ithaca, N.Y.
5. Andrew D. White, *Autobiography*, 2 vols. (New York, 1905), 1:27.
6. Edmund C. Stedman, "George Washburn Smalley," *Harper's Weekly*, 8 November 1890, p. 873.
7. White, *Autobiography*, 1:27.

gratefully. Others, if not Smalley, attributed the high literary standard of his journalistic writing to his sound training in classical languages, and he quoted with approval Sainte-Beuve's remark: "I do not ask that a man know Latin or Greek. All I ask is that he shall have known it." One of Smalley's college accomplishments was the organization of a Yale crew that challenged Harvard, the first American college to engage in boat racing. Smalley was stroke on the Yale crew and Andrew White a member. Harvard beat them by a humiliating margin.

There was no thought in George's mind of a journalistic career, nor probably in the minds of any other of the 108 members of the class of 1853. Yet the class included not only Smalley, Bromley, and Stedman, who were to join the *Tribune,* but Evarts Greene, a leading Worcester editor, Delano Goddard, editor of the *Boston Advertiser,* and Dr. James Morris Whiton, a leading writer for the *Outlook.*[8] The door to journalism was then entered by accident rather than design.

After graduation Smalley returned to Worcester for a year to read law and prepare for the career of barrister. He read in the office of George F. Hoar, afterward U.S. senator and then law partner of Emory Washburn, who became governor of Massachusetts and who lived next door to the Smalleys on Pearl Street. George says that during the year the law occupied his attention "more or less." A local beauty, Susan Gray, to whom he became engaged, seems to have occupied it more. George wrote his friend Andrew White about her and other matters with an exuberance and youthful abandon that make the biographer wish, almost, that he had never grown up. A letter from Andrew describing the charms of a young lady of his acquaintance provoked the rejoinder: "Was there not a concert here last week? . . . Did I not escort the prettiest girl in all this city of Worcester thereto? And has she not the prettiest name of all pretty girls that ever you heard of? And have I not seen Miss Susie Gray every day since? Isn't she an angel and divine and all that sort of thing, ad infinitum? Where are your 'black eyes' and 'merry laughs' and 'little hands' in comparison? Envy me my fortunes, Andrew. I bewail your own

8. Ibid., p. 253.

miserable existence."[9] But Susan's charms, or George's, did not prove lasting. Nor did Worcester's. At the end of the year George was happy to leave "this unloved and unloving city" to enroll in the Harvard Law School. His father had accepted a "call" to the First Presbyterian Church in Troy, New York, and Worcester was no longer George's home.

One incident during the Worcester year made a deep impression. In May 1854, out of curiosity and a desire to see how the legal machinery operated in such cases, he went to Boston for the trial of Anthony Burns, a Virginia fugitive slave on trial for return to his owner. The trial provoked a storm of protest and the threat of violent measures to prevent the enforcement of the Fugitive Slave Act of 1850. Smalley was able to see very little of the trial but like many others he was revolted by the whole affair and moved to deep anger by the sight of troops taking Burns away. "Nothing," he wrote years later, "not even a Four Years' Civil War for Union and Freedom, not even the blood of heroes and martyrs, will ever quite wash from the memory of those who saw it the humiliation of that day. It blistered and burnt and left a scar forever."[10] Shortly after the incident he wrote his friend Andrew White:

And so, in broad day-light, at high charge a citizen of Massachusetts was carried down State St. guarded by Boston troops, and sent into slavery. It's a good thing to tell, don't you think? It doesn't make a man's blood run any faster to know that Massachusetts is nothing but a hunting ground for slave owners. . . .
But that day did its work. For one man earnest in his hatred of slavery before there are twenty now. . . . Men went to Boston this time unorganized and unarmed. The next time they will do better.[11]

For the next two years Smalley pursued enthusiastically the study of law at Harvard where to his great delight, and in sharp contrast to undergraduate life at Yale, there were no restrictions;

9. Smalley to White; 17 October 1853, White Papers; see also *Letters and Journals of Thomas Wentworth Higginson; 1846–1906,* ed. Mary Thacher Higginson (Boston, 1921), pp. 82–83 (hereafter cited as *Higginson Letters and Journals*).
10. Smalley, *Anglo-American Memories,* p. 37.
11. Smalley to White, 23 July 1854, White Papers.

even attendance at lectures was not required. At Yale he got on well enough with the gentlemenly Southerners among the students but at Harvard he was one of twenty-or-so men who constituted the "Anti-Slavery Backbone" in the student body and fought the Southerners and "doughfaces" in the Law School parliament. He rejoiced when Judge Edward Greeley Loring was not rehired as lecturer in law and when Samuel S. Eliot was refused an L.L.B., attributing both acts to the proslavery views of the men.[12] He had little social life, delighting rather in concentration on his studies and in the available lectures and libraries of a city that he determined never to leave. On one memorable occasion, accompanying a nephew of Ralph Waldo Emerson's, who had obtained the invitation, he walked the thirteen miles from Cambridge to Concord for a visit to Emerson's home that he described with rapture. There were many Bostonians, including George's uncle with whom he was to practice law, who then thought Emerson the most dangerous of men, but the Congregational deacons of Worcester had long since lost their hold on the son of Pastor Elam Smalley. Twenty years later, when Smalley was able to render some services to Emerson on a visit to England, he counted them among his proudest moments, and he named his second son Emerson.[13]

In 1856 Smalley was admitted to the Massachusetts bar and became a junior partner of his uncle, W. R. P. Washburn, whose law office was located at 46 Washington Street, Boston. For three long years he was a struggling young lawyer, firmly convinced that his own great talents and his industry would break the barriers to success and financial security. But his was not a success story. In 1858 his father died, leaving George with the responsibility for his mother and sister. "I shall never forget the wretchedness of the first few weeks of such a sorrow," he wrote Andrew White when White's own father died.[14] In the fourth year of his struggles to make a success in the law, Smalley decided to launch out on his own, after first seeking Andrew's advice about the possibility of getting a teaching position in

12. Ibid., 29 August 1855.
13. Smalley, *Anglo-American Memories*, pp. 57–73.
14. Smalley to White, 26 September 1860, White Papers.

a western college. "I am going to dissolve my partnership with Mr. Washburn," he wrote, "and start alone, having become satisfied that I have next to no chance, in connection with him, of building up a business of my own. A young lawyer in partnership with one much older does not get the kind of business which he ought to have; friends think he doesn't need or doesn't want it . . . which in my case is a great mistake. . . . My income this year falls short of my expenses—say nothing of what I ought to do for my mother and sister. . . . It looks a little dismal but try it I will."[15]

After his Harvard years Smalley veered away from his antislavery activities. Doubtless the improvident young lawyer had little time to devote to "causes," and in addition his relatives and friends were Whigs who did not look with favor on the abolitionist movement. There was, too, a lull in Boston in the late fifties during which, as Smalley put it, "the emotions of 1854 had gone to sleep." But on 3 December 1860, Boston came alive when the abolitionists attempted to hold an antislavery convention in Tremont Temple on the anniversary of the hanging of John Brown. For all of his earlier antislavery enthusiasm, Smalley was still hesitant to count himself an abolitionist. It was, he says, the violated right of freedom of speech that led him to write Wendell Phillips to offer his services to Phillips and his abolitionist work. He had heard Phillips speak and had fallen "under the spell" of his "passionate eloquence," but had never met him. Phillips responded with a visit to Smalley's office and an invitation to visit the Phillips home. The incident was a turning point in Smalley's career. In short time he became Phillips's devoted admirer, his bodyguard, and the husband of Phillips's adopted daughter. Through Phillips's influence he obtained employment as a journalist, which ended his career in the law.

The Tremont Temple meeting of 3 December was foiled by an opposition group that packed the hall in advance and managed to oust the abolitionists who met elsewhere that evening to hear Phillips make a speech "red-hot with wrath." During the following fortnight careful plans were made on both sides for

15. Ibid., 23 October 1860.

a showdown on Sunday, 16 December, when Phillips was scheduled for a lecture in the Music Hall with the announced title, "Mobs and Education." Smalley was persuaded with other of Phillips's friends that Phillips's life was in real danger, even though they received assurances that the Boston police would prevent mob violence. They, therefore, formed a bodyguard for the speaker and armed themselves with guns to defend him. The speech was "perhaps the most personal, of all Phillips' speeches . . . . You saw the arrow leave the platform and sink deep in the quivering flesh. . . . There were passages of burning eloquence, of pathos, of invective that tore its way through all defenses." Although the atmosphere in the hall was tense, the troublemakers delayed action until after the meeting. Smalley's account to Andrew White, written the next day, may contain youthful exaggeration of the danger but it conveys the excitement of the occasion:

When Phillips emerged from the vestibule of the hall into the narrow passage leading to Winter Street, a desperate rush was made upon him by the mob, knives and pistols were drawn and some powder burnt, but no harm done. The police fought well, so well indeed that those of us who were at Phillips' side had only to steady ourselves against the immense pressure and did not get into active conflict with the assailants. That they meant to murder him it is impossible to doubt. I saw the whole from the central point of view, having Phillips' arm in mine from the platform all the way to the house. . . . More trouble was expected last night and a half dozen of us spent the night at Phillips' house, but nothing happened it being known that the police were awake and ready with sufficient force to handle any mob that could be gathered. I think we could have stood a siege for some little time without their help.[16]

Smalley's devotion to Wendell Phillips was complete, his admiration unstinted. Phillips, the Boston aristocrat, descended from six or seven generations of Boston Phillipses, a man of small stature but absolutely fearless of mobs or other dangers, appealed to Smalley no less than did Phillips, the fiery and passionate orator. Smalley, a big man, "a trained athlete and natural soldier," as a fellow defender of Phillips described him,[17]

16. Ibid., 17 December 1860.
17. Higginson to his mother, 22 March 1861, in *Higginson Letters and Journals*, p. 83.

thoroughly enjoyed his role as Phillips's friend and protector. The evidence suggests that the young man fell victim more to the personal magnetism of the older man than to his views, though it is a little confusing. Two weeks after meeting Phillips, he wrote Andrew White: "We mean to do our part here toward precipitating secession. I trust you have an equally wholesome sentiment prevailing." In the same letter he spoke as though he had become a Republican,[18] but in his *Memories* he says he was still a Whig. When the break between North and South did come, Smalley says he did everything in his power to persuade Phillips, a longtime advocate of ridding the Union of the slave states, to support the war and try to preserve the Union. In his own opinion, Smalley had a part in the conversion. He felt that Phillips's speech announcing his support of the war was his greatest.

Phillips's protectors of mid-December 1860 felt it necessary to continue the defense for several months. In addition to Smalley the group included James Redpath, Charles Fallen, Thomas Wentworth Higginson, John W. LeBarnes and a man named Hinton. These bravos, says Julian Hawthorne, were as "avid for the opposition's gore as those could be to string our Wendell up to the lamppost."[19] They followed Phillips about the streets, sat on the platform when he lectured, and made a fortress of the Phillips home on Exeter Street. In addition to Phillips's invalid wife, Ann, there was in the household their adopted daughter, Phoebe Garnaut. Phoebe was the daughter of Eliza Garnaut, a woman of Welsh birth who had married a Frenchman and had come with him to Boston in the 1840s. Shortly after their arrival Garnaut died, leaving Eliza without funds and the care of an infant daughter. Eliza Garnaut was clearly an unusual woman. Not only did she manage to provide for herself and a daughter but she became a professional Good Samaritan, a promoter and fund raiser for many of the causes that Phillips

18. Smalley to White, 17 December 1860, White Papers.
19. *The Memoirs of Julian Hawthorne*, ed. Edith Garrigues Hawthorne (New York, 1938), p. 242. See also Thomas Wentworth Higginson, *Cheerful Yesterdays* (Boston, 1898), pp. 230–41.

espoused. Phillips loved her "as a sister and looked up to her as a saint."[20]

Bravo George Smalley found Phoebe a very special reason for defending the Phillips household. Thomas Wentworth Higginson summarized the story in a letter to his mother:

When I saw him [George Smalley] at Wendell's planning with us to mount guard, and then turning to pretty Phoebe—to arrange little plans to keep everybody still and spare Mrs. P's nerves, I thought to myself that the adopted daughter might prove the next attraction, and it now turns out that they are engaged. He is tall, erect, strong, blond, Saxon, and she is a brunette with lovely eyes and a Welsh smile—you know her mother was Welsh; they will be a picturesque couple, and it is quite a chivalrous little affair.[21]

It was all very chivalrous, indeed, and a serious affair of the heart, but George Washburn Smalley, lawyer on his own, had not improved his professional status or his economic position in the many days spent as a bodyguard to Wendell Phillips. Some months later he had not found it possible to balance his accounts and, in September 1861, he wrote to his friend Andrew White asking for a loan of $150 for six months. "A good deal of money I ought to have had July 1st I can't get at present. The deficiency leaves me temporarily embarrassed with sundry claims which I ought to and must put out of the way before the happenings of such an event as marriage. . . . If you will lend it to me for six months it will relieve me from my trouble and clear the way to the greatest happiness this world can ever bring me." White replied that he was not in a position to make the loan.[22] Wendell Phillips came to the rescue by obtaining a job for Smalley on the *New York Tribune*. The marriage of Phoebe and George did not take place until December 1862. In the meantime, G. W. Smalley became a veteran war correspondent and an established journalist with the *New York Tribune*.

20. Carlos Martyn, *Wendell Phillips: The Agitator* (New York, 1890), p. 217.
21. *Higginson Letters and Journals*, p. 83.
22. Smalley to White, 19 September 1861 and 16 October 1861, White Papers. Smalley's letters to White are less intimate and less frequent after this incident. The friendship was cordial, however, throughout the lives of the two men. White was one of the few people that Smalley addressed by his first name.

3. Civil War
Correspondent

When he applied to the *Tribune* for employment Smalley did not imagine he would be sent into the field to cover military activities, but he accepted the offer to go with alacrity. "If my reporting suits the Tribune as well as the 'rough' work will suit me, I shall be content," he wrote Sidney Howard Gay, the assistant managing editor who was shortly to replace Charles A. Dana as managing editor. "I had, of course, nothing of the kind in view, but the adventure is entirely to my taste, and I would not throw away the chance, if it were not."[1]

The new recruit was assigned to Port Royal, South Carolina, where he remained from November 1861 to April 1862. The Union navy had recaptured the forts at Port Royal before he arrived, leaving only minor war activity in the vicinity to be reported. Smalley witnessed and sent in an account of the capture of Fort Pulaski but he made no effort to see a skirmish a hundred miles away at Williamstown, North Carolina. The oversight brought a sharp reprimand from Horace Greeley, the *Tribune* publisher, and a lesson in anticipating events that the neophyte journalist took to heart. The bulk of the news from Port Royal had to do with the "contrabands," as the Negro slaves within the Union-occupied areas of the South were called at the time. The New Englander dutifully filled his reports with sympathetic accounts of the plight of the contrabands, but he could not

1. Smalley to Gay, 16 November 1861, Sidney Howard Gay Papers, Columbia University Library, New York, N.Y.

hide the fact that he was appalled by the backwardness and ignorance of the slaves from the cotton and rice plantations who crowded the camps established for them. "If you were not already a convinced abolitionist, they were not likely to convert you," he declared.[2]

The *Tribune* editors found numerous things to correct in the letters of their Port Royal correspondent, but they were sufficiently pleased with his work to offer encouraging comments and even a few words of praise. What bothered Smalley was their apparent intention of leaving him indefinitely at his uneventful post. By April he could stand the monotony no longer. He announced that he was returning to New York and Boston for a brief visit, explaining that there could not possibly be any military action that would require his presence in Port Royal. "It is of much consequence to me to visit Boston, if I am to be detained here through the summer," he added.[3] As Smalley undoubtedly hoped and probably suspected, he was not sent back to South Carolina. Instead he was assigned to the command of General John C. Frémont in Virginia with whom he remained until the end of June when that ex-explorer, political darling of the abolitionists, and inept general was relieved of his command.

It was still the early freewheeling days of Civil War reporting when the individual correspondent moved about with little restraint—if only he could find means of conveyance and sustenance. What he wrote was determined by what his paper wanted, what he could get from army informants or, failing that, what his ingenuity could provide. As yet there was little censorship, but communications between a man in the field and his paper were beset with uncertainties and delays. Smalley's experiences were typical and his questions to the *Tribune* managing editor illustrated the problems of the field correspondent. Had he paid too much for a horse?—$130 including a saddle, two bridles, and two blankets. Horses were almost impossible to obtain at any price and this was an excellent animal. Everyone envied

2. George W. Smalley, *Anglo-American Memories* (New York, 1911), pp. 130–33.
3. Smalley to Gay, 19 April 1862, Gay Papers.

him the bargain. The previous owner had paid $180! Had his early reports been adequate? Did the *Tribune* want letters when there was nothing really worth writing about? Would the editor please rush him the best and most detailed map of Virginia available; also additional stationery and envelopes. Then there was a very human request from the fiancé of a young Welsh lady in Boston: "May I ask you a special favor? If any accident should happen to me, please telegraph to Mr. Phillips; never to Miss Garnaut. She is not strong enough to bear any news suddenly, or unexpectedly in print, or any way. If Mr. Phillips hears, he will take care that she does not, prematurely."[4]

Politics and the attitude of his paper toward a commanding officer usually affected the position of the field correspondent during the Civil War. Happily for Smalley the *Tribune* was well disposed toward Frémont, a posture that earned its correspondent special favors at the general's headquarters. The *Tribune* man had ready access to officers close to the commander, was allowed to read official communications and even use them in the composition of his reports, and was given as much aid as possible in sending his own telegrams and letters. The censor usually passed his dispatches without reading them. In his first account of a real battle, the engagement in early June between Frémont and Stonewall Jackson at Cross Keys, Smalley performed quite well.[5] He wrote Gay: "I think I saw more of it [the battle] and know more about it than almost anyone on the field. After it was over I went everywhere and saw everybody, compared notes, etc., and was sure I understood it. My horse had 14 hours hard riding and I believe I had about 20 hours pretty hard."[6] Fortunately the account, which pleased the editors, arrived well ahead of reports from other New York correspondents.

While Smalley was attached to Frémont's command, the general had no more enthusiastic supporter, though years later he dismissed the general as a man of promise but "not much more for the purposes of war."[7] Vigorous, unrestrained, some-

4. Ibid., 28 May 1862.
5. *New York Tribune*, 11 June 1863.
6. Smalley to Gay, 13 June 1869, Gay Papers.
7. Smalley, *Anglo-American Memories*, p. 133.

times unbalanced support of people and causes were early characteristics that Smalley was never able to control completely. Not only was he persuaded while attached to Frémont's command of the general's great ability and sound judgment but he was equally convinced that President Lincoln and Secretary of War Stanton were making a scapegoat of his hero for political reasons. His letters to Gay are full of charges against the Washington government and pleas that the *Tribune* use its position to force adequate support of Frémont. When Frémont received word that his troops were to be placed under the command of General John Pope, Smalley lost all sense of proportion and wrote his managing editor:

If the Tribune and the Gen.'s friends, if he has any in Washington—if he has in Washington who have either courage or capacity—don't make Lincoln hear thunder, and don't make him rescind the order, I hope and trust F. will resign. He is removed this time from his Dept. without a shadow of charge against him, and just at the end of a brilliant campaign. . . . I believe Lincoln has gone crazy. Hitherto I have tried to continue to believe him honest, but if you had seen all the dispatches I have for a month past twould tax the strength of your credulity.[8]

There was more in the same vein in other letters but Sidney Howard Gay was an unusually tolerant editor. He simply "failed to receive" some of Smalley's most indiscreet letters, a circumstance common enough at the time to be entirely credible, and waited until the angry young man had cooled his temper and regained something of his balance to remind him, gently, that field correspondents were not always in the best position to determine the editorial policy of a paper. The correspondent's anger gradually subsided and when Frémont resigned, his former ardent supporter felt that the general was not justified in taking that step. A little later the correspondent was entirely mollified when he was assigned to General Pope's command of the army of Virginia, a force ten times larger and far more important than Frémont's army. Also he was given charge of several correspondents who were to aid him in his new assignment.

At Pope's headquarters the position of a representative of the

8. Smalley to Gay, 26 June 1863, Gay Papers.

Tribune was the reverse of what it had been with Frémont. Smalley soon found that his *Tribune* connection, instead of presenting him with an open sesame, stamped him with a suspicion that he had to overcome personally if he were to have anything worth reporting and if he were to avoid humiliation by comparison with reporters of such favored journals as the *New York Herald*. Worse still, he managed to get his ankle in the direct path of a kicking horse, an event that left him lame for several crucial weeks and dependent upon his assistants for news foraging. It was a kind of test for journalist Smalley and he met it with calculated realism. He cultivated the officers close to Pope, especially those who dealt with information for publication, observed all rules carefully, and gave General Pope's opinions prominence in his letters to the *Tribune*. All of the details of the reporter's tactics were made clear to his approving managing editor and he was at pains to see that his own opinions were not confused with those of the general. This tactic, too, met with Gay's approval.

The correspondent's scheme proved successful. In a matter of weeks he was able to report to Gay that he was making numerous friends among the headquarters officers, that he was rivaling the *Herald* man in access to information, and that General Pope, who often read and corrected correspondent's dispatches, had changed only one word in Smalley's latest. Ultimate proof of Pope's favorable disposition toward the *Tribune* man came in connection with an order from General Henry W. Halleck, general-in-chief of the Union armies, to clear the field forces of all newspaper correspondents. Pope delayed enforcing the order for Smalley for two days in an attempt to permit him to report an imminent engagement, but the engagement did not come off and Halleck refused to rescind the order against journalists. In late August, Smalley returned to Washington.

The next phase of Civil War reporting—it had many and the range was wide—forced most correspondents to engage in subterfuge. Unable to attend battles legally, they went as aides-de-camp, medical attendants, or in whatever capacity they could, and they were abetted by generals and officers who knew the value of a good press. For a fortnight Smalley spent his energies organizing the work of four or five correspondents, making arrangements to get information from officers and obtaining what he could through Washington officials. He continued to hope that the order against correspondents in the field be withdrawn. When this did not happen he obtained an appointment as aide to General John Sedgwick, with the rank of captain. Like most correspondents who received appointments of the kind, Smalley took the assignment lightly. He had no specific duties and seems to have worn a captain's uniform or discarded it as the circumstances of the moment dictated; his most important battlefield duties as an aide were for General Joseph Hooker who pressed the amateur aide into service during the Battle of Antietam.

The Battle of Antietam in mid-September 1862, in which General George B. McClellan checked Confederate General Robert E. Lee's northward advance in Maryland, was an important, perhaps crucial, turning point early in the Civil War. From the viewpoint of the Union, the Rebels were checked; from the viewpoint of the Confederacy, an invasion was made with impunity followed by a retreat with losses no greater than those suffered by the enemy. For George W. Smalley, the Battle of Antietam supplied the opportunity for fame. His account of the engagement was possibly the best description of a battle during the Civil War. Certainly it was acclaimed at the time by military and journalistic observers who were in a position to judge as eyewitnesses and it stands up well to the test of time. Henry Villard and A. D. Richardson, both superb reporters, called it the best battle report of the war. According to J. Cutler Andrews, historian of Civil War reporting, the account was reprinted in approximately 1,400 newspapers throughout the country.[9] One of the *Tribune's* rival New York papers, the *Evening Post,* gave the piece high praise: "The only satisfactory account of the last great battle of Wednesday in Maryland is that written by the special correspondent of the *Tribune.* From that truly admirable account, which ranks for clearness, animation and apparent accuracy with the best battle pieces in literature, and far excels anything ever written by Crimean Russell, we

9. J. Cutler Andrews, *The North Reports the Civil War* (Pittsburgh, 1955), pp. 282, 700, 101n.

gather that the contest was, after all, indecisive—the advantage of superior position only remaining with us." The *Evening Post* concluded: "The writer of this letter has filled many columns of this paper, within the last six months, with letters of similar character."[10]

How Smalley got his material and how he wrote the account and got it by train to New York are tales that are rarely omitted in accounts of great feats of war reporting.[11] He won the praise of observers, including General Joseph Hooker, for his coolness under fire. A shell tore off a portion of his coat and the horse he was riding received two bullets in the body in spite of which it was able to continue in service. Smalley first rode to Frederick where he sent off a brief telegraphic message only to have the telegraph operator send it to the War Department in Washington instead of the *Tribune* office in New York. Finally the reporter managed to get on a train for Baltimore and then another for New York. Most of the Antietam account was written while Smalley stood on the swaying train under the light of one dim oil lamp. The *Tribune* issued an "extra" to carry the story on the morning of Friday, 19 September 1862. Few battle accounts by reporters make good reading a century or more later, but Smalley's description of the Battle of Antietam stands up well. It is given at length as Appendix A of this book.

Smalley had speculated that the Confederate forces might withdraw from the engagement, which was what happened. He had assumed that McClellan would pursue vigorously if the Rebels retreated and that did not happen. The correspondent was given no respite in New York but returned to Harper's Ferry on 20 September, the day following the publication of his Antietam story. Several weeks later he was "invalided" home with camp fever and his days as a Civil War correspondent were over. For a brief period he took charge of *Tribune* affairs in Washington and in early 1863 he made a tour of various army headquarters in the East in order to make an appraisal for the

10. Quoted in *New York Tribune*, 26 September 1862.
11. Andrews, *North Reports the Civil War*, pp. 277–82; F. Lewiston Bullard, *Famous War Correspondents* (Boston, 1914), pp. 399–402; Joseph J. Mathews, *Reporting the Wars* (Minneapolis, 1957), p. 82.

Tribune of Union army commanders. But he spent most of the remaining war years in New York writing editorials and other items for the *Tribune*. These writings cannot be identified with confidence and there are only scattered bits of information, mostly of no great interest, about Smalley for the period. In the 1863 riots in New York he was active in trying to protect *Tribune* interests and property; a son of Sidney Howard Gay reported that Smalley taught Mrs. Gay how to use a pistol in order to defend herself against possible rioters.[12] For the most part the late Civil War years for Smalley have to be judged by subsequent performances. The evidence shows that he became thoroughly imbued with *Tribune* policies and practices and developed into a mature journalist.

12. Information supplied by Eben Gay of Hingham, Mass.

4. London Commissioner
of the New York Tribune

During the Civil War Americans lost interest in European affairs other than those related to their own conflict. Almost nothing from Europe appeared in North American newspapers unless it had to do with the attitudes and policies of the European powers toward the Union or the Confederacy. The American Civil War was the first "total" news war; there was little difference between war news and news in wartime. The end of the conflict, at least in the more prosperous North, brought a surge of renewed interest in Europe, all the greater since it had to compensate for a half decade of suspended normal intercourse. Wartime animosities were neither forgotten nor forgiven, at least not immediately. Napoleon III's attempt to take advantage of the Civil War to establish an empire in Mexico embittered Franco-American relations and left deeply imbedded suspicions of France until the emperor was overthrown in 1870. Great Britain's equivocal attitude throughout the war, and the *Alabama* claims quarrel that continued for nearly a decade afterward, prevented genuine and complete amicability.

But whether or not they felt kindly toward Europe, Americans were determined to see and hear about it. The year 1865 marks the beginning of mass tourism to Europe, a dividing point between Americans who crossed the Atlantic for a particular purpose and those who did not try to pinpoint their reasons for going. It was taken for granted that the cultural advantages of a trip to the Old World were obvious and did not have to be defended. The *Anglo-American Times,* founded in 1865, was a London weekly that until the mid-nineties serves as an excellent source of information for and about the travelers. In June 1866 the paper announced that the number of Americans going to Europe had already exceeded that of any previous year and the peak had not been reached for the year. "It is said," the paper continued, "that the number of applications for passports at the State Department, Washington, averages three hundred per week; and it is well known that not one traveller in ten thinks it necessary to take out a passport at all."[1] The *Anglo-American Times's* estimate of the number of American travelers arriving in England during May and June was in excess of 1,800 each month and the money they would spend was guessed to be $38,000,000. The paper thought that before the end of the season an equal number of additional travelers from the United States would bring another needed $38,000,000—to the great joy of English and Continental businessmen.[2]

After 1866 the travel tide increased steadily although there was a brief but decided recession following the panic of 1873. The estimate of the *Anglo-American Times* of American visitors in the summer of 1880 was 30,000.[3] Other papers with similar purposes were founded after the *Anglo-American Times.* The *American Traveller,* also published in London, ran from 1875 to 1890, and the *American Register,* printed on the Continent, offered similar services. Of course the number of Europeans immigrating to the United States far exceeded the number of travelers to Europe. Many of the new arrivals could be expected to take a greater interest in European developments than longtime residents and their children.

After years of disheartening failure the Atlantic cable was completed and secured at Heart's Content, Newfoundland, on 28 July 1866. No one doubted, least of all the American newspapers, that transatlantic news would be revolutionized as a result. One of the better statements was made by the *New York Times:*

1. *Anglo-American Times* (London), 2 June 1866.
2. Ibid., 7 July 1866. These figures are almost certainly too high but estimates only are available.
3. Ibid., 14 May 1880.

To none . . . is the cable fraught with so much significance as the makers of newspapers. The merchant or the financier has but to take one bold step, look the revolution full in the face, and go on making money more rapidly than ever. The journalist may not so easily meet the case. His foreign news arrangements are upset; appliances on which he has relied for years are superceded and a necessity arises for revising and reconstructing on nearly every hand. European mails will be little more than wastepaper. The profound discussions of the Old World press will pass unread; for long ere their receipt, the facts on which they rest will render distant opinions out of date.[4]

The predicted changes did not come all at once. What did come almost immediately was the transmission of brief news items of an urgent nature by cable and the development of a system by the New York papers for collecting the news in Europe rather than waiting for the arrival of the European papers from which the news had traditionally been culled. But the high cost of the cable kept alive for many years the news-letters sent by ordinary mail. The foreign correspondent during this period of transition had to maintain a delicate balance between the old methods and the new. The cable made the task of the American correspondent in Europe far more difficult, but at the same time it increased his importance enormously. He had to find ways of meeting the new demands of speed, brevity, and costs imposed by the cable; he had to plot the directions of the news revolution and could no longer rely solely on the press where he was stationed; he had to get closer to the news sources. He had an important role in bringing the United States more intimately and fully in touch with the European world.

On 28 July 1866, the day of the completion of the Atlantic cable, George W. Smalley was in Europe for the purpose of reporting the Austro-Prussian War. He and Henry Villard had been sent to Europe at once by the *Tribune* on receipt of news of the outbreak of the war, but they arrived after the signing of the armistice. A "Seven Weeks' War" did not allow enough time for word to reach the United States by ship and for war correspondents to get to Europe in time to report it. Smalley stopped off in London to send one of the earliest, possibly the

4. *New York Times*, 30 July 1866.

earliest, news cables dispatched across the Atlantic by a journalist. It was a brief message of forty-nine words, signed S, and sent at a cost of £1 per word. It appeared in the *Tribune* on 1 August: "Peace was certain at Berlin on Saturday. Bismarck and the King return this week. Prussia carries all her points. The Liberals support Bismarck's foreign policy. Austria's naval victory is much overrated. The Hyde Park riots and the movement to form exclusive Reform League meetings have periled the Derby government."[5]

There is considerable uncertainty about the first cabled news to the United States from Europe. Apparently the first news received did not come through regular news channels, but rather through Cyrus W. Field who received word on 27 July from Volunteer Bay, Ireland, of the end of the Austro-Prussian War. He was still on board the *Great Eastern* (the cable-laying ship) and the news was received just before the cable was cut for starting work on the shore end. It still took two days to get news from Heart's Content to New York. But Field's item on the end of the war was the cable news that the New York papers carried on Saturday, 30 July 1866. In his *Anglo-American Memories* Smalley says he thinks he sent the first news from Europe dispatched by cable but he adds to the confusion by referring to a later dispatch from Berlin.[6] The speech of the Prussian king to the Prussian Parliament is often referred to as the first cabled news from Europe but it did not appear in the New York papers until 9 August. By then cabled news was appearing every day in the American papers.[7]

Far more important in establishing Smalley's reputation than his early use of the cable was an interview he managed to obtain with Bismarck. Prussia's success in her 1866 war with Austria established Bismarck as one of the ablest European

5. *New York Tribune*, 1 August 1866. The final comment on the possible fall of the Derby government is almost certainly the first news cabled from Europe of a party-political nature.

6. George W. Smalley, *Anglo-American Memories* (New York, 1911), p. 165.

7. John Russell Young, *Men and Memories: Personal Reminiscences*, ed. Mary D. Russell Young, 2 vols. (New York, 1901), 2:270. Col. Finlay Anderson cabled the king's speech to Parliament at a cost of $6,500 in gold.

statesmen of his day. He had clearly guided the diplomacy leading to the war and more than anyone else he chose the terms of the peace settlement. The interview took place on 13 September, lasted more than two hours and appeared in the *Tribune,* three columns long, on 25 October. It bore the caption "An Afternoon with Count Bismarck." Interviews by journalists with leading European statesmen were so uncommon at the time that one of such length, especially with a journalist unknown to European reporting, had to be a sensation. Smalley said that he obtained the interview through a friend who knew Bismarck well but he gave no hint as to the identity of the friend.

Bismarck must have seen advantages in using an influential New York paper to present a defense of his policies for the four years he had served as Prussia's chief minister. Possibly he had in mind as a part of his audience the large U.S. population of German background. In Europe he was already well known but his policies were not familiar to the people of the United States. John Russell Young, then managing editor of the *Tribune,* considered Smalley's article the American reading public's introduction to Bismarck. He indicated that the "masterful, prophetic articles" led the *Tribune* management to offer Smalley the position of London correspondent.[8] The competence of the article is beyond question. It stands comparison with Smalley's best later reporting. There is in it also the egotistical touch that was a Smalley trademark. He pointed out that he had seen Bismarck "in a way in which I suppose few Americans have seen him" and reminded his readers that there is much "I must forbear to say. To put private matters into print is an offense which I do not mean to commit for any temptation."[9] When Senator Charles Sumner, then chairman of the Senate Foreign Relations Committee and a man to whom Smalley was indebted for favors, asked for further details of the interview, Smalley replied unctiously that he did not feel at liberty to pass on Bismarck's private confidences.

8. Ibid.
9. *New York Tribune,* 25 October 1866. Smalley also gives many details of the interview in his *Anglo-American Memories,* pp. 178–93.

Smalley returned from Europe with a plan for meeting the problem of European news coverage under the new conditions that virtually all the New York dailies were trying to solve. His proposal called for the establishment in London of an office for the collection of news from both British and Continental sources. Since England (actually Ireland) was at the European end of the cable, telegraphic news would be sent to London for transmission to the United States. The man who headed the London office was to appoint and supervise the correspondents on the Continent. It was a novel idea although Smalley had used a somewhat similar scheme for a brief period in Washington during the war.

The Smalley plan was adopted, though with modifications and restrictions that left the representative in London with less freedom than proposed. Managing editor Young in particular was fearful of a move that would decentralize authority and run the danger of creating a European editor whose independence and power might prove too great. And, of course, Smalley was offered the London appointment. As he remembered in his *Memories,* he had not himself in mind for the job. When it was tendered, he at first refused, pleading a lack of experience for so important an assignment; besides, he said, he preferred to write editorials in the New York office of the *Tribune.*[10] Contemporary evidence does not support his memory. Smalley had been in Europe only a few months when Wendell Phillips wrote managing editor Young: "Smalley is in Paradise, and indebted to you, the Pope, who lifted him out of Purgatory to that bliss."[11]

The *Tribune* editors had a difficult time in finding a suitable title for the new position they had created. They tried out several for size and announced the appointment officially as follows: "Mr. Smalley sails for Europe today [11 May 1867] to act as Foreign Commissioner for the Tribune, resident in London." There were few subsequent uses of "Foreign Commissioner," though the high-sounding title was used now and then

10. Smalley, *Anglo-American Memories,* pp. 221–24.
11. Phillips to Young, August 1867, quoted in Young, *Men and Memories,* 1:157.

on special occasions. To his credit, it should be noted that Smalley never used it.

Like most strong American papers, the *Tribune's* European news coverage was a combination of dependence upon special correspondence for travel accounts and the coverage of unusually important events, backed up by more or less regular letters from one or more European natives (usually journalists), and subscriptions from a half dozen to a score of European journals from whose pages the gaps were filled. Horace Greeley's paper took great pride in its "special correspondence," still a catchall term in precable days that included letters from regular and traveling correspondents reporting from distant places. In keeping with the American custom of braggadocio, the *Tribune* proclaimed its superiority. "In this department [special correspondence]," an editorial of 16 October 1866 asserted, "we make bold to say, THE TRIBUNE is surpassed by no other paper of the age, either in this country or in Europe."

The claim was a bit too "bold," at least for comparisons with several European journals, but the *Tribune* had a solid basis for claims to outstanding correspondence. At the time, Bayard Taylor, later U.S. minister to Germany and for many years the chief *Tribune* special correspondent for travel accounts, was sending in a series on the American West. The following year he contributed letters from Germany and Italy that appeared alongside letters by Mark Twain from the Near East. In late 1866 Henry Villard and Smalley were in England, Germany, and Russia, trying to make up for their failure to arrive in time to report the Austro-Prussian War. Clarence Cook, an American art critic, was sending more or less regular letters from Paris and occasional letters were printed from natives in Berlin, Madrid, Rome, and Constantinople.

For the *Tribune*, London letters had to have the right slant to fit the Greeley-*Tribune* view of the political spectrum. In particular that meant a strong pro-Union view of anything related to the Civil War and a John Mill radical approach to politics and economics in general. To fill this bill the *Tribune* received letters from an impressive trio: G. Y. Holyoake, Thomas Hughes, and (occasionally) Justin McCarthy. Holyoake was an outstanding Radical and agitator who had endeared himself to the *Tribune* by his strong support of the North during the Civil War. Thomas Hughes, widely known in the United States as the author of *Tom Brown's School Days,* was also a strong antislavery man and had worked with Holyoake in his pro-Union campaigns.[12] Both were leaders in the cooperative movement. Justin McCarthy was not as well known in the 1860s as later, but he was an Irish journalist who could trim his sails to suit the prevailing winds. In 1866 when Hughes became the *Tribune's* London correspondent he was a member of Parliament from Lambeth. It would be hard to name a journal other than the London *Times* or the *Independance Belge* that had a stronger corps of correspondents than the *Tribune* at the time, although the regular news coverage of a number of papers was more thorough and up to date than that of the *Tribune.*

When Smalley began reporting from London in June 1867, Colonel Finlay Anderson, chief representative of the *New York Herald,* was already well established as a correspondent. "Little Col. Anderson" was an Irishman by origin who had spent a number of years in the United States and like Smalley had made his reputation as a Civil War reporter.[13] He was one of the first journalists to make use of the Atlantic cable and he used it more lavishly than his competitors. According to Benjamin Moran, First Secretary at the American legation in London, Anderson "lived elegantly," and Moran's standards in this respect were not low. He described a dinner given by the American minister, Charles Francis Adams, as "the meanest dinner I ever sat down to in a gentleman's house" and complained particularly that no champagne was served.[14] During the first years of Smalley's work in London, Anderson was his chief competitor and was often ahead of Smalley with the news that

12. Edward C. Mack and W. H. G. Armitage, *Thomas Hughes: The Life of the Author of Tom Brown's School Days* (London, 1952), p. 131.

13. J. Cutler Andrews, *The North Reports the Civil War* (Pittsburgh, 1955), p. 62.

14. Diary of Benjamin Moran, 27 December 1867 and 22 April 1868, Benjamin Moran Papers, vols. 19 and 20, Library of Congress, Washington, D.C.

was most highly valued in the United States. Minister Adams was extremely careful about information he gave to press representatives, but he was more tolerant with Anderson than with other reporters. Reverdy Johnson, who succeeded Adams, was notoriously free with reporters that he favored and they included Anderson, whom he once took with him on a speaking tour.[15]

In the sixties Smalley was less concerned with competition from other American journalists, save on rare occasions such as the first Harvard–Oxford boat race in 1869 when rivalry reached an unprecedented peak, than with the task of organizing the *Tribune's* Continental coverage and with composing his own letters and cables. The idea of making London the central point for European news coverage was ridiculed by other papers and did not really prove itself until the Franco-Prussian War when it enabled the *Tribune* to outdistance all of its competitors. Smalley employed some of the correspondents in the European news centers while others were appointed by the managing editor in New York. Most of the time he stayed in London though occasionally he reported a special event elsewhere such as the meeting of the British Association for the Advancement of Science that met in Dundee, Scotland, in September 1867. In 1869 he went to Spain when the ousting of Queen Isabella made that country a center of intrigue and general interest. Later in the same year he was one of about three hundred journalists who reported the opening of the Suez Canal. The ten lengthy letters he sent to the *Tribune* on this event are well balanced between glamor and significance.[16] Once he rushed madly across the channel to France when the *Tribune's* Paris correspondent, Clarence Cook, notified him that the cost of admission to cover the famous trial of Prince Pierre Bonaparte at Tours would be £100. Smalley's concern was uncalled for: the telegraph operator had translated pounds for francs.[17]

15. Ibid., 24 April 1869, vol. 22.
16. *New York Tribune*, 16, 17, 19, 21, 23, 29 November 1869, and 13, 20, 24, and 25 December 1869.
17. Smalley to Reid, 20 March 1870, Whitelaw Reid Papers, Library of Congress, Washington, D.C.

Letters were still the main concern of the correspondent of an American paper in London. Telegraphic news in the sixties centered on major political developments, market quotations, and the horse races. The Doncaster Races were cable news for four straight days, 11–14 September 1867. The press association took care of most cable news routinely, which made life easier for the correspondent. The correspondent was responsible for deciding what to cable that would be missed otherwise and this was not always an easy decision. But it is worth noting that Smalley's private correspondence from London with the *Tribune,* authorities was filled for more than a decade after his arrival in London with discussions of boat sailings and sea mail time, and included many charges and countercharges as to whose fault it was when the *Herald* or some other rival beat the *Tribune* with a news account—usually by several days or a week. Both Hughes and Holyoake continued to write occasional letters after Smalley took over; and Moncure D. Conway normally took Smalley's place when he was away from London. Smalley also increased an old practice of employing someone of special competence for an unusual subject.

Smalley's own early letters averaged one and one-half columns of about 2,000 to 2,500 words. They appeared once or twice weekly, sometimes got front page space but more often appeared on page two, and were run one to two weeks later than the London dateline. Of first importance in subject matter, though not necessarily in length of treatment, were matters of Anglo-American concern— the *Alabama* claims, the statements and activities of the American minister, English opinions of America, and anything having to do with important visitors to England or to America. Following these came British politics. During the British elections of 1868 one of Smalley's letters ran to seven columns and several others were three or four columns in length. Close behind politics came literary and artistic subjects. The attention given to selected books by American correspondents abroad during the early second half of the nineteenth century is impressive if it reflects American public interest. Smalley gave three of his letters and nearly 30,000 words to the third and fourth volumes of A. W. Kinglake's *Invasion of the Crimea.*[18]

Newspaper publishers were interested then as always in the topics dealt with by their correspondents. *Tribune* publisher Horace Greeley never relaxed in his attention to the subject matter submitted by his reporters; he had special interests, and strong convictions about what his readers wanted. These special Greeley interests gave Smalley more headaches than his publisher's slants and biases. In 1870 Greeley was absorbed with the question of farming and did a series in the *Tribune* entitled "What I know about Farming" that ran for most of the year. Nothing would do but that Smalley write on English crops in spite of the plea that accompanied his first farming letter: "What I knew about farming was not much before this morning."[19] Another frequent command performance was to send more letters in a light, gossipy vain. The word "gossip" always irritated Smalley–he thought it somehow was lower than the dignity of his writings–and he pleaded with the editors to refrain from using the caption "London Gossip" even when he did send gossip. After one of Mr. Greeley's complaints that his letters were "almost exclusively literary and political," Smalley made a count for a four-month period and concluded that only 40 percent of his letters had been literary and political, leaving 60 percent for other topics; also that the *Tribune* had failed to publish a number of his letters, all of the nonliterary, nonpolitical variety.[20]

During his first two years in Europe Smalley's relations with his employers and superiors at the *Tribune* were comparatively pleasant. John Russell Young, the managing editor who appointed him to the London position, was highly pleased with his work in spite of his early concern that Smalley would be too independent of New York authority. But in May 1869 Young was dismissed by Greeley on the charge that he made use of New York Associated Press material in the *Philadelphia*

18. *New York Tribune,* 1, 19, and 23 July 1868.
19. Smalley to Reid, 21 August 1871, Reid Papers.
20. Ibid., 3 February 1872.

Morning Post of which he was part owner. It was alleged that Young had used his position with the *Tribune* to make material available to the *Morning Post*, though the Philadelphia paper had no right to the information.[21]

Young's dismissal was almost as much of a blow to Smalley as to Young. Smalley wrote Young a long letter (twelve pages) in which he declared he was sorry he had ever gone to Europe; that he believed somehow the incident would never have occurred had he remained in New York. "I cannot wonder that H. G. [Horace Greeley] should consent to it, and abide by it, for I know that his love for the Tribune is greater than anything else, and he never could risk a contest which should permit men to say the character of his paper was touched. Well, I too have a love for the Tribune, as you well know, but I never could sacrifice my friend to it. . . . I have had a few friends whom I loved and the kind of affection you extorted from me." Smalley added that the *Tribune* could never again mean what it had meant to him.[22]

Young did not make matters easier for Smalley with the new *Tribune* management by recommending him as his successor,[23] though Smalley asserted emphatically that he did not want the post. Young's successor, though not immediately, was Whitelaw Reid who had joined the *Tribune* staff subsequent to Smalley's departure for London. For several years after Reid took over the management, the *Tribune* was in a state of uncertainty. Reid's own position was never secure until he became one of the chief owners in late 1872. Greeley's relationship to the paper was a trial as well as a source of strength, especially when Greeley ran for the presidency of the country in 1872. Smalley remained in London for four years (until the spring of 1871) without a visit to the United States, which meant that his position and his relationships with Reid had to be worked out

21. Harry W. Baehr, Jr., *The New York Tribune since the Civil War* (New York, 1936), pp. 73–74.
22. Smalley to Young, 29 May 1869, John Russell Young Papers, vol. 7, Library of Congress, Washington, D.C.
23. Young to Smalley, 16 May 1869, ibid. There were public suggestions during the *Tribune* crisis that Smalley would be the best man to manage the *Tribune* (*New York Standard*, 25 August 1870).

by correspondence on a professional basis with none of the leavening that comes with personal acquaintance.

One of Whitelaw Reid's greatest talents was his capacity for appreciating the abilities of others; another was his diplomatic skill in dealing with difficult people. Both of these qualities were needed to keep Smalley as the London representative of the *Tribune* and to establish a working relationship between the two men that was to last for many years. At times the relationship was even one of warm friendship. Reid made it a point shortly after taking over the management of the paper to solicit Smalley's views on the quality of the paper and how best to improve it. Smalley responded with sound advice.[24] Still, the going in the early days was sometimes rough. A minor crisis arose in late 1869 when a private letter from Smalley to Theodore Tilton, in which Smalley complained of deletions and changes in some of his dispatches, was published in another newspaper. Smalley was also outspokenly critical of some of the correspondence to the *Tribune* from the Continent by writers he had not selected, especially of the letters of Clarence Cook from Paris. "The Tribune could have been made to ring with Paris letters," he wrote Reid in early 1870. "All other European politics were tame and dull in comparison."[25]

Smalley was never one of Greeley's favorites, which sometimes made for difficulties. Reid told Smalley years later in 1893: "Even when I was very young on the Tribune, I had to sustain you from two orders from Mr Greeley for your removal—one of which named a successor for you."[26] Reid was simply too good a journalist not to recognize Smalley's contributions to the *Tribune*. He was especially grateful for the London representative's great work during the Franco-Prussian War. A better personal understanding was established between the two men when Smalley visited the United States in the spring of 1871. "If we had any misunderstandings when we were 3,000 miles apart," Smalley wrote, "I am sure there is nothing I could remember after what you have said, and I hope nothing

24. Smalley to Reid, 12 September [1869], Reid Papers.
25. Ibid., 16 December [1869].
26. Reid to Smalley, 25 November 1893, ibid.

you care to remember, after we had once shaken hands. It was my conviction that our meeting would set matters right that brought me over, and my gratification at finding your personal friendship just what it was is very great."[27] In the years that followed the friendship was subjected to many stresses but it survived even the severance of Smalley's relations with the *Tribune*.

27. Smalley to Reid, 17 May 1871, ibid.

5. American Radical
in England

In the eighties and nineties George W. Smalley became notoriously conservative. He was also thought by many Americans to be unacceptably pro-English, so much the Anglophile that he could not see the good points in his own country and countrymen. This later Smalley image has obscured the picture of him in the sixties and most of the seventies. In 1863 he wrote Andrew White: "I hope you bring back with you hearty hate of all things English. My bones will never rest if I die before we have thoroughly flogged John Bull—him and all his belongings. How you could have sojourned in London I cannot conceive."[1] This private, casual remark to a friend was made at a time when relations between the United States and Great Britain were severely strained. Still, it illustrates an attitude that Smalley carried with him when he went to live and work in England. During his first years there he was belligerently American, suspicious of most Englishmen, and critical of Britain's traditions and institutions.

As a "*Tribune* man" Smalley proudly counted himself an American Radical Republican. It should be remembered that the Radical Republicans were held together during the Civil War mainly by their advocacy of abolition and in the Reconstruction era that followed by their determination to make the

1. Smalley to White, 27 September [1863], Andrew D. White Papers, Cornell University Library, Ithaca, N.Y.

conquered South safe for the Republican party and Northern business. Horace Greeley's liberalism did not include free trade, and Wendell Phillips was one of the few Radicals who could be considered prolabor. But the *Tribune* was egalitarian, committed to full male suffrage, inclined to see all political issues as moral ones, and sympathetic to the cooperative movement. It was enough to make Smalley feel at home with most of the left wing of the British Liberal party.

Smalley arrived in London long before there was any disposition on the part of British officials to render aid to journalists. Public men sought to avoid rather than court newspaper representatives. Nor was the American legation inclined to be helpful to American journalists save in exceptional cases. Smalley carried with him a strong letter of recommendation from a good friend of Charles Francis Adams, but the American minister became friendly only after the new arrival declared that he had no favors to ask.[2] It was more than two years later that Benjamin Moran, First Secretary of the legation, took Smalley with him to the House of Commons and introduced him to the chief doorkeeper "who promised to let him in occasionally."[3] Moran was horrified a year before Smalley's appointment when he heard that Thomas Hughes, a member of Parliament, had accepted the post of London correspondent for the *Tribune*. "It is an awful comedown on his part," Moran wrote in his diary.[4] American residents in England rarely moved in circles that gave them access to high social or political figures and could be of little help to a journalist-compatriot. "I know many Americans in London," Charles Francis Adams wrote in the diary, "but I see scarcely any in the places I am invited to. . . . Very certainly if it was not that I came with a position that makes me on an equal footing with everybody, I should never have put my foot on these shores."[5]

2. George W. Smalley, *Anglo-American Memories* (New York, 1911), p. 197.
3. Diary of Benjamin Moran, 18 February 1870, Benjamin Moran Papers, vol. 24, Library of Congress, Washington, D.C.
4. Ibid., 24 August 1866, vol. 23.
5. Diary of Charles F. Adams, 20 July 1861, Charles F. Adams Papers (microfilm reel 76), Adams Manuscript Trust, Massachusetts Historical Society, Boston, Mass.

The London friends and associates of the Smalleys were Liberal newsmen and politicians, writers, European exiles, and visiting or resident Americans. In the early days there were no peers of the realm, or Tories even, and the names of people of prominence that appear in Smalley's private correspondence or on guest lists for dinners that he gave or attended are not numerous. Thomas Hughes was probably Smalley's best early friend and greatest aid. Hughes had many friends in the United States as well as in England and for many years he was a man to whom young Americans presented introductions on their first visit to the British Isles. The novelist Charles Reade was an early acquaintance though not an intimate friend. Publisher Alexander Macmillan, an early dining companion, was a sufficiently close friend to enable Smalley to "commend him heartily to all good fellows in America" when the publisher visited the United States in 1867.[6] Another friend was the French exile, Louis Blanc, whom Smalley firmly believed would be the president of the French republic should one replace the Napoleonic empire. John Bright and Charles Dilke were some of his first acquaintances among the Liberal political leaders. In the early seventies Smalley was frequently seen at informal social gatherings at the home of "Darwin's Bulldog," Thomas H. Huxley. From the American colony in London his closest friends were Cyrus W. Field, the banker Hugh McCulloch, the artist George Boughton, the diplomat Benjamin Moran, and the minister-writer Moncure D. Conway.

"What you say of Smalley is very gratifying to me," Wendell Phillips wrote John Russell Young, Smalley's managing editor, on 12 November 1868. "I think and have for some months, that his style has gained very much in vigor, variety and point. I assure you from quarters where he is personally no favorite, I hear earnest praise of his letters. . . . Dining with Sumner at Motley's the other day, Sumner used almost your own terms in speaking of the [Smalley] review of Bright. He called it 'masterly,' 'a work not an article,' 'one of the finest things in

6. *New York Tribune*, 5 September 1867.

journalism,' in which Motley joined."[7] Senator Sumner wrote
Young about the same time: "He writes admirably and I enjoy
his liberalism."[8] Smalley's liberalism included unreserved support of Gladstone on domestic issues and criticism of the Liberal
leader in 1871 for including in his ministry too many Whigs
rather than genuine Liberals, and too many peers.[9] When three
Fenians were hanged at Manchester, he wrote: "Disguise it
how you will, this is a political execution." The three were
hanged "in order to crush a political movement."[10] In 1872 the
Saturday Review declared that Smalley had "written of all English matters in a tone of contemptuous acrimony" for a paper
that was the constituent enemy of England and an advocate of
Fenianism.[11]

The charges against Smalley and the *Tribune* by the *Saturday
Review* were too strong, though their partisanship was obvious
and the language used designed for the earthy tastes of American readers. In April and May 1868, the reporter's letters were
filled with indignation over a supposedly "drunken speech"
made by Disraeli on the problem of the Irish church. The
Troy leader, Smalley asserted, left the House of Commons at
3:30 A.M. "blind drunk" and did not come to himself until noon
the following day. "Indeed, how can you contradict what 600
eye witnesses testify to? There is no longer any affectation of
reserve in speaking of Mr. Disraeli's condition on that evening."[12]
"England is disgraced by Mr. Disraeli," he declared, "but the
often praised elasticity of her Constitution has not yet enabled
her to throw him off."[13] In a more general condemnation of

7. John Russell Young, *Men and Memories: Personal Reminiscences*, ed.
Mary D. Russell Young, 2 vols. (New York, 1901), pp. 157–58. Curiously
the biographical sketch of Smalley in the *Dictionary of American Biography*
credits him as author of a book entitled *Review of the Speeches of John
Bright.* There is no other evidence for this assertion.
8. Summer to Young, 29 September 1868, John Russell Young Papers,
Library of Congress, Washington, D.C.
9. *New York Tribune*, 24 January 1871.
10. Ibid., 5 December 1867.
11. Ibid., 6 March 1872. Smalley quoted from the *Saturday Review* in
defense of his own radicalism, something he occasionally felt called upon
to do even during the early days.
12. Ibid., 7 May 1868.
13. Ibid., 18 May 1868.

the Conservative leader, Smalley referred to the "power which he gained by life-long hypocrisy, and has upheld by base arts."[14]

Smalley's letters to America tended to magnify the importance of Republican sentiment in England and to be critical of the royal family, especially of the Prince of Wales. He was disgusted with English newspaper "gush" over the prince's typhoid fever in 1872, called its coverage of the illness "flunkeyism," and emphasized that the time had come for the prince to recognize his duties and responsibilities.[15] Two years later he dwelt at length with the matter of the prince's debts in anything but a friendly spirit.[16]

The question arises naturally as to what extent Smalley was speaking for himself and for the *Tribune?* Or, put another way, did his critical views represent a larger segment of American opinion? It can be said, without attempting a precise answer, that Anglo-American relations were edgy, still in a state of convalescence from the wounds of the Civil War period. There were many American critics who thought Smalley and the *Tribune* were soft toward England, especially in regard to the *Alabama* claims. Smalley was charged with having "sold out" to the English when he advocated compromise on the claims. Even Senator Sumner, who usually approved of Smalley's views, got provoked with him when the journalist proposed court dress for the American minister to the Court of St. James.[17]

Smalley was deeply disturbed by the inadequate London press coverage of American affairs. Worse than inadequate, it was highly prejudiced—at least so Smalley thought. Misrepresentation of the Republican party and American radicalism could be expected from the *Times* and the *Standard,* but the presentations in the *Daily News,* the *Spectator,* and the *Star* were equally bad. "It is still the fashion," he wrote, "which *The Times* speaks for,

14. Ibid., 5 December 1868.
15. Ibid., 9 June 1872.
16. Ibid., 23 September 1874.
17. Smalley tried to explain to Sumner: "Mr. Young sent me what you wrote him about my poor little paragraph on court dress—a matter I had quite forgotten and on which I have no very obstinate opinions" (Smalley to Sumner, 2 December 1868, Charles Sumner Papers, vol. 88, Houghton Library, Harvard University, Cambridge, Mass.).

to affect a kind of social contempt for American Radicalism. *The Times* has never learned the secret of the universal strength that lies in belief. It has no convictions; does not feel sure that anybody else has."[18]

The arrows he fired at the *Daily News,* a Liberal paper, were tipped with even stronger acid. Here there were personal as well as political reasons for anger. The "mischievous and even treacherous" American correspondence in the *Daily News* was supplied by E. L. Godkin, editor of the *New York Nation,* with whom Smalley carried on a bitter and lifelong feud. "All the hatred of Republicanism he does not think it prudent to express in his own journal, he scatters with a free hand in the *Daily News* of London," Smalley charged.[19] And, "I suppose this gentleman would describe himself as belonging to the reserve forces of the Republican party. His position gives him the very peculiar advantage of being able to shoot his comrades from behind."[20] To get a hearing in England for his own views and to offset the reports of the *Daily News* and of other American correspondents, Smalley often sent "letters to the editors" of London Journals.

Smalley's radicalism, with its heavy hatred of the Confederacy, led him to a prolonged Rebel witch-hunt in England, and to judgments of people based almost entirely upon the attitude they had taken toward the Union during the Civil War. His admiration for Thomas Hughes was greatly strengthened by Hughes's pro-Northern record. He rushed to the defense of Thomas Carlyle, hardly a Liberal, rejecting the "flippant impertinences of the *Nation*" on the ground that Carlyle had not favored the South.[21] When William Thompson was reappointed American consul at Southampton—a post he had resigned in 1862—Smalley resurrected old charges against him that he had rendered aid to Confederate commissioners in England. A small

18. *New York Tribune,* 24 April 1869.
19. Ibid., 25 June 1868. The *Nation,* 28 October 1869, said that Smalley had asserted that Mr. Walker, *London Daily News* editor, did not know his correspondent was editor of the *Nation;* a malicious falsehood, said the *Nation.*
20. *New York Tribune,* 22 October 1868.
21. Ibid., 4 October 1867.

tempest followed in which Thompson was requested by the secretary of state to clear himself of the correspondent's charges, which he seems to have been able to do.[22]

Nor did the London commissioner of the *Tribune* confine his zeal for preserving the purity of the U.S. foreign services to officials in England. In early 1869 he paid a visit to Spain for the purpose of writing on the revolution that had brought about the ousting of Queen Isabella and created a situation of domestic uncertainty and interest on the part of outside powers. While there Smalley became persuaded of the truth of charges made against the American minister John Parker Hale by Horatio J. Perry, First Secretary of the legation in Madrid. There was no question of a Rebel taint; rather the charges concerned moral delinquency and the minister's abuse of his position owning to his lack of sympathy with the Spanish revolution. In publicizing the affair Smalley wrote with restraint and apparently with sincere regret.[23] The *Tribune* backed him editorially and the journal's campaign against Hale undoubtedly contributed to the minister's recall.

When, shortly after the Hale incident, Consul Morse of London came within the range of Smalley's fire, his longtime enemy, E. L. Godkin, felt that the time had come for strong language in calling down the self-appointed critic of U.S. officials abroad:

This gentleman was accused in the usual style, by the London Correspondent of the New York *Tribune,* of "sympathizing" with the Confederacy, or with Andrew Johnson, or with anti-impeachers, or with somebody or something of an objectionable nature, and was denounced in the columns of that paper accordingly. So Consul Morse goes hat in hand to the correspondent, explains himself and excuses himself, and finally makes it alright with that functionary, who accordingly publishes an acquittal of the culprit, which he supposes a few people, who did not laugh over it, read without blushing at the thought that any American official should be allowed to subject himself publically to such

22. Ibid., 27 April, 11 and 12 May 1869. It was believed that Benjamin Moran, who had a quarrel of long standing with Thompson, was back of Smalley's charges, but Moran says he was not (Diary of Benjamin Moran, 21 June 1869, Moran Papers, vol. 23).

23. *New York Tribune,* 11 and 20 March, and 24 May 1869.

ridiculous humiliation without being promptly sent about his business by his superiors.[24]

Added point was given to the *Nation's* ire and alarm by Smalley's denunciations of Reverdy Johnson who succeeded Charles Francis Adams as U.S. minister to England. Johnson, a native of Maryland, remained loyal to the Union during the Civil War but retained his sympathy for the South and consistently opposed Sumner and the Radicals while a member of the Senate. He worked tirelessly to prevent the impeachment of Andrew Johnson from whom he received his appointment to the Court of St. James. To the disgust of Benjamin Moran he was far more openhanded with the press than his predecessor had been. Moran called his policy one of "open diplomacy," certainly an early use of that term. But this was no boon to the representative of the *Tribune*. Colonel Anderson of the *Herald* was one of those who received favors, including an invitation to accompany the minister when he went to Liverpool to give a speech. There was no doubting Johnson's popularity in England but in the views of Smalley and the *Tribune* he sought and found popularity with the wrong people, including notorious friends of the Confederacy. It was only a question of time before the *Tribune* would shift from a sniper's position into an open attack. On 22 October 1868 it printed a letter from Smalley under the London dateline of 10 October:

It is time to tell the truth about our Minister, truth which I have hesitated to believe, but which becomes only too plain day by day. His extraordinary popularity is not due to the fact that he is an American Minister, but to the fact he is a Southerner.
[Details are then designated to demonstrate his pro-Southern friendships.]
If you care to save the country from further humiliation, summon home its recreant Minister. If you care to preserve so much good will as exists between England and America, summon him home. Mr. Reverdy Johnson has done more in the last six weeks to estrange the two countries than he can undo by a dozen treaties.

The *Tribune* endorsed Smalley's demand editorially and joined him in maintaining a regular fire on the minister until

24. *Nation,* 17 June 1869.

the new president, General U. S. Grant, took office in the following spring. Grant accepted the normal resignation submitted by
a minister and did not ask him to continue in office. Prior to
Johnson's resignation Smalley attacked him in the *London Daily
News* as well as in the *New York Tribune.* The English paper
printed a letter from him in which he asserted that Johnson's
statements with reference to the *Alabama* claims were misleading,
that he did not represent the views of his countrymen, and
that he would shortly be recalled in disgrace.[25] Privately Smalley
corresponded with Charles Sumner, chairman of the Senate
Foreign Relations Committee, urging him to take action against
Johnson. (Presumably Sumner needed no arguments to persuade him of Johnson's wrongheadedness.)

Claims against Great Britain for damage done to U.S. shipping
during the Civil War by the English-constructed *Alabama* was
the most important official issue between the United States and
Great Britain until its settlement in 1872. Great Britain had
constructed several ships for the Confederate government during
the Civil War. The *Alabama* was the most important of these
and alone captured between sixty-five and seventy U.S. ships,
most of which were destroyed. The United States protested
during the Civil War and continued to demand reparation. In
1869 Senator Charles Sumner led a demand for $2,125,000,000
in damages. In 1872 an arbitration committee awarded the
United States claims of $15,500,000. The public, so far as can
be determined by the press reactions, was sporadically interested
in the question which faded into the background for months
only to burst forth in a sudden and surprisingly strong erup-
tion of emotions. For a correspondent who took his duties as
seriously as Smalley, and who viewed his role in Anglo-American
relations as crucial, the problem was a delicate one. For all his
belligerency and partisanship Smalley was pledged to the cause
of closer Anglo-American friendship soon after his arrival in
England. But he wanted to build on the right foundation and
to rest on the good will of what he considered the right, perhaps
righteous, elements in both countries.

25. *London Daily News,* 1 December 1868.

It was easy and natural enough for Smalley to please the palates of *Tribune* readers with vigorous support of the more extreme demands for claims. He could readily blame pro-Rebel sentiment in England for any failure to recognize the legitimacy of the demands. He did support the claims fully, and with arguments that only a man with legal knowledge and strong private views could muster. He backed the near fantastic sum demanded by Senator Sumner in 1869. But at the same time he gave a fair presentation of English views in his letters to the *Tribune*. He wrote letters to the London *Times* defending Summer and wrote Sumner giving him a realistic view of English opinion, assuring him that the anger expressed in the British press was real and representative of the official view as well.[26] The award made in 1872 by the Geneva commission that satisfied neither side, though the British less than the American, gave Smalley an opportunity to work even harder for conciliation. This aim was quite apparent in both his letters to the *Tribune* and private letters to the *Times,* which were treated with respect.[27] Smalley's judgments in the *Alabama* claims case were not always free from heat or consistently logical, but they presented in the main a statesmanlike performance, one of the saner stands taken by any protagonist on either side of the Atlantic.

26. Smalley to Sumner, 18 May 1869, Sumner Papers.
27. See particularly the *New York Tribune,* 1 and 29 March 1872, and the *Times* (London), 15 and 19 February 1872.

6. A Boat Race
and a War

The Oxford-Harvard boat race held on the Thames on 28 August 1869 and the Franco-Prussian War, which produced a united Germany and a new European balance of power, were the most important European news stories in the American press of their period. The *Alabama* claims negotiations, that smouldering hotbed of trouble between Great Britain and the United States, was pushed into the background for both events. The generally accepted importance of the war makes any explanation of its news value unnecessary, but placing a long forgotten sports event that lasted only a few minutes on the same level might seem to require some explanation. All that is really needed, however, is to see how the people of the time viewed the event.

In England the annual race between crews representing Oxford and Cambridge was a well-established event going back to 1829, while in the United States intercollegiate boat racing had less than two decades of history. But almost from the moment in early May 1869, when Oxford accepted a challenge from Harvard after considerable difficulty in reconciling different racing practices, the prospect of a Harvard-Oxford contest aroused the interest of the American public event more than the British. It became in the words of the *New York Times* "more than a boat race. . . . [It was] in every sense an international event." Even the dignified London *Times* let itself go and declared the day of the race "henceforth ever immortal in Anglo-American annals."[1] When a delay occurred in the transmission of the cable news to the *New York Tribune,* Whitelaw Reid could scarcely find words to describe the enormity of the crime committed by the Trans-Atlantic Cable Company. He wrote to Cyrus W. Field: "This was not simply an extraordinary event calling for full and fresh details, such as the death of the Emperor Napoleon tomorrow would be, or the outbreak of a Fenian insurrection in Ireland. On the contrary, it was a topic to which the attention of two continents had been directed for over a month, the interest constantly rising and everybody concerned having had ample time for all preparations for securing the earliest news. The leading newspapers of the United States and Great Britain were known to be looking forward to and making every possible arrangement for it."[2]

The press indeed aroused interest in the great event. Between early May and late September—the race continued to be news for a month after it was run—the *New York Times* devoted sixteen editorials to it, not to mention the many columns of noneditorial material. The expense of cabling, still a restrictive factor in the transmission of most news, was disregarded. Three weeks before the race the *New York Times* noted that "the cable rarely fails to give now a daily bulletin from the seat of the war" on the Thames. Some of the longer cables, including those by Smalley, were little more than chitchat. It was stated that no fewer than fifteen American journals were represented on the press boat that accompanied the competing crews in the race. The majority of these had no regular representatives in England.[3] In its account of the race on 28 August the *New York Times* gave over five of its six front-page columns, including a large map of the course. On other pages there appeared additional news and a column-long editorial. Ten days after the race, the *Tribune* devoted four of its six front-page columns to Smalley's sea mail account of the event. The *Echo,* which got

1. For a detailed account of the race see Joseph J. Mathews, "The First Harvard-Oxford Boat Race," *New England Quarterly* 33 (March 1960): 74–82.

2. Reid to Field, 11 September 1869, Whitelaw Reid Papers, Library of Congress, Washington, D.C.

3. *New York Tribune,* 8 September 1869.

the news first in London, sold 25,000 copies of their "extra" in three quarters of an hour, "a fact probably unparalleled in English journalism," according to Smalley.

Several estimates of the number of people who witnessed the race ran as high as one million. All agreed that it was a much larger crowd than had ever seen an Oxford-Cambridge race. It was noted that for ordinary races eighty policemen patrolled the banks of the river, but on this occasion eight hundred were assigned. Reporters who were not bold enough to make numerical estimates of the attendance referred to the "dense masses" along the banks of the river, to the packed bridges, to the crowded windows and rooftops, and to the horsemen and carriages that endangered life by trying to follow the racing boats. The attendance was the more remarkable in that it was the peak vacation period for London and the South. As the *Illustrated London News* described it:

. . . it is well that our cousins should comprehend that all over the island the excitement was as great as their own. This is the wandering season, when everyone who can get away from London rushes into the obscurist place he can find, rambles beyond railways, beyond coaches. . . . But in remote districts of Yorkshire, in savage valleys in the north, in out of the way nooks in Wales, when tourists came across one another on Saturday last the first eager question was about the race.[4]

The *Tribune* reported that in New York City

along the sidewalks there was but one topic of conversation. . . . doubting ones insisted that there would be foul play. Few, however, gave assent to this. The crowd [before the *Tribune* bulletin board] grew larger as the day advanced, and the excitement seemed to be increased. Mayor Hall ordered the flags to be displayed on the City Hall. Wall St., with a patriotic burst, gave up the legitimate work of the day. . . . Curbstone operators noted bets in their stock books, and one firm went into business on the wholesale plan, betting even on Harvard. The excitement gradually spread over the streets into the alleys and lanes, near at hand. . . .[5]

The day was the warmest of the season. "Panting, and in some cases, half suffocating crowds endured the 95° in the sun temperature." Harvard won the toss and took the Middlesex side.

4. *Illustrated London News*, 4 September 1869, p. 226.
5. *New York Tribune*, 28 August 1869.

The boats started at from nearly opposite the Star and Garter at Putney, and rowed to the winning ship, which was placed opposite the Ship Inn, at Montlake. The crews had a splendid day for the race, and the water, although ruffled by a stiff breeze which was blowing, was in a very good state.

The start took place at 5:10. Mr. Blaikie, of Harvard, gave the signal, and the lead was taken by Harvard, who rowed at forty-five strokes per minute, their opponents doing only thirty-nine and forty. As may be expected, the Americans jumped away at a rapid pace; and, indeed, their speed and time to Hammersmith is the fastest we have on record. As the Harvard Crew led by one-third of a length at Simmonds,' the odds went down to 10 to 8 and even on Oxford . . . the Americans, still rowing the same number of strokes, cleared Craven point half a length ahead. . . . by the time they [Oxford] went by the Soap work their bow was up to No. 3 in the American boat and odds of 2 to 1 were offered. . . . The Harvard Coxwain tried to get his course again and drew once more a few feet ahead; but it was their last grand effort; for the long draw of the Oxford Crew had worn them out; and Darbeshire, calling on his crew . . . much by wish drew up until they came dead heat at the foot of Chiswick Ait. For 200 yards they both went at it with almost super human effort; but the better style of the Oxonians told its infallible tale, and halfway up the Ait the Americans lost ground fast, until off Chiswick Church . . . they were a length ahead. The Harvard Crew made desperate efforts to alter the tide of affairs, and, although the Coxwain threw water over his own men and roused them to fresh exertions, every minute they gradually fell astern. Oxford, preserving the lead . . . won by three lengths, Benson's Chronograph giving the advantage of 6 secs. in regard to time.[6]

No one had made more elaborate arrangements for the fullest and earliest New York account of the race than George W. Smalley. In the slightly more than two years he had spent as the London correspondent of the *Tribune* there had been no test of his mettle quite like it, and he was keenly aware that his reputation was at stake. Like virtually all journalists, he had an appreciation of the importance of a boat race as an international event that is beyond the grasp of most historians and "serious" students of international relations. As a member of the Yale crew first to challenge Harvard he qualified as a knowledgeable reporter in racing matters. His experience was

6. *Illustrated London News,* 28 August 1869, p. 189. Sir Aubrey Paul, the judge, later ruled that Oxford won the race by one-half to three-quarters of a length.

also something of a handicap; he knew that the chances of a Harvard victory were slim and his doubts were obvious in his prerace reports, which made him a natural target for sniping competitors. The *New York Times* accused him of carrying "juvenile grudges into mature life," and he once asked his editor whether it might be better to have someone else report the contest for the *Tribune.*

The answer was in the negative and he proceeded with his careful plans. Fortunately, Thomas Hughes, his friend and *Tribune* contributor, was a racing expert and was made referee for the event. He readily agreed to send letters to the *Tribune.* The novelist Charles Reade, an occasional *Tribune* contributor who had included an exciting boat race in his novel *Very Hard Cash,* also agreed to write a description of the race. Mr. William Blaikie, secretary of the Harvard Boat Club, was persuaded to do a report on Harvard's view of the race, for which he was paid twenty dollars. The plan called for getting Reade's letter off on the steamship *Russia* on the day of the race with the other letters by Hughes, Blaikie, and Smalley to follow later. Every conceivable precaution was taken to ensure the early arrival of Smalley's cable immediately following the race.

But alas, Smalley's cable arrived in New York too late for the Saturday editions, although cables to other New York papers did arrive on schedule, including a lengthy one for the *World* by Moncure D. Conway. Worse still, the *Tribune* did not have a Sunday paper. The journal had to content itself with association dispatches until Monday when Smalley's 2,200-word cable was printed. Smalley's agony was compounded when Charles Reade refused to write his letter because Harvard lost the race. Later he allowed Smalley to quote him: "It could hardly be believed in the United States to what extent I, an Oxford man, sympathize with your gallant fellows."[7]

Smalley was beside himself, blaming anybody and everybody and venting his spleen on all. He complained bitterly to White-law Reid of changes made in his cable dispatch for publication in the *Tribune,* which he said were "as unlike the technical language of rowing . . . as unlike English." He added, "If I

7. *New York Tribune,* 8 September 1869.

should ever send you another telegram, I pray you to have it transmitted unmutilated."[8] A month later his temper had cooled but he had not recovered from his failure. "You may laugh at me if you like," he wrote Reid, "but the disaster was a blow to me which I have not got over. It left me unfit to do anything but sit on the beach at Dieppe and curse the idiot who caused it."[9] Reid was not laughing. He demanded and received compensation from the Anglo-American Cable Company for their failure to send Smalley's dispatch on schedule.

Having determined that the contest between the crews of the leading American and English universities had the qualities and significance of a great international event, the press probed its possible ramifications, used it as a vehicle to compare American and British ways of life, and philosophized about what they found. "For the first time in the history of either people, the nation of England has been brought in close rapport with the nation of America," it was asserted in *London Society*.[10] On both sides of the ocean there was a strong note of snobbery in reporting the event. The *Illustrated London News* made the point by calling the race a "gentleman's business." The *Tribune* quoted the London *Times* with obvious approval:

The Harvard men are of the best families of New England, although one of them nominally "hails" from the Sandwich islands. It is understood that this is due to an accidental migration of his father but three or four years since, and like his comrades, his birth, his education and his descent connect him with Plymouth Rock. . . . Harvard . . . [like Oxford] is the epitome of national history. . . . Harvard has educated the United States.[11]

For those skeptical of the importance of the race, the *New York Times* had some scathing words: "There are, perhaps, a few aberrant philosophers in existence who will look down from their serene eminence on this memorable contest, and smile at what they regard as the folly and vanity of mankind. But philoso-

8. Smalley to Reid, 12 September 1869, Reid Papers.
9. Ibid., 27 September 1869.
10. "Young England and Young America," *London Society* 16 (November 1869): 412.
11. *New York Tribune*, 31 August 1869, quoting the *Times* leader of 30 August 1869.

phers never rule the world, and seldom comprehend the
motive-power by which it is governed."[12] "Without making too
much of a boat race," the *Illustrated London News* declared,
"we say with all sincerity, it is calculated to do more in the way
of producing brotherhood than as many hundred-weight of
important documents as would have sunk both boats in the mud
of Father Thames."[13]

It fell to the London *Times,* however, to sound the greatest
note of profundity and to venture a prophecy:

The victory was a victory of education, and here the advantage was all
on our side. We live—not in rowing only—a closer life. The competition is sharper. The lessons of the past are more searching and more
exact. The margin of our lives is so narrow that every possible economy
of strength has been utilized by successive generations. Rowing is with
us a science; it has been developed bit by bit by men who have made
it their business, and knew that in the contests before them the small-
est "wrinkle" told. Thus it happened on Friday that the Oxford Crew
knew precisely the limits of continuous effort—they knew where to
abstain as well as where to abound. The advantage is, however, perhaps, not without its drawbacks, for it may be that nations, like men,
should have some reserve of natural endowments, which should be, as
it were, not brought into tillage, so as to be better able to meet the
days when the progress of others shall have equalized the benefits of
training.[14]

During only one European war in which the United States
was not a participant did an American newspaperman really
excel in its news coverage. This was the Franco-Prussian War of
1870-71, the paper was the *New York Tribune,* and the man
chiefly responsible was George W. Smalley. It has been claimed
with reasonable justice that the *Tribune's* coverage of the war,
at least until after the surrender of Marshall Bazaine at Metz
in October 1870, was superior to that of any other newspaper.
This is fairly generally recognized in American histories of
journalism, though English accounts tend to play up the coverage of the *London Daily News* which operated under a cooperative agreement with the *Tribune.* No phase of Smalley's career
has received comparable attention and praise. Some of the

12. *New York Times,* 28 August 1869.
13. *Illustrated London News,* 4 September 1869, p. 226.
14. *Times* (London), 30 August 1869, leader.

praise has been overly generous and some has fallen short of the merits of his performance.[15]

When on 19 July 1870 France declared war on Prussia there had been only a fortnight of crisis between the two powers. Newspapers recognized the seriousness of the crisis but could not seem to get into gear for war coverage. Smalley was one of those who engaged in frantic preparation; he, rather than the editors of the *Tribune*, determined that the paper should play a major role. The probable costs frightened Whitelaw Reid and brought from him words of caution and pleas to shorten or omit cables—still, he stopped short of ordering full brakes. Smalley's Civil War experiences had given him not only convictions of how to cover a war but stature even in the eyes of a worried editor (who, incidentally, was also an experienced Civil War reporter). He knew firsthand both the value and the fickleness of the telegraph. The failure of the cable in the story of the boat race was still fresh in his memory and he had not forgotten that his great success in reporting the Battle of Antietam had been achieved by taking his account in person to New York. Reid urged him to leave the London post in other hands and to try to get himself attached either to the French or German army. The idea must have had some appeal for Smalley but he rejected it in the belief that the day of the great individual war reporters like William Howard Russell had passed, at least for the purpose of covering a war in its entirety.

The circumstances, Smalley said, called for a "method" rather than for complete dependence upon individual efforts. He disobeyed an order from New York to report to Prussian headquarters and asked that he either be allowed to follow his "method" or be relieved.[16] His correspondence with Reid for this period does not reveal this dramatic confrontation but it does back up his claim that he set the course for reporting the war. "There are in journalism two ways of dealing with a war crisis of this kind," he wrote. "One way is to send into the field

15. He has not always received full credit for organizational work in London while he has been given too much credit for good judgment in selecting field correspondents.

16. George W. Smalley, *Anglo-American Memories* (New York, 1911), pp. 222–23.

everybody you can lay hands on to cover, *tant bien que mal*, as many points as possible, and to take your chance of what may turn up. The other is to choose the best two men available and send one to the headquarters of each army. I preferred the latter, perhaps because there was difficulty in finding good men, and there were but two from whom I expected much good."[17] Actually, Smalley adopted a combination of the two ways and got better results from his shotgun than with the rifle.

The problem of obtaining good men was a real one. The *Tribune* had few regular correspondents in Europe. With the possible exception of Joseph Hance, who held a diplomatic position in Berlin, none was suitable for a field assignment. Through the good offices of American Minister George Bancroft, Hance was given leave from his Berlin post and sent in several good accounts from the Prussian side.[18] After Sir Henry Hozier, a British army officer who had done distinguished reporting in the Austro-Prussian war, was refused permission by the British government to report for the *Times,* Smalley made efforts to obtain his services but without success. The two correspondents upon whom Smalley counted most were M. Méjanel, who was to report from French headquarters, and Holt White, a recent Oriel College graduate who had joined the staff of the *Pall Mall Gazette* but who accepted also £6 a week and expenses from Smalley to report from the Prussian side. Méjanel was the find of Clarence Cook, and White, whom Smalley had never met, was hired on Cook's recommendation.[19] Gustav Müller, a short-lived but brilliant star in reporting the war, was hired quite casually in London where he stopped briefly en route from New York to the battle front to work in an ambulance unit. The *Tribune's* account of the Battle of Gravelotte (called Rézonville in French reports), which was counted a major scoop, was purchased from an employee of the *London Daily News.*[20]

The relations between Smalley and Clarence Cook were al-

17. Ibid., p. 231.
18. Smalley to Bancroft, 29 July 1870 [copy], Reid Papers.
19. Smalley to Cook, 16 July 1870, ibid.
20. Archibald Forbes, "War Correspondence as a Fine Art," *Century* 40 (December 1892): 293.

ready stained and they broke completely under the pressure of reporting the war. Cook was an able writer, especially in the field of art, but highly sensitive and unsuited to the crash effort demanded by Smalley who bombarded him with orders and with recriminations about reports he had not submitted. Smalley does not appear to have given him credit in the home office for recommending Méjanel and White; nor did he blame him for proposing several people who proved to be duds. "Very easy for Smalley sitting in his London Office with a man to do his copying, clipping and making up abstracts and a boy to run his errands, to give orders," Cook complained to Reid. "A difficult thing for a man with only two legs, no office, and dependent on his own exertions to carry out these orders."[21] The situation became so unpleasant that Cook demanded complete independence from Smalley's authority. Reid could scarcely grant such a request at the time and Cook returned to New York to serve as the *Tribune's* art critic.

The jumble of inexperienced people that Smalley sent into the field for the *Tribune* placed a premium on the observance of his "method." His instructions to the people in the field were explicit and remind one of Smalley's own success in reporting the Battle of Antietam:

Each was to find his way to the front, or wherever a battle was most likely to be fought. They were to telegraph to London as fully as possible all accounts of preliminary engagements. If they had the good luck to witness an important battle they were not to telegraph, but, unless for some very peremptory reason, to start at once for London, writing their accounts on the way or on arrival. If they could telegraph a summary first, so much the better; but there must be no delay. The essential thing was to arrive in London at the earliest possible moment. They were to provide beforehand for a substitute, or more than one, who would take up their work during their absence.[22]

No one at the time appreciated as Smalley did the advantages of bypassing the French Prussia censors and of trusting an important account neither to the telegraph nor the mails. All cable news to the United States had to go through London which made his "method" all the more sensible. It was also far more

21. Cook to Reid (n.d), Reid Papers.
22. Smalley, *Anglo-American Memories*, p. 231.

economical to coordinate the activities of the field writers and put their accounts together in London before cabling any of them to New York. One other Smalley innovation that was to prove invaluable to the *Tribune,* especially late in the war, was his arrangement with the *London Daily News* to share all war reports. Whether it was farsightedness or simply luck, Smalley's pick of the *Daily News* was most fortunate. The paper had no great record for war coverage and no experienced reporters. Probably the liberal character of the paper was the determining factor, though possibly no other London daily would have been interested in an alliance with the *Tribune.* As it was, Sir John Robinson, manager of the *Daily News,* was reluctant to form the attachment and agreed only at the insistence of Frank Hill, the paper's editor.[23]

In one way or another the *Tribune's* record was one of uninterrupted success in its war coverage. Joseph Hance sent in reports of early skirmishes when news of any kind was at a premium. The best and earliest account of General Macmahon's defeat at Gravelotte, on 18 August, was written by Moncure D. Conway, an old friend of Smalley's and an occasional contributor to the *Tribune* but at the time employed by the *Daily News.* Smalley solved the problem by purchasing U.S. rights to the story from Conway. The greatest scoop of the war for the *Tribune* was Holt White's account of the French surrender at Sedan. White, who had done nothing of great merit to this point, was at Prussian headquarters where he witnessed the Battle of Sedan on 1 September and learned of the French surrender the following day. With great difficulty, and with considerable danger to himself, he made his way to London, arriving at 5 P.M. on 4 September, totally exhausted, incapable of further effort, with his story as yet unwritten. But after having something to eat, and under Smalley's relentless prodding, he wrote for nearly seven hours while Smalley copied his near-illegible handwriting and at intervals took copy to the cable office.

It was typical of Smalley that he took the sheets he had copied to the cable office in person to be sure that they arrived and

23. Ibid., pp. 224–27.

were sent without delay.[24] Not all of the story got through that night but the following day the *Tribune* was able to publish four columns on Sedan well in advance of any of its New York competitors. Smalley says it was two days later that any part of the London journals had a full account, though the *Pall Mall Gazette,* with whom White had a special agreement (which prevented the *Daily News* from using his story) printed an abridged account on 6 September that White wrote for the paper. White's story was followed in the *Tribune* two days later by one from the French side, this by M. Méjanel who also came in person to London with his account.

The second great coup by a *Tribune* correspondent was of the surrender of Bazaine at Metz. Again the reporter, Gustav Müller on this occasion, brought his story to London. For this account the *Daily News* was able to profit by its alliance with the *Tribune,* publishing the story on the same day as the *Tribune.* A day later the London *Times* was still without direct news and copied the account from the *Daily News,* giving generous credit to that paper and to its correspondent. The *Tribune* correspondents were one-performance people. White, Méjanel, and Müller produced little of note after their single outstanding accounts; Müller, in fact, was not heard from again during the war. Years later Smalley learned that he had returned to New York rather than to France. After the fall of Metz the *Tribune* was largely dependent upon reporters of the *Daily News,* including the great Archibald Forbes. And for the siege of Paris, the *Daily News* had the incomparable Henry du Pré Labouchère. After the fall of Paris in January 1871 Smalley paid the city a brief visit as the bearer of dispatches from the American ministers in London.[25]

The cable news that appeared in the *Tribune* had already been arranged as to sequence, and in some cases it was edited by Smalley in London. Datelines for the field correspondents were maintained and the accounts of individuals warmly praised

24. Ibid., pp. 236–37.
25. The arrangements were made by Smalley's friend Moran (Diary of Benjamin Moran, 1 February 1871, Benjamin Moran Papers, vol. 28, Library of Congress, Washington, D.C.), who had used one of Smalley's agents in this capacity in September 1870 (ibid., 15 September 1870, vol. 26).

when deemed justifiable. The novelty of the procedure puzzled the *Tribune*'s competitors and aroused their suspicions. When they discovered that most of the *Tribune*'s accounts were appearing also in London papers, they became convinced that dirty work was afoot. The complex arrangements that gave the *Daily News* access to some *Tribune* accounts, but not to others, was confusing, and the *Tribune* seems to have taken pleasure in trying to preserve the mystery. On 8 September the *Tribune* made a slighting reference to its arrangement with the *Daily News* when its hand was forced by the *New York Times*:

Our modesty would have prevented any mention of the matter; but since the *Times* has called public attention to it, we will be pardoned for explaining that THE TRIBUNE has of late been under the necessity of furnishing the news to its English as well as its American contemporaries. The *London News* received the account of the *Tribune* correspondent by virtue of an agreement with our London correspondent, not unlike the business arrangement by which the *New York Times* obtained it from the home office.

Smalley felt that the item was boastful and that it would be harmful to his relations with the *Daily News*. He cabled Reid in language that Reid called "peremptory." Reid said he had not seen the offensive item prior to publication but refused to print a refutation. Smalley sent the *Daily News* an apology, requesting that it not be printed unless another London paper took up the case, which apparently none did. "But for my close personal relations with the Editor and Manager," he told Reid, "our alliance would have ended then and there."[26]

War news in the *Tribune* was impressive in quality as well as quantity for which Smalley's selecting and editing were in part responsible. The prestige of the paper was greatly enhanced and the numerous plaudits received were given generous space in its columns. But it was a costly effort: "The expense of discussing [with the home office] the initial organization cost over $100 a day, while, at the height of the excitement, Smalley's

26. Smalley to Reid, 24 September 1870, Reid Papers. On December 2 the *Tribune* printed another statement on the *London Daily News* alliance that Smalley protested vigorously on the grounds that it was untrue and compromising to him personally (Smalley to Reid, 20 December 1870, Reid Papers).

cable bills in four days amounted to $4000."[27] "The *Tribune*'s telegraphic bill, largely payable in gold, was $85,303.51. Its additional bill for correspondence, also mostly payable in gold, was $43,263.46."[28] These were not small items in the modest newspaper budgets of the time. Harry W. Baehr, Jr., in his excellent history of the *Tribune*, regards the expense as "a small price to pay for the privilege of bearing this *quiet tag*" [italics mine] on the front page: "The TRIBUNE is the only newspaper in the United States fully represented by Special Correspondents with both Prussian and French Armies and at leading capitals; and is the only paper receiving full special dispatches. Thus far the *Tribune* dispatches have been used, in an imperfect form, by the *New York Herald, World, Times* and *Sun.*"[29]

Both during and after the war there was discussion of the impact of "American methods" on British journalism. The extent of the impact is difficult to measure. During the war the London journals all increased the speed of their communications. Before the war's end even slow-moving William Howard Russell had hired a special train to rush him to London with a story. The revolution would have come in any case in all likelihood, but George W. Smalley cannot be denied the role of pacesetter. The *London Daily News* became the acknowledged war news leader among London journals and subsequently published its Franco-Prussian War correspondence in two volumes. Little was said then or later by those who extolled the success of the paper about its debt to the *New York Tribune*. Smalley and Robinson, the *Daily News* manager, did not get on well together; Robinson referred to Smalley as a "very Napoleon of journalism,"[30] but the remark may have been more of a barb than a compliment. Smalley was not the man to view his own accomplishments with undue modesty but he openly admitted his indebtedness to

27. Harry W. Baehr, Jr., *The New York Tribune since the Civil War* (New York, 1936), p. 79.

28. From a speech delivered by Whitelaw Reid and reproduced in the *New York Tribune,* 20 June 1879.

29. Baehr, *New York Tribune since the Civil War,* p. 79. The paragraph was run regularly for some months with the final sentence varied to fit the copyists of the preceding day.

30. Joseph Hatton, *Journalistic London* (London, 1882), p. 56.

others; in none of his writings about the Franco-Prussian War did he fail to acknowledge the contributions of the correspondents of the *Daily News* and he was especially generous to Archibald Forbes.[31]

31. Smalley, *Anglo-American Memories,* pp. 225–26.

7. GWS—An Anglo-American Institution

Eighteen seventy-two was a crisis year for the *Tribune*. Horace Greeley's unsuccessful candidacy for the presidency of the United States on the Liberal Republican–Democrat tickets alienated many old friends of the paper and left it in strained relations with the Republican party. Greeley's death late in the year brought on a period of chaos in ownership during which Whitelaw Reid and John Hay resigned temporarily from the editorial staff. Before the end of the year, however, a new group of stockholders returned Reid to the editorship and initiated a period of several decades in which Reid, as publisher and editor and later chief owner, dominated the policies of the paper. Through the seventies the question of costs in operations was a crucial one in determining most of Reid's decisions.[1]

In its European news coverage in the seventies the *Tribune* faced major problems, some of which could not be solved satisfactorily without spending more than Reid was able or willing to spend. Reid was proud of the position of leadership the paper had attained in reporting the Franco-Prussian War but he could not see how to keep up the lavish expenditures necessary to maintaining it. The first solution attempted was a complex arrangement by which Smalley tried to reduce the cost of European news by obtaining European advertisements and by continuing the wartime scheme of control from London. This was

1. Harry W. Baehr, Jr., *The New York Tribune since the Civil War* (New York, 1936), pp. 105–74.

66

Smalley's idea and he gave himself to the work with abandon. His correspondence with Reid on the subject would fill a good-sized volume. In letter after letter he urged the need of maintaining at least a skeleton staff to be ready for another war or major crisis. He reported that the partnership with the *Daily News* could not be continued indefinitely on a basis of gratitude for services rendered in the Franco-Prussian War and that the *New York Herald* was making attractive financial proposals to the *Daily News* for an agreement to replace the unprofitable one it had made with the *Daily Telegraph.* And he defended the costs of the new venture on the ground that the first years of the experiment should not be used to judge the ultimate benefits.

For several years Smalley maintained two offices in London and for a briefer period one in Paris. In his bookkeeping he tried to make a clear distinction between the advertising venture, the newsgathering from the Continent, and his own reporting activities, but the three were difficult to separate. Reid did not help matters by employing an occasional Continental correspondent on his own initiative and by responding to Smalley's plea for a salary increase by authorizing him instead to deduct personal expenses from other accounts. The hope for success of the advertising campaign was based largely on the increasing number of American tourists. Efforts were made to make copies of the *Tribune* available to them on eastbound ships from New York, in hotels, and in other places in London and on the Continent.

Increasing attention to the needs and purchasing power of travelers was apparent in the seventies and even more pronounced in the eighties. An account in the *Tribune* on 4 April 1878 on how to travel in Europe economically could have been entitled "How to See Europe in Some Elegance (Including Ocean Fare) on Less than Five Dollars a Day." London banking houses, which had once served as meeting places and reading rooms, were replaced by organizations that catered specifically to the tourists. The favorite of these organizations was Messrs. Gillig and Company, an American agency located at Charing Cross, West Strand, where Americans were certain to meet fellow countrymen and, for a nominal fee, could "loaf" as much as they liked over a good collection of U.S. papers, have their luggage received and held, and arrange almost any sort of commission.[2] In 1880 Gillig and Company merged with the American Exchange and shortly had ten departures, on six floors of a building, with Henry F. Gillig as managing director. In addition to devoting itself to American travelers in Europe, the firm gave attention to British visitors in America and to migrants to the United States. One estimate of American visitors to Europe in the summer of 1880 was 30,000, guessed to be spending $100,000,000; the estimated number of emigrants from Europe landing in New York City in the first half of 1880 was 177,362.[3]

Other New York papers, the *Herald* included, made efforts to serve the American tourists and to make copies available to America-bound Europeans, but no European press representative abroad had Smalley's faith in the prestige and gain to be had from tourists and emigrants and probably no one worked as hard as he to make something of the potentials of the situation. Before there were adequate facilities elsewhere, he kept files of American newspapers in the London *Tribune* office and encouraged Americans to make use of them. The advertisements in the *Tribune* that resulted from Smalley's efforts constitute an amusing comment on what were presumed by European advertisers to be interests of American travelers. In the *Tribune* on 12 June 1875 there appears a half-page of ads from a variety of London tailors, gunsmiths, ladies' perfume and hat dealers, Madame Tussaud's, a New York magazine, and a person ready to provide secretarial help. From the Continent there were advertisements for the Antwerp Zoo, for six Belgian, two French, ten German, and fifteen Swiss hotels. In another issue for 1875 space was taken by the wine merchants, by S. J. Spark's Anglo-American Agency in Paris (specializing in houses and flats, to be let furnished or unfurnished), by Sunderland and Crane, London, whose specialty was "Gentleman's Drawers, the famous **BELT DRAWERS** that impart in the wearer the most remarkable comfort. Their use, too, has in various ways an unmistakably

2. *New York Tribune,* 1 November 1878.
3. *Anglo-American Times* (London), 14 May and 9 July 1880.

healthy tendency. Efficacious as respects the spare and the corpulent." Two of the largest space buyers were a Turkey and Axminster carpets dealer and Lamplough's "Pyretic Saline, proved to be the best preventative of SMALL-POX, FEVER, AND SKIN DISEASE."

Not least among the many problems the scheme presented was the bookkeeping difficulty. Reid had an audit made for the period from 20 January 1871 to 24 February 1874 by which Smalley was charged with a cash outlay of $69,723.79, which apparently included his salary, but which was incomplete regarding income. On this point Smalley's records and Reid's did not tally. Who was to pay for the supply of copies of the *Tribune* placed on ships sailing from New York and who should bear the costs of the papers sent to the European hotels and advertisers were questions that produced endless disagreement between Smalley and Reid. Smalley was greatly disturbed by the many complaints he received from advertisers who had never received copies of the *Tribune* issue in which their ads appeared. In late 1875 a plan was adopted to systematize the whole arrangement by giving Smalley responsibility for all *Tribune* operations in Europe and a fixed sum of $15,000 annually. This scheme did not work, either. There seemed no way to agree on the space and placement of the advertisers; at least the advertisers were dissatisfied with the treatment they received. Smalley was gradually divested of the business side of his journalistic activities, though he was not at all happy about it.

For roughly two decades—from the *Alabama* claims arbitration in 1872 until the second Cleveland administration beginning in 1893—Anglo-American relations were smooth and relatively friendly. One historian of Anglo-American diplomacy entitles this period "Inactive Relations."[4] Nor were there Continental developments during the time that were unavoidable subjects for coverage by European representatives of the American press. The evolution of the Bismarckian alliance system followed by the Franco-Prussian counter-alliance supplied an abundance of material for thoughtful essays but few dramatic moments. Under

4. R. B. Mowat, *The Diplomatic Relations of Great Britain and the United States* (London, 1925), chap. 20.

such circumstances American newspapers and their European representatives exercised greater choice in their selection of material than when they were faced with major wars, controversies between the United States and European countries, or other exciting affairs. An exception in the way of a major effort at coverage was the Vienna Exposition of 1873, which was so elaborate and carefully planned that it deserves special notice. Reid wanted Smalley to go to Vienna, but Smalley begged off on the plea of heavy work in London. Instead, he persuaded the able art critic W. J. Stillman to go from Italy, Reid sent E. V. Smalley (no relation to G. W.) from the New York office, and Bayard Taylor, diplomat, well-known man of letters, and longtime contributor to the *Tribune,* agreed to attend as star performer for the occasion. Smalley undertook the direction of coverage from London with the same vigor with which he had directed the flow of news in the Franco-Prussian War. He made arrangements as to what should be telegraphed to London, he provided for the rental of a suite of *Tribune* rooms for five months in Vienna, and he tried to use the occasion to strengthen his scheme of advertisements and circulation. "I want to make the paper felt in Vienna as well as Vienna felt in the paper," he wrote Bayard Taylor.[5] The Vienna Exposition brought on a journalistic rivalry not unlike that which attended the coverage of a war, though it is not easy to see why. The great star war reporters of the day, Dr. W. H. Russell and Archibald Forbes, represented the *New York Times* and *London Daily News,* respectively. The *New York Herald* sent Edmund Yates and John Russell Young, along with two German-language writers for the New York German population, in an effort to offset Bayard Taylor.[6]

As indicated earlier the *Tribune*'s policy of financial retrenchment limited its foreign news coverage. It made no attempt at direct reporting of the Russo-Turkish War of 1877-78 and the Congress of Berlin that followed. The alliance with the *London*

5. Smalley to Taylor, 8 April 1873, Bayard Taylor Papers, Cornell University Library, Ithaca, N.Y.

6. Edmund Yates, *Recollections and Experiences,* 2 vols. (London, 1884), pp. 276–84. Yates thought that the *Herald* scored a decided victory over other papers, including the *Tribune* which used the Atlantic cable sparingly.

Daily News had come to an end and the *Tribune* had no corps of available war correspondents of its own. But in George W. Smalley the *Tribune* had the Special Commissioner for the United States for the Paris Exhibition of 1878. It was scarcely an accident that the *Tribune* gave approximately as much space to the exhibition as to the Congress of Berlin. Smalley spent six weeks in Paris writing about the exhibition and the International Literary Congress that followed.[7] Seemingly, Reid tried to rationalize his shortage of reporters. He told the editorial associations of Ohio and New York "that the field for advantages through enterprise in the mere getting of news is about exhausted." The success of the future, he declared, "lie with the story better told; better brains employed in the telling."[8] But if in fact he was allowing circumstances to shape his philosophy of journalism, Reid did make a determined effort to employ people who would present "the story better told." He tried unsuccessfully to persuade John Hay to take Clarence Cook's place in Paris after Cook left during the Franco-Prussian War, but managed to employ Arsène Houssaye who, by his own description, wrote nothing but letters of "worldly gossip," which John Hay and others in the New York office grudgingly translated. On matters of society, art, and literature, Houssaye was the answer to Reid's prayers. Houssaye had been head of the national theater under Napoleon III and he continued to occupy a position of prominence, entertaining lavishly in a princely residence, "a Moorish and Renaissance Mansion" on the Avenue de Friedland. The *Tribune* gave his letters front-page space, headlined his name, and for good measure added his initials at the end of his letters.

Houssaye's letters seem out of place under such an impressive build-up; one suspects that the *Tribune* was consciously playing

7. The "Association Litteraire Internationale" assembled in June 1878 under the presidency of Victor Hugo with only five Americans in attendance, only one of whom had published a book. The American delegation was greatly strengthened by the subsequent arrival of George W. Smalley and Andrew D. White (Thomas Wentworth Higginson, *Cheerful Yesterdays* [Boston, 1898], pp. 311–12).

8. Whitelaw Reid, *Some Newspaper Tendencies: An Address Delivered before the Editorial Associations of New York and Ohio* (New York, 1879).

him up to compensate for the weakness of its political reporting in the seventies. The Paris political correspondent for the early seventies was W. H. Huntingdon, whose letters were often not printed by the paper. Impressed by the talents of Mrs. Crawford, wife of the *Daily News* correspondent in Paris, Smalley hired her to replace Huntingdon, but Reid was not pleased with her writing. On John Hay's recommendation, Reid employed Henry James to write a series of letters from Paris during 1875–76. Reid and other *Tribune* officials thought James's letters moderately successful. Reid was sufficiently happy with them to offer to continue the arrangement though he was unwilling to pay more than twenty dollars a letter. The editor felt that his readers liked a change now and then "except in the case of a few men like Smalley who are perennial favorites. . . ."[9] Then James decided to move to London, which left no place on the paper for him. Besides, he "claimed to have found the *Tribune* task a dreadful bore, supportable only for the money he earned" and he thought that insufficient. Two critics who collected and republished James's *Tribune* letters gave them high praise. Another critic wrote: "All this sort of thing is hardly James the First, let alone James the Second or the Old Pretender; it is Bonny Prince laying about him with a fine careless swing, and all who are interested in James will be grateful for these early yet surprisingly up-to-date by-products of his genius."[10]

Although Henry James wrote his letters for the *Tribune* during a period when Smalley held prime responsibility for the *Tribune*'s European news coverage, he was employed by Reid from New York and was considered outside Smalley's province. So was the novelist Thomas Trollope (Anthony Trollope's brother), who contributed letters from Florence and Rome. Smalley rarely objected to the "extra-help," save on occasions when he was asked to pay these correspondents from the always-short funds at his disposal. Their employment by the editor, however, emphasized the complexity of European news control

9. Reid to Hay, 27 July 1875, in Henry James, *Parisian Sketches: Letters to the New York Tribune, 1875–76,* ed. Leon Edel and Ilse Dusoir Lind (New York, 1957), p. 211.

10. Anonymous review of Edel and Lind's edition of James, *Parisian Sketches,* in the *Times Literary Supplement,* 4 July 1958.

for the *Tribune*. In the last analysis, the editor determined policy, a fact that Smalley did not forget. In the seventies Smalley was grateful for any help he could obtain in finding suitable writers of occasional letters. He was unable to cover the whole front, even in Great Britain. He did not feel qualified to write about some topics, others he did not care to write about, and on others still the *Tribune* editors wished to print views different from those he held. Even though harmony prevailed in the seventies—nothing in the way of opinion differences approached the bitter quarrels over Home Rule in the eighties—the *Tribune* still felt the need to supplement, and even occasionally to offset, its great correspondent.

In spite of Smalley's fondness for writing on the subject of English journalism, the *Tribune* ran a series of letters on the subject, beginning on 5 July 1882, by an English "occasional correspondent" that gave a very different slant from Smalley's. The correspondent was laudatory in his remarks about the *Daily Telegraph*, a paper GWS referred to as "that unspeakable journal." It was quite usual for others to do travel accounts, descriptions of tourist attractions and transportation facilities, and to offer advice to traveling Americans. William Winter, dramatic critic for the *Tribune*, made several trips across the Atlantic to give presumably fresher accounts of English attractions than Smalley could offer. Occasionally, too, there were letters of English gossip of a less sophisticated sort than Smalley was willing to write. In 1882 the *Tribune* ran a series of letters on rural England by Captain Mayer Reid, and, in the following year, Robert P. Porter wrote some thirty letters on "Industrial England," followed by a similar series on "Industrial Germany." Smalley dealt quite knowledgeably and at length with the war scare of 1875 between France and Germany, but he turned over the Balkan crisis the following year to an English writer who was clearly better informed than he. Although Smalley usually paid close attention to prominent Americans who visited England, he did not consider the visiting American evangelists, Messrs. Dwight L. Moody and Ira. D. Sankey, deserving of a single line from his pen. The evangelistic team was too popular in the United States for the *Tribune* to ignore, however, and the paper resorted to printing accounts of the large English audiences and general success of the preachers written in New York and based on information in other New York papers.

The core of the *Tribune*'s problem in European news coverage was the cost of the cable. For a time Reid seems to have thought that if he ignored the question long enough it would go away. Smalley was under orders for several years not to cable any long messages unless explicitly instructed to do so. Dependence upon the cabled news of the press associations was not a satisfactory solution for a journal that prided itself on its individuality and early distinction in cabled news. Smalley complied dutifully though not always gracefully with the imposed restrictions, but he asserted "whether we like it or not the telegraph is our master."[11] Reid often complained about receiving letters containing information already published in the *Herald,* or in some other New York paper, and Smalley just as often replied with a detailed listing of ship sailings and New York arrival times to prove that any tardiness was not his fault.

In late 1879 the *Tribune* launched a Sunday edition, something that the paper had not published since the Civil War. The event marked an important change in Smalley's work. He began a lengthy, regular cable for the Sunday edition, at first entitled "Yesterday in London." Though it subsequently appeared under various headings, it was to continue for most of Smalley's period of service with the *Tribune.* The Sunday cable was often more than a column in length, usually received the left column position on the front page and sometimes appeared in large print. It was published in addition to the several letters Smalley sent each week.

The Sunday cable did not wholly solve the problem, and for several years there was considerable correspondence containing suggestions for other measures. Reid thought Smalley might reduce his letters sharply and try his hand at a daily cable, but to this idea Smalley—the vigorous advocate of the telegraph—strongly objected, chiefly on the ground that it would involve light work for him. "If I am to undertake it myself," he wrote

11. *New York Tribune,* 11 June 1874.

Reid, "it would upset all my present work, all my associations, the growth of so many years, and put an end to all or nearly all letter writing and to opportunities for getting the information on which much of the value of my work depends."[12] Later, in 1886, when Reid ordered a regular Wednesday cable ot 600 to 800 words, Smalley replied sadly from the Durdons, Epsom, one of the residences of Lord Rosebery: "I go to London in the morning to do your dispatch." The truth was that Smalley had become what would later be called a columnist. The transition was gradual, but he had lost interest in trying to stay on top of the latest news, or even of serving as the head of a news-gathering organization. Although Smalley's position was dictated largely by personal considerations, it was professionally sound. The Associated Press left a good deal to be desired in its handling of immediate news, but Smalley could not have competed with it successfully, even if he had wanted to do so.

Smalley reached the age of forty in 1873, and in many respects the forties were the best years of his life. Although he worked hard, his health was generally excellent. His eyes, however, gave him difficulty even then—eventually he became blind—and on one occasion he took a lengthy vacation in order to "recruit" from overwork and strain. Smalley was a big man, blond, with large hands and feet. Julian Hawthorne wrote that "George, even in peaceful London, looked more like a professional bruiser than Tom Gribb and Tom Sayers did."[13] Harry Furniss, who was capable of exaggeration in such matters, reported that Smalley "considered himself a great dandy" and told a story of a visit by Smalley to Poet Laureate Tennyson on which occasion Smalley was dressed "in the pink of fashion; a silk hat of dazzling newness, light summer overcoat, lavender trousers, and patent leather shoes."[14] In 1881 Mrs. Henry Adams, who had an even sharper tongue when talking about the Smalleys than her husband did, remarked that "there is a jaunty, ci-devant young-

12. Smalley to Reid, 2 January 1880, Whitelaw Reid Papers, Library of Congress, Washington, D.C.
13. *The Memoirs of Julian Hawthorne,* ed. Edith Garrigues Hawthorne (New York, 1938), p. 43.
14. Harry Furniss, *My Bohemian Days* (London, 1919), pp. 140–41.

man-of-fashion air about him which riles my sweet temper."[15]

One of the curious things about Smalley is how differently he appeared to different people. In sharp contrast to the portraits presented by Furniss and Mrs. Adams, others show him as conservative in appearance and aloof in manner; still others as warm and modest. The fancy-dress whim could not have lasted long. R. R. Bowker, an American writer associated at the time of his description (1881) with the new *Atlantic Monthly* but earlier with the *Nation,* thought him a "cold-blooded, self-centered man, not taking the trouble to say much but relying on reserved ability."[16] Young Richard Henry Dana, son of the author of *Two Years before the Mast,* was impressed by Smalley's friendliness and refusal to accept credit that he did not consider to be owed him. He was especially struck by Smalley's knowledge of politics in the United States when he predicted rightly that Rutherford B. Hayes would be the Republican party's nominee for president in 1876, but even more impressed with his modesty when he stated that the prophecy had really been that of Mr. Washbourne, then U.S. minister to France.[17]

In fairness to George W. Smalley—since many of his contemporaries delighted in telling and retelling the anecdotes that do not show him in a favorable light—it must be said that he had a considerable capacity for doing favors for his friends. One can wonder how he found time to render so many little services during his busiest periods—to peddle an ode of Bayard Taylor's; to purchase books for Charles Sumner and to arrange for Sumner's entertainment on a London visit in 1872; to carry out some of the whimsical and erratic requests of Emerson on his last visit to England; and to find a temporary manservant for Andrew D. White when he came through London in 1879 on his way to Berlin to serve as U.S. minister to Germany. These, to be sure, were favors to friends, but there are other good deeds in George Smalley's storehouse of grace. He could

15. *The Letters of Mrs. Henry Adams, 1865–1883,* ed. Ward Theron (Boston, 1936), p. 404.

16. English Journal of R. R. Bowker, 1880–81, 22 February 1881, R. R. Bowker Papers, New York Public Library, New York, N.Y.

17. Richard Henry Dana, *Hospitable England in the Seventies: The Diary of a Young American, 1875–1876* (London, 1921), pp. 309, 334–35.

reach into his own pocket to leave funds anonymously at the American legation for an elderly western American ex-judge who was a bare acquaintance and down on his luck. Or, he could devote the time and energy in trying to get financial help for G. Y. Holyoake when he was old and penniless.

Phoebe Garnaut Phillips Smalley was a petite brunette. People who commented on the appearance of the Smalleys together noted the contrast. Most observers thought that Mrs. Smalley was unusually attractive. Even Mrs. Henry Adams, who had tea at the Smalley's home in London in 1879, remarked on the "very pretty house and charming hostess—adopted daughter of Wendell Phillips with whom I went to school at Miss Houghton's before the Deluge."[18] (Several years later, she called Mrs. Smalley a "silly, stout bore.") Julian Hawthorne thought she helped "Bruiser Smalley" in society. Bowker, who seemed determined to find nothing good to say for any member of the family of an old-time enemy of the *Nation*, described her as "an unprofessional beauty, one of the willowy-mosaic-face types," and declared that on a second meeting he talked to her for five minutes without being able to place her.[19] There were five Smalley children, two boys, Phillips and Emerson, named after the two people George Smalley admired most, and three girls, Evelyn Garnaut, Ida, and Eleanor.

In 1873 the Smalleys moved to 8 Chester Place, Hyde Park Square, into a house of sufficient distinction for Moncure D. Conway to describe it at length in an article on English houses:

A hall in which gray and brown shades prevail in dado and paper, where a soft light prevails, and the garish light and noise of the street can hardly be remembered. . . .
To the suite of drawing rooms every excellence must be ascribed. They consist of two large rooms and a large recess, all continuous, whose decorations adapt them to any domestic or social purpose whatever. It is an apartment in which the finest company that could be gathered in London would feel itself in an atmosphere of refinement and taste; it is a place where the mind can equally well find invitation to society or solitude. Perhaps it is the rich Persian Carpet that gives

18. *Letters of Mrs. Henry Adams*, pp. 158–59, 404.
19. English Journal of R. R. Bowker, 22 February and 7 April 1881, Bowker Papers.

such grace. . . . [The wall] paper is of a French tapestry pattern; the golden thread, which is its basis, weaves the colors that are rich but always subdued, and every shade.

The wood used in Mr. Smalley's drawing room is ebonized, and of it there are several cabinets—one displaying some fine specimens of china—pieces supporting beveled mirrors, framed with shelves which display porcelain and other ornaments.[20]

As Edmund C. Stedman wrote in 1890: "For years his [Smalley's] London life at his residence in the select region of Hyde Park Square has been of an ideal type. Many of the foremost men and women of Great Britain, and of his own country, have there received the hospitalities in which he is assisted by the tact and grace of an accomplished wife."[21] A. W. Kinglake, the historian of the Crimean War and a well-established figure in London society, used even stronger language than Stedman: "Years ago it [the *Tribune*] established in London a kindly, highly gifted correspondent, whose charming house has done more than the stateliest embassies could well have achieved toward dispersing old, narrow prejudices, and creating and maintaining good will, affection and friendship between the two great English nations."[22]

Though he became one of the highest paid of all American journalists, Smalley was never in really comfortable financial circumstances. When Reid offered him a chance to buy *Tribune* stock he replied that he could not afford to buy the stock and take a house, too. The costs of leasing and furnishing the Chester Place house were heavy, as was the entertainment that the Smalleys undertook. In repairing and furnishing the house he got into the hands of dishonest people who overcharged him and he had to write to Reid requesting the editor to "strengthen his balance." Reid sent a note to Mr. Ford who handled such

20. Moncure D. Conway, "Decorative Art and Architecture in England," *Harper's New Monthly Magazine* 50 (December 1874): 38–40. The American expatriate artist, George Boughton, whose house is also described by Conway in the same article, is said to have advised his friend Smalley on the decorations, particularly on the choice of woods.

21. Edmund C. Stedman, "George Washburn Smalley," *Harper's Weekly*, 8 November 1890, p. 873.

22. A. W. Kinglake, *The Invasion of the Crimea*, 6th ed. (London, n.d.), 7:499.

affairs for the *Tribune:* "The Herald has been trying to get Smalley away from us and on this account as well as because he is a good fellow who has done us faithful service and has never been highly paid, I would be glad to do this if it isn't too difficult."[23] A few years later Smalley responded indignantly to Reid when the latter, in his reply to another request for funds on account, suggested that Smalley might be living beyond his means. "You say that I am obviously embarrassed financially," he wrote. "It is to the extent of the deductions referred to in my previous letters—no further. I have no debts, properly speaking. The few hundred pounds which I owe for current expenses I should not owe if you had adopted my views. That is all. I am not harassed by creditors, as you seem to think. But I hate being behind hand at all, and I have harassed myself no doubt. When you contrast your expenses with mine, you don't put in the larger family I have on my hands. . . ."[24]

It is virtually impossible to be precise about Smalley's income, judging it from the Smalley-Reid correspondence. The main problem is that sometimes expenses, at least some expenses, were included in the salary arrangements and sometimes they were not, and it is not always possible to tell when they were and when they were not. Also sometimes they talked in dollars, sometimes in pounds gold, and sometimes pounds sterling. The puzzle is even more vexing during the period when Smalley was handling European advertisements and circulation for the paper; as previously noted, Smalley and Reid were thousands of dollars apart in their books. Almost certainly Smalley's salary, exclusive of *Tribune* expenses, exceeded $10,000 annually by the end of 1875. In the eighties it got as high as $14,000 (both figures in gold). In addition, Smalley added to his income by the sale of magazine articles.

Aside from any personal inclinations, virtually all representatives of foreign newspapers in London tried to live well and to achieve a position of acceptable social standing for professional reasons. Max Schlesinger, who died in 1881 after many years of representing the *Cologne Gazette* in London, was a member of

23. Undated note, apparently late 1873, Reid Papers.
24. Smalley to Reid, 9 August 1878, ibid.

the Garrick Club and entertained widely in English and foreign literary and artistic circles. A number of American correspondents had to give up their London posts because they could not make ends meet. When Dr. G. W. Hosmer of the *New York Herald* left London in 1873, Benjamin Moran reported that he was the third *Herald* man to leave in seven years for financial reasons: "These gentlemen come here to live quietly but they end up living at the rate of about £5,000 a year and Bennett then recalls them. Not one of them has been proof against the temptations of London Society to live beyond their means."[25] Smalley survived the demands of London through his own wits. Neither he nor his wife had an inheritance worth mentioning. It was Smalley's belief that the social position of a journalist depended upon the journalist himself. "He will not be admitted (to any level of society) because he is a journalist, nor excluded because he is a journalist. If a man really cares for society, and has good manners, he may go almost anywhere he will, on condition of making himself agreeable."[26] Throughout the seventies Smalley's associates continued to be journalists, liberal politicians, men of letters, and an occasional actor, artist, or academician. His first close friend among the leading peers was Lord Rosebery and his first visit to Dalmeny Park, the ancestral Rosebery home near Edinburgh, was in November 1880. During Smalley's time there was no tendency on the part of the Americans in London to constitute an American colony—as there was, for instance, in Paris—which made mingling with the English as natural as it was professionally advantageous. When in 1881 U.S. Minister James R. Lowell gave an all-American dinner in honor of his own and George Washington's birthday, Mrs. Smalley said it was the first time in their fourteen years of residence the Smalleys had attended an exclusively American dinner party.

At no time in his career was Smalley freer to choose his own topics and voice his own slants than in the seventies. He was moving gradually toward the right in his views but so was the

25. Diary of Benjamin Moran, 26 September 1873, Benjamin Moran Papers, vol. 36, Library of Congress, Washington, D.C.
26. *New York Tribune,* 27 December 1877.

Tribune. He was still liberal but somewhat more cautiously so than he had been earlier; he was still critical of the Tories but more temperate about them than he had been earlier. Fate had been kind to him. "To be both foreigner and a journalist is . . . to combine as many advantages and immunities as this world can be expected to afford one man," he declared.[27]

More specifically regarding his views, GWS was still critical of the royal family, especially of the Prince of Wales. In the London letters of the *Tribune,* the prince appears as an amiable wastrel. When Edward made a voyage to India, Smalley commented "the six month's journey will enable the Prince—living all the while at public costs—to economize nearly half of his year's income, and that this half will benefit his creditors."[28] He was disgusted with the eulogies of Theodore Martin in his "introduction" to the memoirs of Prince Albert, unable to see how a man with a respectable literary reputation "could sink so low."[29] Nor did Queen Victoria entirely escape his acid pen—he often noted her playing of favorites, especially her slighting of Gladstone and her generous treatment of Disraeli. Few subjects aroused the American's ire more than that of Bonapartism, and he felt that the Queen was noticeably pro-Bonaparte, even after the death of Napoleon III. He called Napoleon III "the crowned assassin who kept France under his heel for nigh twenty years,"[30] and declared with satisfaction on the death of the emperor's son, "We have never had much liking in America for the bastard Bonapartism of which this unlucky boy was . . . the representative."[31]

Still, Smalley was at his best, or near best, in his description of events that included royal pageantry. The *Tribune* gave him special praise for his account of the opening of Parliament in 1880:

Our accomplished London Correspondent is seen at his best in describing the recent pageant at Westminster. His letters to the *Tribune*

27. Ibid., 24 October 1877.
28. Ibid., 31 July 1875. See also ibid., 23 September and 5 October 1874.
29. Ibid., 26 December 1877.
30. Ibid.
31. Ibid., 3 January 1884.

have been recognized by so high a literary authority as *The Spectator* as models of newspaper correspondence on contemporaneous history, and American as well as English readers fully appreciate the merits of his descriptive work and political philosophy. This account of the opening of Parliament contains the evidence of his eyes, rather than the conclusions of his judgment respecting the tendencies of English politics. It is a graphic picture etched by a strong hand. The moral is pointed in the quizzical quotation at the end: "It is a comfort to think what a jolly smash we shall make some day of this Japanese mummery."[32]

In 1875 Disraeli received words of praise from Smalley over the purchase of the Suez Canal shares. GWS declared this act "probably the most important step in British foreign policy since 1815" and considered it strange that Gladstone, "so acute in perceiving other things can never perceive what the rest of the world is thinking." But this did not really mark a departure in Smalley loyalties. "A man must write what he believes," Smalley declared, "and for my part, I find it impossible to believe in the sincerity of Lord Beaconsfield. To me he is the most sinister figure in English political life since Lord North; and being a man of incomparably finer abilities than Lord North, is capable of incomparably more mischief than George III's head clerk."[33]

The editors of the *Tribune* occasionally roused themselves to use strong words—they called Disraeli as "unscrupulous as Machiavelli" in his acquisition of Cyprus in 1878, but they had no great interest in the Near East and were content to do an occasional mild echo of Smalley's strong views. Smalley was consistently pro-Russian and quite worked up about the English "war mongers." In summing up conservative foreign policy in 1879 he declared:

The Government have brought Parliament into discredit by withdrawing in great measure the whole foreign policy of the country from the control and knowledge of Parliament. In every important matter of foreign policy, Lord Beaconsfield, and his satellites have determined what should be done. They have refused to let the country or its representatives to their councils until it was too late for remonstrances or

32. Ibid., 22 February 1880. In his letter Smalley identifies the author of the quotation only as a "Member of Parliament of much distinction." See also Appendix C.
33. Ibid., 6 June 1878.

opposition to alter the course of events. The Berlin Treaty, the Afghan War, the Zulu War, the Egyptian troubles, have all been dealt with in accordance with Lord Beaconfield's views, some as far as they were modified by popular feeling. Public meetings and the public press have had more influence than Parliament has had.[34]

When it became apparent that Lord Salisbury would succeed Lord Beaconsfield as leader of the Conservatives, Smalley wrote: "I believe the Toryism of Lord Salisbury is impossible."[35] That was in 1881. When a new Tory journal called *London* was launched in 1877, the future "Tory squire" wrote: "If I were a Tory, I should read it with horror; for every form of mental activity must be, in the long run, deleterious to conservatism. Not being a Tory, I find it extremely amusing . . . and I should like above all things to know who are the men who have hidden their light so long under a Tory bushel."[36]

Smalley supported the Liberals consistently though in varying degrees of warmth. He favored Gladstone over the old Whig leaders and found occasional opportunities to correspond with the Liberal leader. Once he wrote to ask for clarification on several points in a speech Gladstone had delivered, again to quote private statements on the attitudes of Gladstone and Disraeli toward the Confederacy during the American Civil War, and once to send the Liberal leader copies of his letters to the *Tribune* on the Midlothian Campaign of 1879.

When he criticized a Gladstonian speech he wrote: "It is with sincere regret that I have felt called upon to attack . . . a Liberal statesman for whose splendid services to the Liberal cause I have the most profound respect."[37] The *Tribune* correspondent was never more enthusiastic over Gladstone than in his reports of the Midlothian Campaign of 1879 which he followed from beginning to end. In one cable he asserted: "It is the universal admission that never did an English statesman evoke equal enthusiasm. No public demonstration during this

34. Ibid., 30 August 1879.
35. Ibid., 2 April 1881.
36. Ibid., 24 February 1877.
37. Smalley to Gladstone, 16 February 1872, William E. Gladstone Additional Manuscripts, 44433, f186, British Museum, London.

generation has approached this Scotch uprising."[38] From Edinburgh he wrote: "Mr. Gladstone has now delivered three elaborate orations on three succeeding days, each of great length, each a masterpiece, each a distinct and well-considered execution of a separate part in an elaborate programme, a programme which, as a whole, aims at nothing less than the overthrow of a powerful government by *an appeal* to the sovereign people."[39]

No topic was more of a certainty for the American correspondent in London than the activities of the U.S. ministers to the Court of St. James. Since Smalley viewed his role as that of an unofficial ambassador of sorts, he was even more committed to watching over the activities of the ministers than were others. He was delighted in 1869 with the appointment of John Lothrop Motley, a friend and classmate of Wendell Phillips at Harvard, and wrote Charles Summer to express his pleasure: "I suppose we owe Mr. Motley's appointment to you. I beg to thank you for sending us a minister who will really represent America."[40] When Motley was abruptly dismissed the following year, an act usually regarded as a thrust at Sumner by President Grant, Smalley was unable to say much because the *Tribune* sided with Grant in the controversy, but he did not forget. Motley's death in 1877 gave him an opportunity to reopen the question with sufficiently strong charges against Grant's unfair treatment of the minister to cause the then ex-president to issue a public statement in his own defense accusing Smalley of unjust and inaccurate statements.[41]

For Motley's successor, General Robert C. Schenck, Smalley had no good words, and he reported at length on the minister's connection with the infamous Emma Mine. Happily, he and the *Tribune* were in agreement concerning General Schenck. Editors and correspondent were again of like mind in 1876 in denouncing the U.S. Senate for rejecting the nomination of R. H. Dana as minister to Great Britain. From London Smalley had to play

38. *New York Tribune,* 7 December 1879.
39. Ibid., 10 December 1879. Smalley's reports give excellent evidence of the atmosphere and public reactions to the speeches.
40. Smalley to Sumner, 14 May 1869, Charles Sumner Papers, vol. 92, Houghton Library, Harvard University, Cambridge, Mass.
41. *New York Tribune,* 23 February 1878.

second fiddle to the bitter denunciatory language of the *Tribune* editorials,[42] though he reported all the evidence he could find in the British press that disapproved of the Senate's action, and wrote a letter to the *Times* in language so strong that the editor omitted portions of it.[43]

In his comments on Edwards Pierrepoint who received the appointment, Smalley was correct and noncommittal. He was more kindly disposed toward the elderly John Welsh who came next in the rapid parade of U.S. ministers in the seventies. The great appointment for Smalley during his whole period of service in London was that of James Russell Lowell in 1880. The two men were already acquainted, but the great intimacy between them came after Lowell's appointment as minister and lasted long afterward. Their friendship included the two families as well, and more properly belongs in a narrative focused on a later period.[44]

Ex-President Grant's European tour beginning in mid-1877 presented Smalley with a plethora of delicate problems. Foremost was the obligation to uphold the dignity of an ex-president of his own country, a responsibility that he felt keenly. Yet he was committed to the *Tribune*'s and his own critical attitude toward Grant the politician, especially during Grant's second administration. Smalley had railed at the British press for the relish with which it had reported the scandals of that administration but had agreed fully with his own paper's anti-Grant position. To further complicate matters, Grant on his travels was in the hands of the rival *New York Herald*, and was being squired about by Smalley's old and dear friend, John Russell Young, now an employee of the *Herald*. As Smalley described the situation, Grant had captivated "the versatile and fertile journalist who had acted as a sort of civil and political aide-de-camp in his recent journeys, and who works the press for him with untiring energy."[45]

42. See editorial, 20 March 1876, ibid.
43. *Times* (London), 14 April 1876.
44. Smalley's letters to Lowell are in the James Russell Lowell Papers, Harvard University, Cambridge, Mass, and Lowell's letters to Smalley (the few that were preserved) are in the Henry E. Huntington Library, San Marino, Calif.
45. *New York Tribune*, 17 July 1877.

Smalley could report with detached amusement a dinner given by journalist Young for Grant at which the guests were nearly all journalists. But he became incensed over any hint in the British press that the ex-president was not being given proper deference or accorded proper preference in entertainment. He could do a tongue-in-cheek performance if necessary, as when he denied with unnecessary vigor a rumor that Minister Pierrepoint had had to solicit dinner invitations for the visitor. The death of ex-Minister Motley in London just after Grant's arrival was embarrassing to everybody. Grant and Pierrepoint did not attend the funeral but they attended the memorial services at Westminster Abbey where Dean Stanley, unaware of their plans to attend, delivered a eulogy on his late friend Motley. All in all, Smalley walked the tightrope during Grant's visit successfully. A few years later, when Grant himself died, Smalley served on the committee to arrange memorial services in Westminster Abbey and took special pains to assure the attendance of prominent Englishmen, including William E. Gladstone.

8. *American Tory in England*

Radical in the sixties, moderate Liberal in the seventies, Tory in the eighties and after—that is the way George W. Smalley appeared to his contemporaries. As labels go, these are more accurate than most. He changed his position on some basic issues and got credit for changing on others by the time-honored practice of standing still. He shifted markedly in his attitude toward the British royalty and nobility, for example, but did not change his views perceptibly on labor questions. He was never really sympathetic with anything that could be called socialistic but he became violent and even irrational on the subject. In the sixties he did not object to the cooperative movement; in the eighties he called Lord Rosebery socialistic for a mild proposal to reform the House of Lords; and in the early nineties he called Sir William Harcourt a Socialist for proposing a budget that was slightly harder on the rich than had been customary in English budgets. There was some justice in the charge that Smalley had become more Tory than the Tories.

It is no great rarity for a man to shift his political convictions and allegiances in the course of a lifetime. Smalley was sufficiently complex—he had all sorts of attitudes that do not fit into a neat pattern of liberalism, or toryism, or under any of the large political umbrellas—to make his case of some interest. He was a vigorous defender of American protectionism even when it strained Anglo-American relations. Also, his transition from one camp to another was erratic and often unpredictable. But his views are important because they were the focal point of controversy and aroused widespread interest. As the best-known American journalist resident in Europe, he attracted attention that other correspondents could not rival. Although the *Tribune* did not have a circulation sufficiently large to rank it as a paper of mass appeal, its readers included many persons of influence. In addition, Smalley was often quoted in other journals.

The issue that brought on Smalley's shift in party allegiance in England was Irish Home Rule, a matter hard to define in terms of theoretical political principles. He broke with Gladstone and the Liberal party on the point, endorsed the Union-Conservative coalition, became critical of Gladstone from many angles, and ultimately became a wholehearted supporter of the Conservatives. The Irish question was not a burning issue in the seventies and Smalley had little to say about it. He was critical of the "filibustering methods" of the Irish members of Parliament, but he supported Gladstone's Irish Relief Bill in the mideighties. By 1882, however, he was sufficiently anti-Irish in the tone of his reports for James Redpath, writing for the *Tribune,* to charge: "G.W.S. is cordially disliked by Irish in America, and he seems to reciprocate their unfriendship. His testimony ought, therefore, to be entitled to great weight with American believers in the English system of rule in Ireland, of which, I think he is not only the most zealous, but by far the ablest exponent either in the American or British Press."[1]

The charge brought on a spirited though polite exchange of letters in the *Tribune* in which Smalley denied that he was anti-Irish or hated by the Irish, at least the "right kind of Irish." Redpath, founder of the Redpath Lyceum, and Smalley had known each other as fellow correspondents in the Civil War, and during 1880–81 Redpath had been designated by the *Tribune* to make an extensive examination of conditions and opinions in Ireland. This was only one of a number of attempts by the *Tribune* to counter its London correspondent's views on the Irish question by finding someone else to give a different view. Justin McCarthy, journalist and M.P. for Ireland, pre-

1. *New York Tribune,* 29 May 1882.

sented the case for the Irish in a series of letters in 1882.[2] Later, T. P. Gill, another Irish M.P., wrote for the *Tribune* during a considerable period for the same purpose. Once Smalley "retired" for several months while Henry Lucy took over his weekly cable and letter.[3]

Actually, Reid and his *Tribume* associates had little interest in Home Rule for its own sake. Their concern was with the effect of the paper's attitude on the Irish Americans. Probably the number of Irish American subscribers to the *Tribune* was very few, but their importance lay in their political strength. They must not be alienated by a journal that took seriously its political influence and whose editor-owner developed political ambitions. Goldwin Smith believed that "there is no chance for either party in America if the Irish vote is thrown solidly against it,"[4] and his view, rightly or wrongly, was generally held. The correspondence between Reid and Smalley on the correspondent's treatment of the Irish question was boring and endless. The two men covered the same ground time and time again. Reid complained, cajoled and sometimes commanded his reporter either to say nothing on the subject or at least to refrain from interpretation. Occasionally, not often, the *Tribune* took an opposite stand to Smalley in editorials. This happened in 1887 when Smalley presented the Balfour Coercion Bill as essential to the preservation of law and order while the *Tribune* editorially opposed it. More frequently, passages or entire letters thought to be offensive to the Irish were simply not printed.

At best it was an awkward and unsatisfactory situation for everyone, and Smalley was not willing to be helpful. He simply refused to admit that he was biased in his reporting. When Reid told him that *Tribune* office opinion considered his reporting of the 1886 Home Rule Bill "bitterly anti-Irish," he answered that the charge was simply not true. It may be, he admitted, that a

2. Ibid., 11, 18, and 25 June 1882.
3. Henry W. Lucy, *Sixty Years in the Wilderness* (New York, 1909), pp. 93–94. Lucy is in error about the time this occurred and the immediate reason for it. He says it was during the Home Rule campaign of 1886 and that Reid was then a candidate for the vice-presidency of the United States. Actually the substitution took place in 1890.
4. Goldwin Smith in the *Spectator* 62 (1889):566.

"word or a phrase indicating my doubt of the wisdom of Mr. Gladstone's bill escapes me at times, but the dispatches on the whole are rigidly impartial."[5] A year later when Reid cabled, "Anti-Irish partisanship in your dispatches again becoming offensive and damaging," Smalley replied that he had been asked by men who had seen his dispatches whether he "had become a Home Ruler." It should be said for Whitelaw Reid that he never questioned the sincerity of his correspondent's views. Nor did Smalley deny his private opinions; he simply insisted that he was reasonably impartial in his reporting.[6] Compared to some British critics of Home Rule, Smalley was indeed mild. He criticized the *Times,* for example, for the rancor of its denunciations of Home Rule and he was far too good a lawyer to be taken in by the forged letters that the *Times* accepted as valid Parnell documents.[7]

Most Smalley critics who took the trouble to try to explain his anti-Home Rule views drew inferences that questioned the correspondent's honesty and integrity. He had succumbed to the allurements of the "aristocratic drawing rooms," or he had been subverted by social recognition. It is a fact that the Home Rule issue created a bitter social as well as a political split in the ranks of the Liberals and that, in general, the more aristocratic elements broke with the party to become the Union wing of the Conservatives. It is equally true that Smalley became more openly snobbish in the eighties and that he delighted in invitations to the homes of the aristocrats and in his club memberships. Even Reid, himself a snob, liked to twit Smalley about his social life. But to use these facts as the explanation of Smalley's views not only discredits the man but makes little sense. Possibly there was something of the Boston Brahmin's contempt of the Irish in Smalley and possibly his Protestant upbringing left him with a lack of sympathy for Roman Catholicism. There is no reason to assume that his Irish views were anything less, or more, than opinions honestly arrived at.

5. Smalley to Reid, 19 June 1886, Whitelaw Reid Papers, Library of Congress, Washington, D.C.

6. Reid to Smalley and Smalley to Reid, 6 April 1887, ibid.

7. *New York Tribune,* 22 January 1888.

For some time after Smalley had become antagonistic to Gladstone's Irish policy, he continued his appreciations of the Great Liberal on other scores. In December 1882 he wrote: "Liberals of other countries than England are hardly less indebted to you than those of the Empire on which you have conferred such vast and various benefits. Pray allow me to say how much delight I have personally in the recognition and homage which came to you from all over the world, and believe me, dear Mr. Gladstone, with deep regard and respect."[8]

In 1884 Smalley was present at Brechin Castle when Gladstone made some apparently casual remarks indicating his high regard for George Washington and his desire to promote good relations among the English-speaking peoples. Smalley saw in the remarks both an excellent journalistic opportunity and chance to improve Anglo-American relations, and wrote Gladstone asking permission to quote him. The request resulted in a carefully drawn, remarkably laudatory statement on Washington:

When I first read in detail the Life of Washington, I was profoundly impressed with the moral elevation and greatness of his character; and I found myself at a loss to name among the statesmen of any age or country many, or possibly any, who could be his rival. In saying this I mean no disparagement to the class of politicians, the men of my own craft and cloth, whom, in my own land and my own experience, I have found no less worthy than other men of love and admiration. I could name among them those who seem to me to come near even to him. But I will shut out the last half century from comparison: I will then say that if, among all the pedestals supplied by history for public characters of extraordinary nobility and purity, I saw one higher than all the rest, and if I were required for a moment's notice to name the fittest occupant for it, I think my choice, at any time during the last 45 years, would have lighted, and would now light, upon Washington.[9]

Smalley was elated, of course, as were the *Tribune* editors, but there were complications that held up the publication of the document. When Gladstone gave his statement to Smalley in early October 1884, the presidential campaign was in full stride.

8. Smalley to Gladstone, 18 December 1882, William E. Gladstone Additional Manuscripts 44478, f125, British Museum, London.

9. Extract copy of letter, Gladstone to Smalley, 4 October 1884, Gladstone Add. MS, 44487, f258. I do not know the location of the original.

The *Tribune* was ardently supporting James G. Blaine, the "Plumed Knight" whom American jingoes counted on to pursue a hostile policy toward the British Empire. Blaine, moreover, had Irish blood in his veins, a fact that appealed to the Irish Americans. When E. A. Hamilton, Gladstone's secretary, wrote Smalley after three months to ask for the cause of delay, Smalley answered rather lamely that it had seemed wise to let the "effervescence of the Presidential campaign subside."[10] When the Gladstone letter was finally published in February it was accompanied by comments from Smalley urging stronger ties between the English-speaking peoples. There was some favorable comment but the whole thing was too much for the *Times*. The "Thunderer" declared that it was incongruous to associate the name of Washington, who had led the disruption of the empire, with talk of an alliance, and pointed out that the larger half of the English-speaking people "exclude by rigid tariff" the commerce and intercourse upon which an alliance would have to be based; finally, the leader declared that no policy could appease the hatred of the Irish, also an English-speaking race.[11]

In his writings about Gladstone's later years, Smalley allowed his emotions to get the upper hand of his judgment. "Down to 1885," the correspondent wrote, "he was content to be a Liberal, and the English Liberal was just as conservative as the Tory on social problems; often more so." True perhaps, but, the correspondent continued, eventually Gladstone became "open to every new problem behind which there were any votes." If he had but followed his best instincts, he would have been a "bulwark against the rising tide of radicalism." Instead, "he drifted away from his anchorage. His perfidy to the cause of the Union drew other perfidies in its train."[12] Some of Smalley's strictures were unnecessarily petty. When the one-time Latin student at Yale reviewed the Liberal leader's translations of the odes of Horace, he concluded that the translator neither knew Latin nor understood Horace. He even indulged in slighting

10. Smalley to Hamilton, 16 January 1885, Gladstone Add. MS 44489.
11. As reported in the *Anglo-American Times* (London), 20 February 1885.
12. *New York Tribune*, 12 June 1892.

remarks about Gladstone's poor game of whist.[13] Still, compared to the radicals in his party, Gladstone was a "giant among pygmy followers." When the Grand Old Man retired, Smalley wrote his friend Andrew White: "Gladstone is a weight off the Radical neck,—a rope off as one of them described it to me, and the pace is distinctly faster since he withdrew. Liberalism is a spent force. Socialistic Radicalism has shoved it in a corner."[14]

One of Smalley's specialties was describing men. In the early nineties when the bugaboo of socialism replaced Home Rule in Smalley's mind as the greatest danger of the time, few of the radicals in the Liberal party escaped attack and even old friends who were not radicals came under fire with absurd charges. Lord Rosebery was called "this young socialist of the peerage who has no censure for socialism and nothing but censure for Lord Salisbury."[15] He wrote about Sir William Harcourt's budget of 1894: "I do not believe that ultimately the Liberal Party will have much cause to be grateful to the Chancellor of the Exchequer for his socialistic finance. No state can base its financial system permanently on spoilation, or even on avowed discrimination against certain classes and flagrant injustice to minorities."[16]

Happily, the friendship between Smalley and both Rosebery and Harcourt survived such remarks. The official biographers of each man quote from Smalley appraisals.

There are scores, possibly hundreds, of biographical sketches in Smalley's newspaper letters, many of which were republished in his book, *Studies of Men* (1895) and *Anglo-American Memories* (first and second series, 1910 and 1911). Most of the newspaper sketches were sufficiently well done to be reprinted without change. They are admirably drawn and there is rarely a dull one. He wrote from the viewpoint of the personal observer, told when and under what circumstances

13. Ibid., 13 May 1894.
14. Smalley to White, 8 July 1894, Andrew D. White Papers, Cornell University Library, Ithaca, N.Y.
15. *New York Tribune,* 15 May 1892.
16. Ibid., 5 August 1894.

he knew the person, and usually managed to suggest the importance of the teller of the tale. "What may be learnt from his sketches," the *Times Literary Supplement* reviewer of the second series of his *Memories* declared, "is the art of introducing the relevant detail, the characteristic note."[17] Godkin's *Nation*, which almost never had a good word for Smalley, says that the author appears "oracular and omniscient" and "sometimes patronizing," but even the *Nation* felt that the sketches were superior.[18] In the *Library of American Literature*, published under the editorship of Smalley's friend E. C. Stedman between 1887 and 1899, two of the three Smalley writings included are biographical sketches (of Louis Blanc and Bismarck). Smalley was given more space in this publication than any other journalist.[19]

Aside from Theodore Roosevelt, whose many-faceted character and varied policies kept Smalley in a continual state of uncertainty about him, Joseph Chamberlain seems to have been Smalley's greatest puzzle for biographical treatment. When the man from Birmingham became a British national figure, Smalley was alarmed over his views, and Sir Charles Dilke became concerned over the way the *Tribune* correspondent was presenting Chamberlain to the Americans. Dilke, at the time a friend of both Chamberlain and Smalley, tried unsuccessfully to effect a reconciliation. Chamberlain responded to Dilke's invitation to meet Smalley with "he may be as cantankerous as he damn pleases for ought I care, especially as he writes in American papers which I never see."[20] For his part, Smalley remained skeptical, believing Chamberlain to be engaged in a "calculated effort . . . to foment that struggle between classes to which he looks forward with eagerness." A meeting between the two men was arranged in Dilke's study, but even Dilke felt that the accomplishments were negligible. Later, when Chamberlain

17. *Times Literary Supplement*, 25 April 1912.
18. *Nation*, 20 June 1895, p. 482.
19. Edmund C. Stedman and Ellen Mackay Hutchinson, eds., *A Library of American Literature*, 11 vols. (New York, 1887–89).
20. Memoirs 113, Charles Dilke Papers, vol. 62, no. 43935, British Museum, London. This incident occurred in 1881.

broke with the Liberal party over Home Rule, married an American, and began publicly advocating closer Anglo-American ties, Smalley changed the tone of his public comments though he never relinquished some of his earlier suspicions.[21]

Although political figures were Smalley's most frequent subjects for biographical treatment, his descriptions included people in a wide variety of fields—explorers, churchmen, artists, musicians, schoolmen, poets, historians, and actors. He was never happier than when reporting on the London state, especially if his subjects were Sarah Bernhardt and Sir Henry Irving. He got to know Sarah Bernhardt on one of her early London visits and never recovered from her magnetic spell. She gave him permission to make the first announcement of her 1880 visit to the United States, and he undertook to pave a golden way for her with private messages to friends and by letter after letter in the *Tribune,* all written in ecstatic admiration.

Visits to the United States by leading English or Continental figures were natural topics for discussion for European representatives of the American press. Matthew Arnold consulted Smalley about numerous details on the occasions of both of his visits in the 1880s. Smalley's admiration for Arnold was unstinted. "His friendship was a possession impossible to value too highly," he wrote, "but to the influence of his writing I owe more than to almost any of his time. This debt I share with others—with at least a whole generation." It was in large part because of his high regard for Arnold, and his belief that whatever Arnold said should be taken with utmost seriousness, that he took greater umbrage than did most Americans at Arnold's critical remarks about the United States and proceeded to take him to task in his letters to the *Tribune.* Their private correspondence, rather more amiable on Arnold's part than on Smalley's, ended with Arnold's sudden death in 1888. It was published in part by

21. *New York Tribune,* 28 October 1887 and 2 December 1888. Smalley vigorously denied the charge of W. T. Stead (*Pall Mall Gazette* [London], 27 October 1887) that he was serving as Chamberlain's mouthpiece when the latter was appointed chief commissioner to try to settle the fisheries dispute between the United States and Canada, but wrote up Chamberlain's marriage as a great step forward in bettering Anglo-American relations.

Smalley in his *Tribune* letters and later, in its entirety, in his book, *London Letters*.[22]

James G. Blaine's visit to Europe in 1887 was the occasion for a Smalley plunge into American domestic politics. Blaine's unsuccessful campaign for the American presidency in 1884 had only blunted temporarily the *Tribune*'s hope that he would succeed ultimately, a hope that Smalley shared fully. As John Hay, who was also in England in the summer of 1887, wrote Reid: "Smalley gave all of his time to him [Blaine] and you know his range of acquaintance."[23] Smalley's pleasure at being able to introduce Blaine to his "range of acquaintance" was sometimes greater than that of the acquaintances. "I dine at the Garrick with Smalley to meet some man who (Smalley says in his note) is to be the next President of the U.S.," Lord Wolseley told his wife, but he added, "He does not mention the name, but if he did it would convey nothing to either you or me."[24] Smalley could not ignore the fact that Blaine was regarded on both sides of the Atlantic as anti-British, but he persuaded himself that with the proper tutelage both Blaine and leading Britishers would become more appreciative of each other. He also thought that the American public, or perhaps only the "best element" of the public, would be favorably impressed with a good reception by Blaine in England. His dispatches during the period of the visit overflow with accounts of Blaine's successes with the "best English people": "No doubt Mr. Blaine is pretty generally regarded here as a strong political opponent of England. But the best English people are delighted

22. *New York Tribune*, 6 and 13 May 1888; George W. Smalley, *London Letters and Some Others*, 2 vols. (London, 1890), 1:337–52. As usual the *Nation* found Smalley's role amusing: ". . . public attention has been drawn to the modern Damon and Pythias, and to the estrangement threatened by the untimely publication of the [Arnold] article. One could hardly resist the conviction that if Mr. Arnold had submitted his manuscript to Smalley beforehand, the distressing consequences would have been avoided" (*Nation*, 10 May 1888, p. 377).

23. Hay to Reid, 6 August 1887, *Letters from John Hay and Extracts from His Diary* (printed but not published, 1908).

24. Lord Wolseley to Lady Wolseley, 8 April 1887, in *The Letters of Lord and Lady Wolseley, 1870–1911*, ed. Sir George Arthur (London, 1922), p. 246.

to see him and the personal impression he has made is very great. Indeed, I will take the liberty of saying that no American holding no official position has within my recollection been more warmly received or so much liked and admired."[25]

Smalley was not only Blaine's social guide and reporter but his semiofficial spokesman. He assured the American public of Blaine's good health and intention to remain abroad "until next year," despite rumors to the contrary on both counts, and continued to give authoritative information even after Blaine, accompanied by John Hay, had gone on to the Continent. He reported Blaine's reception by the Prince of Wales in Hamburg—though he was not present—and declared that the prince had gone out of his way to greet Blaine in public parks no less than three times. Blaine was in Paris in December when President Cleveland in his annual message to Congress took a strong antitariff stand. Although an avowed protectionist, Blaine had not emphasized his position and he now chose to deliver a blast against the president, taking a strong protectionist stand. Smalley, who inferred that he helped to persuade Blaine to make a public statement, went to Paris, obtained a stenographer, planned his questions carefully, and cabled a three-column interview to the *Tribune*.[26]

The *Tribune* was as overjoyed as Smalley and declared that the interview was an "immense sensation"; that the general Republican reaction was to the "trumpet sound of a magnificent victory in 1888 . . . that they were willing to talk it over [Blaine's statement] as a lecture on political economy or as a letter of acceptance of the nomination in '88—it was all the same to them."[27] The build-up was impressive. The *Tribune* felt certain of its candidate. The interview was a striking triumph for Smalley. But alas! Blaine subsequently decided not to be a candidate for the party nomination.

One of Smalley's most admired accounts was his description of Queen Victoria's jubilee celebration in 1887. John Hay thought it gave a better idea "than if you had seen it yourself."

25. *New York Tribune*, 1 July 1887.
26. Ibid., 8 December 1887.
27. Ibid., 9 December 1887.

By the mid-eighties Smalley was leaving the coverage of spot news almost entirely to the Associated Press, which had made London its European headquarters and had improved its trans-Atlantic service enormously. Although Smalley occasionally sent cables other than his Saturday cable for the Sunday edition, he was not required to and had more freedom of movement and of topic selections than he once did.

Periodically he went to the Continent for some special event, such as the death of Emperor William I in 1888, or the French elections of 1889 and, again in 1889, for the arrival of Whitelaw Reid as the new U.S. minister to France. In 1893, accompanied by his daughter Evelyn, he spent several weeks in Germany, a part of the time as the guest of Count Herbert Bismarck with whom he had become friendly during the latter's diplomatic service in London. There was a luncheon with the retired Iron Chancellor, which Smalley refused to call an interview, but Evelyn took careful notes and her father used the material not only for his dispatches but for an excellent article.[28] Smalley's German reports rank with his best work. The *Tribune* went out of its way to give prominence and praise to his accounts of the end of Emperor William's reign, and his discussion of Bismarck's retirement in 1890 is a gem compared to most of the journalistic accounts of that significant event. He had always admired Bismarck and expressed concern that the "wild young Emperor" might direct the German state into dangerous channels, but he managed to write about it with perception and balance.

English society fascinated the one-time American Radical almost to the point of obsession. London society with all of its nuances found a regular place in his letters and he did a series in 1888 that included such captions as "Functions of a Social Mentor," "Spencer House, the Queen and the Prince," "Politics in the Drawing Room," and "From Epsom to Ascot—the Gospel of Invitations." He was greatly annoyed at what he considered American misconceptions about the social acceptability of such visitors to England as Colonel William F. Cody (Buffalo Bill) and John L. Sullivan, and made vigorous efforts to correct the

28. George W. Smalley, *Studies of Men* (London, 1895), pp. 107–50.

naïve views of his compatriots.[29] He was impressed with the determined social ostracism of the Home Rulers not only by the Tories but by many of the Whigs. He professed not to approve, but his attempted humor regarding the matter was a bit strained: "Let us not be too tragic about it. Dinners and parties are no great matter; they do not, or do not always, settle the fate of empires; nor will the fate of Ireland be settled in a drawing room."[30]

The Smalley family often spent the summer vacation at Dieppe, then at the peak of its fashionable popularity, though sometimes Smalley went alone while his family spent most of the summer at Whitby. It was Smalley who was invited to the "great houses" in the country, acceptance being easier with his more relaxed writing schedule in the eighties. The American's London clubs included the Devonshire, Beefsteak, and Garrick, a sufficiently exclusive group to illustrate his social acceptability. An English writer referred to him as "an oracle with the peers and publicists of Mayfair."[31] His highly prized collection of autographed photographs included Lady Minto, Lady Rothschild, Lady Curzon, Lady Langtry, the Duchess of Sutherland, and the Duchess of Marlborough. They also included such celebrites as Bismarck, Girabaldi, and Sir Henry Irving. A story that went the rounds in America after Smalley's return to New York was told earlier to Andrew D. White by Sir Morell Mackenzie, the Emperor Frederick's doctor, and Smalley's, "that a certain sort of mixed gathering was now called instead of 'Small and Early,' 'Earl and Smalley'—a hit at the tuft-hunting propensities attributed to our common friend, G. W. Smalley."[32]

There was no doubt in Smalley's mind that his social life complemented his career as a journalist. "You suggest, in very kind terms," he wrote Reid, "that social life and journalistic work together are perhaps too exhausting. . . . The society I do see—not much of it fashionable—is for the most part and

29. *New York Tribune,* 13 November 1887.
30. Smalley, *London Letters,* 2:18.
31. T. H. S. Escott, *Masters of English Journalism* (London, 1911), p. 243.
32. Entry for 17 November 1888, in *The Diaries of Andrew D. White,* ed. Robert Morris Ogden (Ithaca, N.Y., 1959), p. 287.

often in an important way, most helpful with the work. A great deal of my work could not have been done at all without it: which is the main reason for living the way I do and cultivating a certain sort of society, which I might not think otherwise I could afford."[33]

A reviewer of Smalley's *Anglo-American Memories* portrays the social journalist at work with a strong hint of sarcasm:

"The group of people in the smoking room were talking as is the habit of groups in smoking rooms. Sir Edward stood on the hearth-rug listening, reflecting, weighing opinions and characters." Substitute Sir Edward for Mr. Smalley himself, and this passage from his second series of *Anglo-American Memories* may serve to describe the book. . . . We are taken . . . to the Gaity, but it is in a hansom with Lord Hartington. We also go the the Lyceum, but in company with "Sarah" and to sup with "Irving." We dine once at a restaurant; but it is the Ritz and the room was thronged with well known people. . . . For the rest we meet the great people in the great houses.[34]

Time and again Smalley rationalized his taste for associating with recognized persons, whether they were of the social great or had attained their positions through achievement, on the ground that such association was essential to his profession. Never did he admit that the associations he chose might have warped his views and limited his vision. The general influence of his associations is obvious, but it is more difficult to determine the value of his social contacts in specific instances. There are a few examples in his correspondence when he was asked for the source of his information, or was requested to support a particular revelation with more substantive evidence than he had offered, but they throw little light on anything other than unique cases. The accepted rules of discretion of the time ruled out the revelation of sources in all delicate matters and Smalley was pretentiously discreet.

Smalley was interested in conversation to the point of writing about it as a special art, and he became something of an authority on the conversational talents of public figures. He was also counted an uncommonly good judge of public speaking. In 1885 young Lord Rosebery sought his counsel on his progress

33. Smalley to Reid, 31 December 1880, Reid Papers.
34. *Times Literary Supplement,* 25 April 1912, p. 166.

as a speaker. Smalley responded at length, critically but so perceptively that Lord Crewe included his entire comment in his official biography of Rosebery.[35] Smalley himself was a reluctant speaker, avoiding all invitations that he could. Once when U.S. Minister Lowell made a special plea to Smalley to substitute for him on an occasion when he could not appear, Smalley agreed but reminded Lowell that he spoke "poorly" and therefore seldom spoke in public.

Few things were more upsetting to Smalley than suggestions, even if made in jest, that he was losing his Americanism, or had become English in the course of his long residence in London. He was so sensitive on the point that he sometimes asked Reid to tell him if he detected anything in his dispatches that was not "American." His earnest desire to promote Anglo-American friendship did not weaken his championship of the American side of any question. His long advocacy of elevating the U.S. minister to the Court of St. James to the rank of ambassador was based on the argument that the United States suffered in a very practical sense from the lower rank of its representative. He was overjoyed when the step was taken in 1893 with the appointment of Thomas F. Bayard as ambassador.

Smalley's skepticism of Bayard, a southerner, marked a change from the attitude he had held for some years toward the official representatives of his country. Between James Russell Lowell and Smalley there was a more intimate friendship than the correspondent enjoyed with any other American minister. It included close family relationships as well. Smalley once considered publishing a volume of Lowell's letters to him though he gave up the idea. The letters included many of Lowell's comments on literature and also demonstrated the usefulness of a good working relationship between a diplomat and a journalist of stature. Smalley felt that Lowell was a good minister in part because of his Americanism. "He has been throughout the most patriotic of ministers," Smalley declared. "He has, indeed, little inducement to be anything else. Thorough Americanism is—it cannot be said too often—whatever may be thought

35. Marquess of Crewe, K.G., *Lord Rosebery*, 2 vols. (London, 1931), 1:249—50.

out West, one of the things the English most admire in an American Minister or any other American."[36] Smalley got on well with Lowell's successor Edward J. Phelps (1885–89), after an initial period of coolness. Robert Todd Lincoln (1889–93) was largely ignored in the *Tribune's* dispatches from London.

When the *Tribune* felt the need of closely reasoned arguments in support of tariffs, it called upon its London correspondent. It even called on him when it wanted a telling phrase: "Mr. Smalley, who is one of the most consistent of American Protectionists, sums up the case in a single lucid sentence in his cable letter: 'Open your markets to British manufacturers with English labor at half the American price and the British will soon ruin the Americans.' "[37] Smalley returned to the United States for visits every other year or so, partly in the hope of keeping in touch with his native land. He sent both of his sons and one of his daughters back for a part of their education, wishing them to become "Americanized." He had become an American Tory in England, yes, but an *American* Tory.

36. Smalley, *London Letters,* 1:268.
37. *New York Tribune,* 19 June 1892.

9. *From the* Tribune
to the Times

The wonder is that a parting of ways between the *Tribune* and the "Tory Squire" who was said to edit the paper from London did not come before 1895. So long as Whitelaw Reid was the active director of the *Tribune,* he was willing to tolerate a great deal of independence on Smalley's part in recognition of the correspondent's great value to the paper. But there were, even so, occasional crises in relationships in addition to constant differences of opinion on such subjects as Gladstone's policies and Irish Home Rule.

One crisis grew out of an attempt in 1886 to make wider use of Smalley's dispatches by syndicating them for publication in other American papers. Smalley returned to the United States to help work out the details and to visit editors who expressed interest in the project. Reid felt that it was necessary for Smalley to tone down his personal opinions and to place greater emphasis on news, but he agreed readily that it would be out of the question for Smalley to offer opinions that he did not hold. The scheme never worked well. Smalley was furious when the North American Cable News Company used his dispatches without including his initials: "It breaks into my relations with the paper and the public. My initials are, so to speak, my stock in the trade."[1] Reid concluded that the project was failing because Smalley was not giving enough news, to which charge

1. Smalley to Reid, 25 December 1886, Whitelaw Reid Papers, Library of Congress, Washington, D.C.

Smalley responded with a sermon on the nature of news. He focused particularly on Reid's inference that sources might be given more often and cited two examples of confidential information he had recently offered without identifying the sources. He gave the sources privately but warned: "Neither would have opened his lips had he dreamed that he was in danger of being quoted by name. To have given their names or their very words would have been a gross breach of faith and fatal in every way. I should never have heard a word from either again or ever entered either house where I met them."[2]

Reid's censure was so severe in one letter that Smalley replied a week later that he had not recovered from the depression it produced. "I have dropped every other sort of work to devote myself to dispatches—have broken my promise to the XIX Century and other engagements. But I am conscious that I have done no better and probably not so well. Worry is fatal to me."[3]

In 1889 when Reid became U.S. minister to France he appointed Donald Nicholson, his private secretary, managing editor of the *Tribune*. Nicholson had only a limited appreciation of Smalley's contributions and no toleration for deviations from *Tribune* policies. Smalley did not conceal the fact that he regarded Nicholson as an upstart and that he would rely upon his long service with the paper and upon Reid's intervention if it should become necessary. For a time Smalley's view of his security proved correct, though in late 1890 he agreed reluctantly to take a vacation for three months during the Parnell trial. Sir Henry Lucy, who took over Smalley's cable dispatches during his temporary retirement, had done special assignments for the *Tribune* for many years and had often served as a replacement when Smalley took his annual vacation. Lucy was adept at avoiding controversy and sent dispatches that were light, gossipy, and generally innocent of any effort to deal with major British or Continental problems. The vacation effected no visible change in Smalley. He began his first cable on returning to duty: "In resuming, after some months, this review of the

2. Smalley to Reid, 10 March 1887, Reid Papers.
3. Ibid.

week, I am struck by nothing so much as the foolish monotony of human affairs."[4] Shortly he aroused Nicholson's ire—it must have given him pleasure, for wanting in humor as Smalley was, Nicholson was completely devoid of it—by taking a critical stand on French foreign policy regarding Bulgaria and reporting at length British anger over the activities of Patrick Eagan, U.S. minister to Chile. In the latter instance Nicholson was not only concerned that the American Irish would resent Smalley's remarks, but he thought it downright unpatriotic for an American correspondent to criticize an official fellow-citizen. In his remarks on French foreign policy—Smalley called Foreign Minister Ribot's Bulgarian policy a "blunder of the first magnitude"—Nicholson felt that the correspondent had committed a shameful act of disloyalty to his employer. It must be admitted that the editor had imagination, at least in regard to the position of the U.S. minister to France. He wrote Smalley:

Just think of the situation for one moment. Here is Mr. Reid meeting daily the French cabinet members and engaged in delicate negotiations for treaties with France, and yet the paper which he owns, permits its chief European correspondent to take the extreme English view of the [French-Bulgarian] quarrel, and to ridicule France in general and M. Ribot, in particular. Can you conceive of anything more likely to embarrass Mr. Reid in his relations with the French Cabinet, or better calculated to prevent the success of the work on which his heart is set?[5]

The dispute was soon enlarged to include all aspects of what Nicholson considered objectionable in Smalley's work. It would be difficult to find a better example of the rigidly pragmatic view of the proper functions of a newspaper than that contained in Nicholson's letters to his London correspondent.

In a letter from you, just received, you want to know why we cut out a paragraph respecting the American mails. We did it simply because it contained a severe and unnecessary attack upon the Cunard Steamship Company. There is no reason why you should be attacking the company in the columns of the Tribune, and paying off, as is commonly understood here, personal grudges at the Tribune expense. Your

4. *New York Tribune,* 15 March 1891.
5. Nicholson to Smalley, 9 February 1892 [copy], Reid Papers. Nicholson produced no complaints from Reid, much less Ribot, neither of whom had seen the offending dispatches.

last attack on the Cunard people cost the Tribune an amount nearly equal to your month's salary. We were negotiating with them for some special advertising, and the bargain was nearly made when your attack appeared, and they at once refused to complete it. From a business point of view, such attacks are entirely unwarranted, and I have, consequently, instructed the Day Editor to strike them out of any future letters or dispatches.[6]

Nicholson objected to "the whole tone" of the dispatches from London and began using the blue pencil on almost every letter and cable. Then in July Reid was nominated as the vice-presidential candidate on the Republican ticket, which from the editor's viewpoint gave him a mandate to enforce conformity.

Now that Mr. Reid has been nominated for the Vice Presidency, it is necessary—and in fact absolutely imperative—that the London despatches and letters be brought promptly into harmonious relations with the editorial policy of the paper, and that nothing appear in them which *directly or indirectly irritate, offend or alienate a single voter* [italics inserted]. We want to elect Mr. Reid this Fall, and we must all co-operate to that end. There is, at present, in the Democratic ranks a good deal of dissatisfaction with the Democratic ticket, and there is, therefore, an excellent opportunity for Republicans to secure an unusually large Irish vote next November. But we cannot do it by belittling or attacking Home Rule or Mr. Gladstone, or discussing these important subjects from the Lord Salisbury point of view. We cannot do it by printing in the Tribune anti-Irish and anti-Home Rule correspondence from London. Work of this kind would cost Mr. Reid a good many votes, and might, indeed, defeat him; and, therefore, as you will readily see, it would be a fatal mistake to allow anything of this nature to appear in the paper—to allow, in reality, the Tribune to be used, however unintentionally, as a club to kill politically its editor and owner. Hence, the immediate necessity of over-hauling and adjusting your letters and despatches, and making them helpful instead of harmful to Mr. Reid's prospects of election.[7]

The London correspondent responded to the arguments, admonitions, and commands of his editor with a combination of lofty appeals to principle, denials of some charges, occasional petty countercharges, and expressions of willingness to conform insofar as he honestly could. He was incensed at the blue-pencil-

6. Ibid.
7. Nicholson to Smalley, 5 July 1892, ibid.

ling, especially by a "Day Editor" he did not know, and rightly furious when the *Tribune* apologized for one of his dispatches, which had been severely censored, by stating in an editorial that the paper welcomed Mr. Smalley's "letters on any and every subject," however much they might differ from the views of the paper. This, Smalley pointed out, not only placed him in a position "which could become impossible," but was clearly dishonest as well. He warned against efforts to court an Irish vote "which you will never get," and declared that "an editor who tries to offend nobody might end by offending everybody."[8]

Nicholson's stupidity makes it hard to sympathize with the difficulties of his position; moreover, he went from bad to worse, making next a proposal for which there was no moral defense: namely, that Smalley should drop for the duration of the campaign the use of his initials at the end of both letters and cables, at least those dealing with "dangerous and delicate topics." "This," he wrote, "would relieve you of all personal responsibility for them, and might enable you to support Home Rule and Gladstone without stultification." He made alternative suggestions including one to eliminate altogether the "dangerous and delicate" topics, which could be handled by someone else who sympathized with the policies of the *Tribune,* while Smalley dealt only with harmless subjects.[9]

No agreement seems to have been reached but Smalley did, at least for the duration of the campaign, manage to soften his words and avoid expressing in most of his dispatches views of the sort Nicholson felt to be fatal to Mr. Reid's chances. The temporary compromise simply postponed the inevitable. Late in the following summer Nicholson demanded Smalley's resignation, a move which, curiously, seems to have surprised the correspondent. He appealed to Reid, of course: "I have a letter this morning from Mr. Nicholson requesting my resignation on the ground that two letters of mine to him express views of my relations to the Tribune of which he disapproves. That seems an inadequate reason for terminating a connection which has lasted 32 years." Smalley offered to go to New York to talk to

8. Smalley to Nicholson, 15 [?] February 1892, ibid.
9. Nicholson to Smalley, 5 July 1892, ibid.

Reid and reminded him that in 1886 he gave twelve months' notice when there was talk of terminating Smalley's services: "If it [what Nicholson writes] represents your real purpose, [it] means nothing less than the break-up of my life, not very far from its end, and the rearrangement of a future which is, of course, all uncertain. I never thought to part from the Tribune in this way."[10]

But Reid had made up his mind not to intervene. After several weeks' delay, he replied:

When your letter about your latest difficulty with the office reached me, I had just returned from a six weeks' absence in the Adirondacks, and Mr. Nicholson was himself absent on his vacation. I had little knowledge of the circumstances, and had not even known that Mr. Nicholson had sent his letter calling for your resignation, until after my return. I did know, however, and had long known that you were straining your relations with him and with the office to the point of breaking, and on most of the points involved, so far as they came to my knowledge, had thought you in the wrong. Several times I had tried to make you see that no other newspaper in New York, and none other known to me elsewhere would endure from a correspondent the line of conduct which you adopted, and that you were heedlessly, as well as deliberately, a source of loss and enmity to your employers.

When, however, during my stay in Paris it required three letters and a fortnight's time to induce you to pick up at a London newsstand and forward me three English trade papers, which I vitally needed at the moment, and when you took pains at last in sending them to give me notice that I had no right to call upon you for them, since Mr. Nicholson was now your superior and not I, I made up my mind that unless I should again resume the active and minute control, which I had given up on going abroad, I should leave you henceforth in Mr. Nicholson's hands. I have done so ever since, and ought not now to interfere—as I am not interfering otherwise in the personnel of a staff, which he organizes as best he can for the purpose of making the newspaper success which I require.

It pains me, however, to see how you have drifted into this position, and in view of the friendship which has subsisted between us during nearly the whole of our mature lives, I cannot close this without a frank word or two such as I think a true friend owes you.

You had the best position on the American Press, and it was maintained for you largely because of a personal regard (even when I was

10. Smalley to Reid, 15 September 1893, ibid.

very young on the Tribune, I had to sustain you against two orders from Mr. Greeley for your removal—one of which named a successor for you). You have taken a tone towards Mr. Nicholson and perhaps others in the office, which self-respecting gentlemen will not endure, and an attitude towards the newspaper you serve which implies not service but mastery. There has been no principle involved in it. With the least tact you might have had every man in the office whom you have alienated, your warm friend, as every one was anxious to be; and with a little consideration you might, without sacrifice of principle, have avoided a long warfare upon the policy and interests of the paper, which you seem to be striving to make as ugly and as injurious as possible.

I know that Mr. Nicholson values a great deal of your work highly, and will be glad to buy it. He points out to me, however, that you some time ago formally repudiated the title of Correspondent of the Tribune and reminds me that he has since said to you that while he will be ready henceforth to buy your copy, he will only buy what he wants. I cannot quarrel with him as to the justice of this conclusion, and do not see how you can. I believe, in the very wide liberty of discussion we always allow, you can write for him enough acceptable matter to secure you a good income. I should hope you might be able to continue the cable letters, so as to avoid the necessity of sending over another correspondent, but I know he has been considering and preparing for a change there, if necessary.

I know that no personal visit will change his decision. It would therefore be, as he says, a needless waste of time and money. He and all the office have the highest admiration for your brilliant abilities, and will be glad to see them continued in the service of the Tribune. You know well enough my wishes; and you must know also how deeply I regret that such disagreeable matters are forced to the front at a time when you lack the old physical vigor to deal with them.

Earnestly hoping that you may see your way to what I think a common sense conduct of your correspondence with Mr. Nicholson, I am

Whitelaw Reid[11]

One wonders how much of the actual correspondence—especially of Nicholson's letters to Smalley—Reid actually saw and how much he accepted Nicholson's word for. Certainly Nicholson had stepped over boundary lines of principle that Reid had always been careful not to step over. Reid's letter was clear enough in calling for a new relationship between Smalley and the *Tribune,* a demand that Smalley evaded. In his reply

11. Reid to Smalley, 25 November 1893, ibid.

to Reid, he referred to the "trying situation" and said that if he left the *Tribune* he hoped it would not permanently affect their friendship. There ensued only a vague understanding of a termination in a process of fulfillment at some undetermined time. There is nothing in the correspondence to substantiate Nicholson's statement to Reid that Smalley had "repudiated" his position as *Tribune* correspondent. Perhaps there was hope that time would provide a solution more acceptable than the one Reid indicated. At least the *Tribune* did not cut off Smalley's regular salary and Smalley avoided "delicate and dangerous" subjects, though he occasionally inserted remarks in his letters that must have angered Nicholson. "A journal which sells its editorial opinion betrays the public," he wrote. "Are we to go a step further and say, So does a journalist who expresses an opinion not his own. If we take one step how can we refuse to take the other?"[12] It was a strange and anomalous situation. In January 1895, when Smalley went to the United States on personal business, he asked Nicholson whether he cared to have a talk with a man who was no longer a *Tribune* employee. Both Reid and Nicholson were surprised. They thought the matter was still undecided.

In February 1895 Smalley received an offer from E. F. Moberly Bell, manager of the London *Times*, of a position as *Times* correspondent in New York at a salary of £2,000 a year.[13] Discussion of the appointment had been going on for at least as long as the *Tribune* had been engaged in firing its London correspondent. This helps to explain Smalley's rather curious attitude toward the *Tribune* during the preceding year, but it is not easy to understand why he seemed genuinely indecisive about accepting Moberly Bell's offer. The only possible explanation is that he believed he could continue his old relationship with the *Tribune* if he chose. Before accepting the offer he told

12. *New York Tribune*, 11 February 1894.
13. Moberly Bell to Smalley [copy], 21 February 1895, Letterbook, no 10, Printing House Square, London. Some of Smalley's correspondence, preserved in the archives of the London *Times* at the paper's headquarters, Printing House Square, is numbered letterbooks. Other correspondence is uncatalogued. Letterbooks are cited when applicable and other items are simply listed as in Printing House Square, London.

his old friend Andrew D. White that he was reluctant to return to the United States and asked for White's adivce. "I have always felt that I ought to go home to die if not to live," he said.[14] Although the *Times* offered him a generous expense allowance in addition to his salary, the move did not appear financially rewarding, especially since Smalley's lease on his London house had several years to run.

One thing that undoubtedly appealed to Smalley was the idea of having more satisfactory American news in the English press. He had long complained of the poor quality of American news in the London journals, including the *Times*. There had been a time when he had little that was favorable to say about the *Times*, but that had changed. In speaking of *Times* foreign correspondents, he wrote: ". . . a correspondent of the Times has an advantage. It is worth far more to a statesman or financier that the intelligence of which he wishes the public to be in possession should be in the leading journal than in all the others put together."[15] Still, for all of the weighing of pros and cons, Smalley joined the *Times* because his position on the *Tribune* had become an unhappy one.

From the time in 1890 when Moberly Bell became assistant manager of the *Times* he worked diligently at reorganizing and strengthening the foreign news coverage of the paper. He was aided in the task by Mackenzie Wallace who became head of the *Times* foreign department in 1891, but it is clear that Smalley was a Moberly Bell selection. The manager had far greater interest in the United States than did the head of the foreign department.

Curiously Smalley had spotted Moberly Bell's work and accorded him high praise when he was a novice reporter in Egypt in 1882. "He goes everywhere, sees everybody, knows pretty much all there is to be known," Smalley wrote. "He does something more than report facts, more than comment on them, more than criticize the Commanders whom he serves. He argues with them and with the Government at home. . . . He inveighs,

14. Smalley to White, 9 October 1894, Andrew D. White Papers, Cornell University Library, Ithaca, N.Y.

15. George W. Smalley, *Studies of Men* (London, 1895), pp. 341–42.

expostulates, rebukes—sternly condemns delay and thunders forth menaces and warnings. . . ."[16] Moberly Bell was Smalley's kind of man.

For many years the *Times* representative in the United States had been Joel Cook, financial editor of the *Philadelphia Ledger,* whose irregularly submitted dispatches were meager and undistinguished. Certainly he made a poor comparison with Blowitz in Paris, Valentine Chirol in Berlin, Dr. George E. Morrison in the Far East, and J. D. Bourchier in the Balkans. The *New York Times* declared that Smalley's appointment had "settled the question of whether the U.S. has news value for London papers. In the past the London papers have ignored the U.S."[17] One of the common remarks was that Smalley would have no competition worth mentioning in New York. This proved to be the case. Bradford Perkins, a recent historian of Anglo-American relations, estimates that from the mid-to-the-late nineties "perhaps ninety percent of the information published in England came directly or indirectly from George W. Smalley."[18]

The traditional policy of anonymity for *Times* correspondents was even more of a myth in Smalley's case than usual. His appointment was reported by papers on both sides of the Atlantic, and several farewell dinners for him in London received notice in the press. Smalley even gave out a statement for publication: "My motives for making the change are my long exile from America and my desire to return there to stay. My experience in London has taught me how American life ought to be represented in order to interest the British public, and to do this I shall devote myself."[19]

Smalley went to New York in June. There was a note of fatigue, almost the spirit of an old horse being turned out to pasture, in some of the correspondent's comments about returning home, but once in the United States he demonstrated renewed vigor and was soon working as hard as he had ever worked in his life. He was only in his early sixties and in good

16. *New York Times,* 7 July 1895.
17. *New York Tribune,* 13 August 1882.
18. Bradford Perkins, *The Great Rapprochement: England and the United States, 1895–1914* (New York, 1968), p. 23.
19. *New York Times,* 9 March 1895.

health. In addition to his work for the *Times* he accepted an associate editorship on the *New York Herald,* long the *Tribune's* chief rival in foreign news. He wrote occasional editorials for the *Herald* and for a time did a weekly letter on English topics. In addition, he found time to do articles for both American and English magazines.

Predictably one of his first *Herald* letters—a review of James Bryce's *American Commonwealth*—was the occasion for considerable controversy. Smalley gave Bryce poor marks and Bryce's friends were aroused to anger. The author, he declared, was pedantic, dull, and tiresome; in any case, he was a radical. His work on the United States was inferior to the studies of Paul Bourget and Goldwin Smith and simply not in the same class with Tocqueville's. The *Speaker,* edited by Sir Wemyss Reed, declared that Smalley's *Herald* articles should be entitled "Backshots at Old Friends." The *Daily Chronicle* said: "Mr. Smalley is pursuing in the *Herald* his reminiscences of his English bete noires. They appear to be somewhat numerous, and promise to keep his pen amiably employed to the utmost limit of a green old age."[20]

Smalley's transfer brought out some interesting comparisons between English and American journalistic aims and practices. A host of petty differences over matters of style provided irritants for both Smalley and his editors. The *Times* foreign editor, Mackenzie Wallace, at once objected to the American's use of the pronouns "you" and "we," a practice the correspondent insisted enabled him to "get hold of the reader." Moberly Bell said he never supposed it would be necessary for him to correct his new correspondent's English, a statement that brought on heated arguments. Smalley never conceded that he was wrong—only that the editor had final right of decision in such matters.

More important, how did British interests in the United States compare with American interests in Britain? Measured by the information the *Times* called for and that which their correspondent sent, the British readers were interested almost exclusively in political matters with economic and financial affairs

20. As quoted in the *New York Herald,* 1 October 1895, p. 11.

running a poor second. There was by this measurement no reciprocation of American interest in Old World culture—in literature, art, and music. If Professor Bradford is right in his conclusion that 90 percent of the U.S. news published in England came through Smalley, this is a point of considerable significance—as are Smalley's many biases, oversimplifications, and omissions.[21]

21. Perkins, *Great Rapprochement,* p. 23.

10. Journalist-Diplomat
in an International Crisis

When Smalley chose New York as his headquarters the *Times* editors saw no reason to object. Most Europeans thought of New York as the hub of the United States and there was no question regarding its superiority as a news and communications center. Smalley had both personal and professional reasons for his preference. He had more acquaintances in New York. The social life was more appealing to him, the climate, at least compared to Washington's, was the lesser of evils, and he was in a good position to perform his services for the *New York Herald* while composing his dispatches to the *Times*. Also, he thought New York was the best spot from which to judge American moods. He had no appreciation of the American West or South and thought that New England no longer counted for a great deal. When the Venezuelan crisis took him to Washington for a visit early in 1896, he declared that Washington influences on U.S. policy were direct and important to know, but he added: "Washington is probably not now, any more than it usually is, a place where the opinion of the country as a whole is formed or where it is readily to be ascertained."[1]

After Smalley had been in the United States for six years his London employers concluded that they had made a mistake, that their correspondent should live in Washington, that in New York he was under the influence of unrepresentative people, or

1. *Times* (London), 21 January 1896

at least that he did not listen to the right people. This point was made by Smalley critics from the beginning of his stay in America. Senator Henry Cabot Lodge, who was traveling in Europe in the latter part of 1895, kept a close watch on Smalley's dispatches to the *Times*. On the whole he was pleased, especially with the praise for Theodore Roosevelt, but he wrote Roosevelt urging him to take Smalley in hand: "His dispatches are invaluable to us here," but he "is making one error because he has not seen people enough I suppose—I wish you would set him straight. He keeps saying that there is no general interest in the Monroe doctrine, that only a few jingoes talk about Venezuela. . . ."[2] Roosevelt replied: "I have spoken to him as plainly as a mortal can and told him, not only that my own feeling, but also the general sentiment of the country was rather hostile to England and was very strong in support of the Monroe Doctrine; but he does not meet the men who share our views."[3] Both men became increasingly concerned about Smalley's failure to see the right people. Lodge scarcely needed to tell Roosevelt that Smalley's "dispatches have great weight here [in England]—they are quoted on every side and the tone he takes on these points can only encourage England in a policy which will surely lead to trouble if persisted in."[4]

The dispute between Great Britain and Venezuela over the British Guiana–Venezuelan boundary line, which had never been satisfactorily established, worsened in the mid-nineties with an increasingly determined attitude on the part of the United States to defend Venezuelan claims. On 17 December 1895 it burst suddenly and shockingly into a real crisis when, in a special message to Congress, President Cleveland proposed, and the Congress immediately authorized, an American commission to determine the facts in the case and gave unequivocal assurance of American backing in carrying out the decisions of the commission. Support in the United States for the president's posi-

2. Lodge to Roosevelt, 10 August 1895, in *Selections from the Correspondence of Theodore Roosevelt and Henry Cabot Lodge, 1894–1918*, 2 vols. (New York, 1925), 1:163 (hereafter cited as *Lodge-Roosevelt Correspondence.*)

3. Roosevelt to Lodge, 27 August 1895, ibid., 1:168.

4. Lodge to Roosevelt, 10 August 1895, ibid., p. 163.

tion was stronger than Cleveland or Richard Olney, his secretary of state and the chief architect of the offensive, had anticipated. British reactions were a mixture of puzzlement and stubborn unwillingness to back down before a Yankee threat that, rightly or wrongly, seemed to the British to break the rules of sportsmanship.

In his dispatches to the *Times* Smalley essayed the role of the detached statesman. He urged both sides to consider the issues carefully and pleaded for time to allow heated tempers to cool. He continued to insist that American opinion in general did not support the jingoes, that the only real Anglophobes were the American Irish, and that Cleveland's policy was not popular with religious and academic leaders and with New York bankers. The *Times* was pleased. Moberly Bell wired him: "For your impartial and statesmanlike treatment of the present unfortunate situation you deserve the thanks of both nations."[5] Lodge and Roosevelt were not pleased. Lodge wrote Moreton Frewen: "The good man has quite lost his head lately and has been sending over the most ridiculous account of things here and has, so far as I can make out, totally misrepresented American feelings."[6] Roosevelt was even more upset; he told Lodge that "Smalley's whole attitude is contemptible beyond words."[7]

Smalley's position in the crisis would have been of considerable importance had he remained simply the reporter of the *Times* from the United States, but circumstances pushed him into the center of activities and into the dual role of amateur diplomat and journalist. In the days of the Old Diplomacy it was not too unusual for correspondents, especially the representatives of the *Times,* to serve as intermediaries in diplomatic negotiations or sometimes as voices of diplomats. The Venezuelan crisis was a particularly favorable situation for the use of indirect diplomacy and amateur negotiators. In a nutshell, neither Great Britain nor the United States wanted war and neither wanted

5. Moberly Bell to Smalley, 19 or 20 [?] 1895, Letterbook, no. 10, Printing House Square, London.

6. Lodge to Frewen, 9 January 1896, Moreton Frewen Papers, Library of Congress, Washington, D.C.

7. Roosevelt to Lodge, 27 December 1895, *Lodge-Roosevelt Correspondence,* 1:204.

to retreat too far or too fast from its original position. The circumstances called for probing and prolonging the dispute without going too far in the way of commitments.

Contrary to common belief, both at the time and later, Lord Salisbury, Britain's prime minister and foreign secretary, had a keen appreciation of the power of public opinion in foreign affairs and considerable skill in dealing with the press, usually through his private secretaries. There were a few journalists with whom he could work closely. Alfred Austin of the *London Standard* was one and in 1895 Salisbury rewarded him for his services by creating him poet laureate. After Austin's retirement to literature, G. E. Buckle, editor of the *Times,* was probably Salisbury's closest journalistic acquaintance. The two men understood each other's positions: Buckle knew the limits to the information he could expect to get and the requirement of secrecy regarding his relations with the foreign secretary; Salisbury knew the strong wish of the *Times* to be helpful to the government in power while maintaining at the same time a sufficiency of independence. Joseph Chamberlain, British colonial secretary and the cabinet member who had more to do with the Venezuelan crisis than any official other than Lord Salisbury, was relatively openhanded with the press. He expressed his views on public opinion forcefully in asking Sir Frederick Pollock to prepare for publication a statement of Great Britain's case against Venezuela:

. . . in the preparation of what is a great state document—on which large interests hang—I think it will be desirable to remember that Demos is King, both here and in America, and that a popular presentment of a case, including an appeal to well understood and generally accepted principles, is of at least as much importance as technical ideas and legal subleties. It is because I am convinced that you will enter upon the task in this . . . spirit that I have so much confidence in asking you to undertake it.[8]

Richard Olney, himself an amateur in the field of diplomatic negotiations, was less schooled in the subtle uses of indirect channels of diplomacy than were the British officials, but he

8. Chamberlain to Pollock, 27 December 1895 [copy], Joseph Chamberlain Papers, University of Birmingham.

was no less willing than they to make the best use of journalists and the news media. His earliest venture during the Venezuelan crisis into this area was with Henry Norman, correspondent and subeditor of the *London Daily Chronicle,* who left England for the United States on the first available ship after the publication of President Cleveland's special message to Congress. "Our Special Commissioner" is "on a mission—we may say an embassy—of peace," the *Daily Chronicle* declared. Armed with letters of introduction, including one from Reginald Brett (later Lord Esher), who was a friend of the Prince of Wales, Norman soon after his arrival in Washington was in touch with Secretary Olney, among other officials. Olney, at first pleased to be able to use Norman as spokesman in a London journal, became angry when he felt Norman had gone too far in stressing American desires for peace. Sir Julian Pauncefote, the British ambassador in Washington, was doubtful about Norman and told Salisbury in a private letter, "I am rather suspicious that he is 'anguis in herba'" [a snake in the grass].[9] When Norman tried to see Lord Salisbury on his return to London, he was blocked by the minister's secretaries.

Smalley was in a stronger position than Norman to get on the inside of the crisis negotiations. He had lived in England long enough to understand English relationships between journalists and officials and he knew both Chamberlain and Salisbury, though not on an intimate basis. He had met Sir Julian Pauncefote through Lord Rosebery when Pauncefote became minister (later ambassador) to the United States, and, in the crisis, Pauncefote assured Salisbury that Smalley's cables were reliable.[10] Before leaving England for America, Smalley saw U.S. Ambassador Bayard who wrote a letter of recommendation for him to Cleveland, assuring the president that Smalley "now occupies a position very much in line with that for which you have done so much since 1893. I believe that with his long experience and

9. Pauncefote to Salisbury, 3 January 1896, Lord Salisbury Papers, Christ Church, Oxford. Details of the use made of amateurs in the Venezuelan crisis are given in Joseph J. Mathews, "Informal Diplomacy in the Venezuelan Crisis of 1896," *Mississippi Valley Historical Review* 50 (September 1963) : 195–212.

10. Pauncefote to Salisbury, private, 31 January 1896, Salisbury Papers.

diminished partisanship, he will do great service to both countries."[11] Smalley had only met Olney once and unfortunately had been rather patronizing in his tone toward the secretary early in the crisis. Still on 21 January, the day following his arrival in Washington in order to be closer to the center of activity, Smalley began cabling dispatches to the *Times* that were essentially statements of Olney's views. How Smalley and Olney were able to form a working partnership so quickly is a matter of conjecture. Smalley was obviously persuaded that Olney was ready to seek an acceptable compromise and Olney must have felt that Smalley had the proper credentials to be of service to him.

Actually, the British initiated the use of private channels. For several weeks in early January 1896 the British government had on its hands a second crisis growing out of the abortive Jamison Raid and the German Kaiser's congratulatory telegram to Paul Kruger, president of the Transvaal, that seemed a greater threat than the Venezuelan affair. The dual pressure encouraged Lord Salisbury to authorize Chamberlain to approach Ambassador Bayard through Lord Playfair, a distinguished English chemist who had married an American wife. The informal proposals were for negotiations based on the exclusion from arbitration of areas in the disputed territory already settled by the English and for the calling of a European conference on the Monroe Doctrine with Great Britain's assurances that she would back recognition of the Monroe Doctrine.

Olney was pleased that the British were willing to make proposals but he did not find the proposals acceptable. Instead of taking up the Chamberlain-Playfair-Bayard packet of suggestions he chose to open a new channel with proposals of his own. On 24 January Smalley cabled counter-proposals to Buckle, assuring him that he had official backing for the withdrawal of the American commission and for the establishment of a joint Anglo-American commission to be composed of two British and two American members who would report separately to their

11. Quoted in C. C. Tansill, *The Foreign Policy of Thomas F. Bayard, 1885–1897* (New York, 1940), p. 746n.

respective governments. If the commission should fail to agree, a fifth member would be appointed by a neutral government. The conclusions of the joint commission were not to be binding "unless perhaps . . . on matters of fact," but were to serve as a basis for subsequent negotiations or for a decision by a tribunal composed of the chief justice of each of the two countries and a neutral appointee.

When Salisbury received these propositions from Buckle he was deeply impressed—so much so that he came up to London on a Saturday from his country home to talk to Buckle and Arthur James Balfour and to have the proposals (labeled "Most Secret") circulated to members of the cabinet with the request that he be informed at once if there were any objections to the terms offered. The cabinet members who replied were enthusiastically in favor of acceptance, and on 27 January Buckle cabled Smalley: "Your suggestions if proposed officially will be acceptable here. This is authoritative." For a moment it appeared that a basis for negotiations had been found. Instead a fiasco followed. Either Smalley had not fully understood Olney's position before cabling Buckle, or Olney had been guilty of a lack of caution in formulating the suggestions. Smalley took the blame in explaining the misunderstanding to Buckle—he had little choice—but the evidence, while not conclusive, suggests that the secretary of state had seen the cable to Buckle before it was sent.[12]

The response to Buckle's statement followed his acceptance of the Smalley proposals was another cable from Smalley listing some alterations and modifications that would have to be accepted. Individually they were not important but taken together they left no graceful way out of arbitration should the commission fail to agree, and Salisbury was determined not to take a position where he might be forced to arbitrate. He considered briefly the idea of trying to get an agreement to return the Smalley proposals to their original form but decided instead to take his stand on excluding settled areas from any arbitration. This was the central point in the Chamberlain proposals made through Playfair and Bayard and it was now clear that they

12. Details and citations given in Mathews, "Informal Diplomacy," pp. 200–201.

122 · *George W. Smalley*

were getting nowhere. The resort to amateurs had produced some amateurish and ineffectual diplomatic action. In addition to more than the usual amount of correspondence in this type of activity, there had been numerous private meetings between Buckle and Salisbury and Smalley and Olney. But the real impasse to progress was not inept negotiations: it was owing to the fact that the principals were not sufficiently close in their ideas to make agreement possible.

The columns of the *Times,* of course, did not reveal these behind-the-scenes operations, but both the leading articles of the paper and the dispatches of "Our Own Correspondent" from the United States assured the readers that statements presenting official views were authoritative. In his dispatch in the *Times* of 22 January, Smalley asserted that he quoted nobody and imputed no responsibility. He insisted that "there is in the White House and in the State Department a strong and cordial wish for an early and complete settlement of the Venezuela Controversy with Great Britain on terms involving no discredit to Great Britain or the United States." The *Times* replied in a leader with expressions of pleasure and assurances that the British government, too, was ready to find a solution acceptable to both sides. This public exchange of generalities continued for several weeks with a stiffening of tone on both sides as it became clear through private communications that the British were unwilling to include settled districts in any kind of arbitration while the Americans were flatly opposed to excluding them.

Smalley, perhaps a bit influenced by being on the inside of the American position, became increasingly vigorous in his support of Olney's views. On 7 February Buckle cabled his correspondent: "I hardly think cause of peace will be served by negotiations conducted in the spirit of your last communication. . . . I have had reluctantly to omit tonight and yesterday some of your strictures on this Government which seem to me undeserved and not conducive to success of negotiations."[13] In forwarding a private Smalley letter to Salisbury, Buckle begged the prime minister to remember that it was intended only for

13. Buckle to Smalley, 7 February 1896 [copy in Smalley's handwriting], Richard Olney Papers, Library of Congress, Washington, D.C.

the editor's guidance—"otherwise you might be offended by his bluntness." At the time, the *Times* editor was having greater difficulty in defending Salisbury's position than his American correspondent was in serving as Olney's advocate. Buckle's personal views were more conciliatory than Salisbury's; he even urged the acceptance of Smalley's modified proposals of 26 January. But Salisbury would not budge from the position he had taken on "settled districts," even when his attorney general strongly advised against it.[14] He told Pauncefote that he had no real confidence in the impartiality of neutral arbiters who would carry the decision and added: "Even when we get an award the U.S. will not execute it."[15] If he would not retreat on this point, the only course open to Salisbury was a policy of calculated procrastination while presenting an appearance of conciliation.

In Washington the impasse was clear enough and Smalley, disappointed and disheartened, told Buckle he was returning to New York. The editor approved, expressing the hope that in New York his correspondent might regain his former tone. But Smalley did not return. Instead, he lingered on for a fortnight until on 17 February he and Olney launched a new offensive that was a real shocker to the British. In his cable to the *Times* of that date, he presented, with a few elaborations, the modified proposals he had made to Buckle in secret on 26 January, and asserted emphatically that the plan was acceptable to the U.S. government, or would be proposed by it, if there were reasons to believe that the plan would be accepted by Her Majesty's government. He added, but in less positive language, his belief that the Americans would be disposed to agree in advance as to what constituted "settled districts." He did not say there was a disposition to exclude such areas from arbitration. The evidence that the decision to publicize the formerly secret proposals was a joint Smalley-Olney one is clear enough, though there seems to be no indication which of the two initiated the idea.

Editor Buckle decided to publish the dispatch as received

14. Sir Richard Webster to Salisbury, 4 March 1896, Salisbury Papers.
15. Salisbury to Pauncefote, 7 February 1896 [copy], Salisbury Papers.

without consulting Lord Salisbury. Buckle liked to demonstrate his independence, even when working in close cooperation and support of the foreign secretary. He explained to the prime minister: "It seemed to me that if their government wishes to let it be known in public that they were ready to make overtures, they were the best judges." He added: "You will recognize some of your thunder in the leader, which I hope may help both to promote the cause of peace and strengthen your hand."[16] The *Times* leader of 18 February to which Buckle referred welcomed the proposal "which for the first time places before the public the outlines of a definite and intelligible plan for effecting practical agreement between this country and the United States." There were notes of caution in the leader—"Salisbury's thunder" may have been the complaint over the vagueness regarding the matter of settled districts—but the general tone was sufficiently optimistic to place the *Times* among those who were exerting pressure on the prime minister for a settlement: "We recognize with unqualified satisfaction that the plan sketched by our correspondent is in many of its features such as this country can honorably accept, and further offers, on points which may seem a little doubtful, excellent prospects of ultimate agreement."

Lord Salisbury could not fail to recognize that the unorthodox Olney-Smalley move had placed him in a delicate position. The American proposals met all of the demands that he had publicly advocated; for all of his private insistence on the exclusion of settled districts from arbitration, he had not made this demand in public. Leaders of the Liberal opposition, Sir William Harcourt in particular, were becoming suspicious and restive. Under sufficient pressure Salisbury could also play an unorthodox and unprecedented game, which he now proceeded to do by transferring the defense of the British position to Buckle for several days. In effect, he allowed the negotiations to be handled in the columns of the *Times,* with the editor serving as his spokesman and Smalley acting for Secretary of State Olney.

There can be no doubt on this point. Both editor and correspondent said as much in their published statements, and their

16. Buckle to Salisbury, 18 February 1896, Salisbury Papers.

private correspondence bears out what they said in the *Times*. The language of the exchange was that of journalism rather than professional diplomacy, tightly expressed and resembling a brilliant sparring match. Smalley sought to impress *Times* readers with the importance of the American initiative and the gravity of taking such a step publicly: "I cannot express too strongly my sense of the firmness required and shown by the Executive," he cabled on 18 February. "It is no light thing to let such suggestions as those of yesterday come before the American public without any assurance of their acceptance by the British Government." On 21 February a *Times* leader reviewed the proposals in great detail and seemingly gave assurance of British official acceptance of them:

A turning point seems to have been reached in the Venezuela Controversy. . . . A point must be reached in the treatment of the matter where the informal suggestions to which the efforts of newspapers are necessarily limited must give way to negotiations of a more regular kind. That point, in our judgment, has been arrived at now. . . . If these are the views of the Washington Administration . . . it is only requisite to embody them in a dispatch and send them to our Government. . . . We do not say that necessarily they would command instant assent in all details in this country. . . . We do say, however, without the slightest hesitation, that they would be received with the greatest possible respect and with an earnest desire to accept them as the basis for a prompt and complete agreement. . . . It is quite understood in this country that the project of the Washington Government stands or falls as a whole.

Olney was pleased but skeptical and asked Smalley to cable Buckle for direct assurance that the views expressed in the *Times* leader really represented Salisbury. Buckle replied: "I may say in general terms and without committing my friend to exact expressions leader mentioned represents his views."[17]

Salisbury's precise knowledge of the *Times* leader of 21 February and his responsibility for it are impossible to ascertain. It is inconceivable that Buckle would have given Smalley positive assurance that the leader represented the foreign secretary's views without having solid grounds for his assurance. At the same time, the evidence is very strong that Salisburn never in-

17. Buckle to Smalley, enclosed in Smalley's note to Olney, 26 February 1896, Olney Papers.

tended to proceed with negotiations on the basis of Smalley's published proposals. The day before the appearance of the *Times* editorial he indicated as much to the cabinet.[18] On 21 February he wrote Chamberlain that he was shifting the negotiations to Washington with proposals for a general arbitration agreement and added: "This attempt by Smalley to negotiate in print is absurd." Chamberlain agreed and remarked that "Smalley is getting mischievous and has certainly ceased to be useful." His later comment was more kindly but less flattering when he said "Smalley meant well but made a mess of it."[19]

As he had declared to Chamberlain he would, Salisbury hastened to transfer the negotiations to Washington and took steps to speed up the presentation of a general arbitration treaty. Even an old professional in diplomacy like Pauncefote was puzzled by these devious maneuvers and he cabled the foreign secretary to ask whether the *Times* leader of the twenty-first had had his sanction. Salisbury replied evasively that he did not remember expressing approval of any of Smalley's telegrams except the first which was promptly withdrawn. Recalling Salisbury's aversion to being connected in any official way with the press, Pauncefote requested the Foreign Office to remove from the official records any references to unofficial negotiations.[20]

Since Salisbury's proposal for an arbitration treaty excluded the Venezuelan dispute, the transfer simply meant the continuation of procrastination in Washington rather than in London. The Smalley-Olney offensive galvanized him into action and demonstrated that he could play an adroit press game himself. There are even hints that he offered to pay Buckle for his cables to Smalley but he was not as forthright with the *Times* editor as Secretary Olney was with the paper's correspondent. Smalley was again discouraged by the failure of his efforts and,

18. Duke of Devonshire to Salisbury, 21 February 1896, Salisbury Papers.
19. Salisbury to Chamberlain, 21 February 1896, Chamberlain Papers.
20. Pauncefote to Francis Bertie, 22 June 1896, Foreign Office S/2290, P.R.O., London. When a communication that contained references to unofficial negotiations (Playfair's as well as Smalley's) came to Salisbury from the American embassy, he had his secretary return the communication with the request that the reference be deleted (Salisbury Memo for Mr. [Eric] Barrington, 28 February 1896, Salisbury Papers).

after assuring Olney that he would come to Washington if he could be useful, returned to New York.

Smalley was under personal attack in the American press for his effort to serve the American government scarcely less than he had been for his earlier criticism of it. In Washington his colleagues were jealous of his access to the secretary of state. His longtime enemy, E. L. Godkin, censured him, and John Hay recorded with amusement: "We have to open and shut doors, as in an old-fashioned farce, to keep them from meeting each other." Godkin's *Nation* criticized the "Smalley plan" and urged the American government to make use of wider communications. "In the multitude of newspapers there is safety, and no plan which has only one newspaper behind it can command the confidence of a great people."[21] Other papers expressed the view that Smalley had concocted his proposals out of thin air and that he had no official backing for them. Even the *New York Evening Post,* which was anti-jingo, joined the attack on Smalley, as did the *New York Sun,* in spite of the fact that Dana, the editor of the *Sun,* was one of Smalley's old friends. Obviously the American press did not approve of the Smalley-Olney joint enterprise.

In April the American secretary of state tried another approach. "Am I to infer," he asked the British ambassador in what was strong language even for Olney, "that negotiations upon the Venezuelan boundary question are no longer occupying the attention of the British Foreign Office?"[22] He then sent for Smalley, who had said little in his March dispatches on the dispute, and tried once again with the correspondent's cooperation to bring pressure on Salisbury through the columns of the *Times.* In the new offensive Smalley made use of several themes, the chief of which was expressed in Olney's question to Pauncefote: Did the British Foreign Office still have an interest in a settlement? "In lieu of further negotiations upon Venezuela," Smalley declared in his cable to the *Times* on 21 April, "Lord Salisbury has embarked upon a scheme of general arbitration." Two days later he asserted, "Lord Salisbury, so far as it is known

21. *Nation,* 27 February 1896, p. 169.
22. Olney to Pauncefote, 10 April 1896 [copy], Olney Papers.

here, has simply dropped the subject. How can this Government revive the negotiations?" Somewhat surprisingly he repeated the earlier proposals for a joint Anglo-American arbitration commission, but it was not his idea. He proposed to Olney that they try something new such as an Anglo-Venezuelan commission, but the secretary rejected the idea. Lastly, Smalley rang the alarm bell: "The uncertainties are many, the perils grave in the present course of reaction."

For a variety of reasons the April American offensive failed to strike many sparks. Pauncefote assured Salisbury that Smalley's foolish telegram had "only temporarily disturbed the American calm." Interest in the question in the United States was fading in part because the Cuban crisis was creating a diversion. In England Harcourt, who had a low boiling point on the issue, again became excited, but most Englishmen felt that the danger point had been passed and that in due time the controversy would be settled somehow. Salisbury knew that the Cleveland administration was anxious to close the books on the matter before the November elections and that this desire was an additional lever in his hands. Initially, the *Times* responded tolerantly to the April activities of its correspondent, and Smalley assured Olney that the paper would go as far as possible in support of "our view." But the paper lost patience as Smalley persisted and his criticisms became sharper. The Foreign Office objected when Smalley declared that it had not complied with a request for information from the U.S. government. It was all a misunderstanding, declared the Foreign Office, owing to a key communication having been sent by sea mail rather than cable, but the *Times* did not accept the explanation readily. Not long afterward Buckle ordered Smalley to omit references to Venezuela in his communications until further notice.

The order for a taboo was given in early June and virtually ended Smalley's participation in the Venezuelan boundary dispute on both the private and public levels. He stayed away from Washington though "tempted by more than one letter" to return. In July he went to England for his vacation. Observers were surprised when Lord Salisbury warmly greeted his recent journalistic critic at a garden party, and Henry White, a young American diplomat who already knew the British well, was taken aback when he learned that Salisbury had invited Smalley to the Foreign Office for a long talk.[23] Smalley was not surprised; that was not his nature.

The Venezuelan controversy was settled finally in November in a manner reasonably acceptable both to the Americans and the British. Salisbury succeeded in excluding settled districts from arbitration but only managed to limit settled areas to those that had been settled for fifty or more years. Some aspects of the part played by the press in the crisis were not unusual while others were quite unprecedented. Smalley's role was unique only when considered in conjunction with editor Buckle's role in April. The Smalley-Buckle efforts are especially impressive because there has rarely survived such substantial evidence of journalistic-diplomatic cooperation in a crisis. Few newspapers and few journalists have kept records of their collaboration with officials while for their part diplomatic officials have been careful to keep such cooperation out of the official records and often to destroy their private papers.

To some, Smalley may appear to be a bungler in the Venezuelan crisis; to others, he is a journalist who gave up his integrity for access to inside news and a chance to participate in an international crisis. Such views would be unfair on both counts. Smalley's bungling was, in strong probability, the result of Olney's ground shifting. Smalley made no effort to camouflage his position as spokesman for the American authorities. As he told Moberly Bell, he felt that the English people should understand the official American position whether it was right or wrong. Of course he came to believe it was right, in general, and lawyer Smalley is more in evidence in some of his communications than journalist Smalley. Still, both he and Buckle tried to use their respective positions to influence the principals in the direction of moderation. The crisis gave Smalley the greatest opportunity of his life to have a key part in diplomatic negotia-

---

23. Henry White to Richard Olney, 29 August 1896, Olney Papers. In reporting the conversation to Chamberlain, Salisbury mentioned only Smalley's views on the American attitude toward a general arbitration treaty (Salisbury to Chamberlain, 18 August 1896 [copy], Salisbury Papers).

tions, and obviously he enjoyed the part. At times in his dispatches to the *Times* he pushed too hard and labored points until they lost force. Even so, he acted in the crisis with dignity, skill, and perception.

11. American Jingoes and Times *Policy Makers*

The presidential election of 1896 held a fascination for many Englishmen nearly as great as it held for the American public. During the summer Alfred Harmsworth sent his young star reporter, George W. Steevens, to canvass America and send back letters for the new mass circulation paper, the *Daily Mail*. The Prince of Wales asked Smalley to cable him the results of the election. When the election results were coming in, *Times* manager Moberly Bell stayed at his office for thirty-six consecutive hours, getting only one hour of sleep in the thirty-six.[1] On the evening of the election Smalley cabled the results to London at three-to-ten-minute intervals from 5 P.M. to midnight. To most Englishmen, including the editors of the *Times*, William Jennings Bryan's silver policy posed a genuine threat to British and world security. They saw little difference in the foreign policies of the two parties on other counts. While they did not like Republican William McKinley's high-tariff record, they felt it could be tolerated as the lesser of evils. As George W. Steevens put it: "I don't suppose that England would welcome a new McKinley [tariff] Bill with illuminations and votes of thanks. But if it hit Germany harder than it did us, we might receive it with the more Christian resignation."[2]

1. E. H. C. Moberly Bell, *The Life and Letters of C. F Moberly Bell* (London, 1927), p. 189.
2. George W. Steevens, *The Land of the Dollar* (Edinburgh, 1897), p. 175.

Before going on vacation in July Smalley reported the Democratic National Convention in Chicago from New York. He characterized the meeting as an insurrection rather than a convention and declared that "Democratic Jacobinism has taken for its motto the Jesuitical maxim that the end justifies the means." He paraphrased parts of Bryan's famous "Cross of Gold" speech but did not give it very high praise. He wrote that Bryan has "youth, energy, some real capacity, knowledge and enthusiam, and all these with his gift of eloquence he is ready to put at the service of the most abominable political creed ever adopted by a political party in America." Smalley concluded that Bryan was chosen by a combination of Silverites and Communists—to him the Populists were Communists. The leaders in the *Times* were even less charitable than the paper's correspondent toward the candidate of the Democratic party: ". . . when he [Smalley] says that he believes him to be sincere, it is only at the expense of his intelligence and good sense that we can accept this vindication of his morality."

During the summer campaign the *Times* was dependent on the arid and not very informative cables of Reuter. When Smalley returned from his vacation he accompanied Chauncey Depew to Canton, Ohio, where he was able to spend several hours with the Republican candidate. Smalley's irresistible urge to appraise and analyze men met an inexplicably severe test in the relatively uncomplicated McKinley. He began and ended his initial appraisal of McKinley on a note of uncertainty and continued to show puzzlement in the years that followed. John Hay, a strong supporter of McKinley from the outset, wrote his friend Henry Adams in 1898 that Smalley changed his mind weekly about McKinley. "Sometimes he admires him more than I do, and sometimes less. I think he is wrong both times."[3] After McKinley had been in office for more than two years the *Times* correspondent could still write such un-Smallian passages as "I try not to think of myself as one of his friends, and if I do not proclaim it or extol it as a virtue I record it without comment, just yet." The *Times* man dutifully reported the last

3. Hay to Adams, 9 May 1898, in William Roscoe Thayer, *The Life and Letters of John Hay*, 2 vols. (Boston, 1905), 2:167.

stages of the campaign from the Republican viewpoint, emphasized the desertion of the Cleveland Democrats from Bryan, and went to Washington in February 1897 to describe the inaugural ceremonies adequately but without special distinction.

Like almost everyone else Smalley was concerned about the composition of the new cabinet, and he defended it rather unenthusiastically as one that "could pass muster." The appointment that gave him the most unhappiness was that of Senator John Sherman of Ohio as secretary of state. On 12 March, he reported to the *Times* a lengthy interview with the new secretary of state:

After a long conversation last evening with the Secretary of State, I bring away the impression that he either has no very definite and settled opinions on general questions of foreign policy, or that, if he has, he does not hope to make them strongly felt by the Senate. . . . He does not feel himself in his true place as Secretary of State and and does not think foreign affairs of the first importance, or even of very high importance. The country, in his judgment, can get along pretty well without any foreign policy. . . . "We have enough to do at home. . . ." It has been a week since the President and Secretary took office. They have not found time to confer on a single subject of foreign policy.

The one appointment by McKinley for which Smalley expressed unrestrained enthusiasm was that of John Hay as ambassador to the Court of St. James.

Smalley could never get out of range of the fire of the jingoes even when he was working closely with Olney for a policy that most of them supported. For some years his favorite word for his critics was jingo, and he took it for granted that all jingoes were Anglophobes. This interpretation aroused the ire of Theodore Roosevelt. He called up from his full bag of expletives such unflattering characterizations of Smalley as "copper-riveted idiot" and "exceedingly pernicious idiot," and he made references to Smalley's "guinea-pig brain." Smalley had "simply infested the London *Times* and other English papers with the theory that when I speak of the Monroe Doctrine I have especial reference to England, whereas the fact is that as things now are the Monroe Doctrine does not touch England in any shape or way. . . ."[4] The correspondent was sometimes denounced for unflattering but really innocuous remarks about popular figures such as Gladstone and Bryce.[5] When he said that it was necessary to do research in England in order to write American history, he was attacked for belittling American libraries.

Now and then a Smalley episode gave amusement to his friends as well as welcome copy for the gossipy press. At a dinner of the New England Society of New York in December 1897, Smalley responded to the toast "New England and Old England" by praising both the new and the old. At the same time he expressed concern that the belligerence of American policy and jingo spokesmen was endangering American friendship not only with England but with other European countries as well. His statements were moderate enough and were delivered in a mild conversational tone. (Smalley never spoke publicly in any other manner.) At the conclusion of his remarks, Senator Joseph R. Hawley rose and in a "quiet dignified way" said: "Not with a wish to disturb the delightful harmony of this occasion but merely from impulse, I wish to express my sincere and profound regret that our distinguished friend misunderstands his own country to such an extent." Smalley and Hawley were old friends and the correspondent refused to take the incident seriously, but portions of the press made the most of it. The *Boston Herald* even dug up the story for Smalley's obituary in 1916. The mildly critical *New York Times* commented that "Mr. Smalley had more than one experience which should go far to convince him that if he does not knowingly misrepresent American it is only because, in Senator Hawley's words, he fails to understand it."[6] When John Hay, the U.S. ambassador in

4. Roosevelt to Arthur Cecil Spring Rice, July 1901, in *The Letters of Theodore Roosevelt,* ed. Elting E. Morison, 8 vols. (Cambridge, Mass., 1951–54), 3:109.

5. Smalley had long believed that American idolatry of Gladstone was beyond explanation. His own criticism of Bryce, which continued for six or seven years after he came to America, puzzled Bryce and Bryce's friends. They puzzle the present writer as well.

6. *New York Times,* 23 December 1897, editorial. See also the *Brooklyn* (N.Y.) *Daily Eagle,* 27 December 1897.

England, sent an account of the incident to Henry James, the latter replied: "I return you Smalley with thanks and with a certain amount of disappointment, I confess, at not finding his speech quite so explosive as I had supposed. But doubtless it 'did' for that; for utility it is quite as certain that he would or might be better if he were more insidious."[7]

A more serious affair than the New and Old England incident occurred a few months later and came to be known as Smalley's "music hall" interview with President McKinley. During a talk with the president the *Times* correspondent showed him a dispatch from England that suggested that English opinion was veering toward Spain in the rapidly heightening crisis over Cuba. The president was surprised and expressed both his concern and his unchanged attitude of friendship toward England. In his account of the interview for the *Times* Smalley elaborated at length on the president's friendly attitude, being careful as usual not to quote McKinley directly and to take personal responsibility for all phraseology, but he commented quite gratuitously and pointlessly: "America, as everybody now concedes, wishes to be friends with England, but friendship must be on terms consistent with self respect. The verdict of the Music Hall is not sought nor accepted as an expression of English judgement."[8]

The "music hall" reference was completely uncalled for, but it was not in itself very damaging. It certainly did not seem to be an adequate explanation for the wrathful and drastic reaction of the *Times* authorities. The day following the printing of the dispatch, manager Moberly Bell cabled Smalley: "At the request of Editor the Foreign Editor and several friends outside office with whose opinion I concur I beg that you will not continue discussion of Anglo-American relations. The less they are discussed the better they are likely to be and your initiation of discussion by writing President's opinion on feeling of and on music halls has already done much harm."[9]

7. James to Hay (dated only Monday), John Hay Papers, Library of Congress, Washington, D.C.
8. *Times* (London), 29 April 1898.
9. Moberly Bell to Smalley, 30 April 1898 [copy], Printing House Square, London (hereafter cited as PHS).

Smalley naturally had difficulty in believing that the *Times* really meant to exclude from his dispatches the most important topic of all. "Your view perplexes me," he replied. "Silence on that ever recurring subject to be permanent? It is continually discussed here." The implications of Moberly Bell's answer to this inquiry were clear enough: "We do not mean to bar any reference on your part to Anglo-American relations. We only decline to consider those that in any way depend upon music hall gossip. Mutual instances of good will between governments may fittingly be recorded and warn us privately of anything likely to disturb excellent feeling now existing."[10]

Unlike the *New York Tribune*, which had only certain likes, dislikes, and prejudices in foreign affairs, the London *Times* had—or at least tried to have—a foreign policy. Because it was not always easy to ascertain precisely what the policy was, it was frequently impossible for a foreign correspondent to hit the exact note that would please the editors. These facts made working for the *Times* more difficult than for the *Tribune*. When Smalley displeased the *Tribune* editors he knew in advance what he was doing and could calculate the risks. He obviously knew most of the time when the *Times* would be displeased with him, too, but more than once, as was true with the music hall story, he was genuinely surprised when the *Times* editors reacted in anger to what he had written. The story was reprinted in some of the New York papers, including the *Tribune*, without attracting much interest, and it drew only an occasional unfavorable comment in the London journals. It was really a case of poor judgment rather than cause for alarm. Moberly Bell's references to it for some weeks following, which exaggerated the importance of the item and perversely misrepresented the account itself, demonstrate the unusual sensitivity of the paper on the matter of Anglo-American relations. Smalley thought that his very good friend Ambassador Hay had probably complained to the *Times*. One also strongly suspects that the Foreign Office may have objected, but there is no evidence that either Hay or anyone connected with the Foreign Office was among the "friends" who told Moberly Bell they were disturbed.

10. Ibid.

It is difficult to overemphasize the seriousness with which the *Times* regarded its own foreign policy. Financial difficulties and declining circulation did not affect the belief of the editors that the paper spoke with an authority second only to that of the government. Manager Moberly Bell thought that the foreign editor of the *Times* was, or at least should be, one of the four or five most influential men in the British Isles. Donald Mackenzie Wallace, the foreign editor when Smalley joined the *Times,* was a respected, scholarly journalist, but not very influential and far less aggressive than Valentine Chirol who replaced him as foreign editor in 1899. The *Times* took delight in demonstrating its independence on occasions as in the instance of its refusal to replace its correspondent who had been ordered out of Russia in spite of indirect pleas by the Russian government and some pressure from the British government. The paper's feeling of concern over British isolation predated that of the government, as did its promotion of Anglo-American friendship. It even smiled tolerantly on the Anglo-American-Saxon cult of the period though it did not go so far as to support openly the idea of a formal Anglo-American alliance. In 1898 almost everyone was convinced that Anglo-American relations had never been better. The British ambassador to the United States wrote Salisbury of a "sudden transition in this country from Anglophobia to the most exuberant affection for England and Britishers in general."[11] Even Smalley was impressed. "Attacks on England have ceased to be thought useful even by jingoes. . . . Good will has never been so marked."

Under such circumstances Smalley's task should have been an easy one. And so it would have had Smalley only been willing to play softer notes and to steer clear of some touchy subjects. In the Alaskan boundary dispute he expressed approval of the conciliatory attitude of the British but emphasized more than was necessary to intransigence of the Canadians. He opposed the idea of war with Spain, and, until the war actually broke out, continued to denounce the jingoes and the yellow press as warmongers. The editors of the *Times* rarely challenged the

11. Pauncefote to Salisbury, private, 28 May 1898, Lord Salisbury Papers, Christ Church, Oxford.

validity of his views; it simply did not fit their policy for him to express them. In 1900 when the argument between correspondent and editor over Smalley's expressed views had been going on for several years, Chirol wrote him:

You will doubtless notice that we have thought it desirable to prune down to some extent your message concerning Mr. McKinley's attempted intervention. Your criticism is unquestionably legitimate, but is it not more politic to refrain from it? It seems to me that by displaying irritation, we should only be playing into the hands of those who want to irritate us. Tail twisting, one may hope, will lose most of its charm if the tail refuses to squirm. That is the view taken by Downing St. and for once it seems to be a sound one. At any rate for the present we are inclined to adopt it.[12]

After a visit to the United States in 1901 Moberly Bell was more sympathetic with Smalley's problems. When he returned he wrote an American acquaintance:

One of the most puzzling problems that I have carried away with me from your country is that nine out of ten people I met talked privately exactly as Mr Smalley talks publicly, and then assured me that Mr Smalley did not represent their opinions! This makes correspondence from America peculiarly difficult. The province of a correspondent is to describe facts as they are, and not as he wishes they were, and in no country of the world have I found so much frankness in describing things as they are in America, combined with a unanimous desire that they should be described as they are not.[13]

Wickham Steed, one of the great *Times* correspondents of the period, thought it impossible for a journalist to maintain genuine independence in a foreign country over a long period of time. For that reason, he said, he never planned to remain permanently as a foreign correspondent but to use the experience as a stepping-stone to other journalistic work.[14] Smalley's problem was something of an inversion of Steed's in that his long residence in a foreign country had increased his critical attitude toward his own. The added fact that he was endowed with

12. Chirol to Smalley, 16 March 1900 [copy], Foreign Department Letterbook, no. 5, PHS.
13. Moberly Bell to an unidentified American, 29 October 1901, in E. H. C. Moberly Bell, *Life and Letters of C. F. Moberly Bell*, p. 222.
14. Personal statement to the author.

a strong measure of cantankerousness made it certain that he would irritate many fellow Americans by his candid reporting. And Moberly Bell, for all of his fine talk about reporting things "as they are, and not as he [the reporter] wishes they were" was, like Chirol, more interested in placating the Americans at the turn of the century than in having conditions described candidly.

Efforts to cover the Spanish-American War gave the *Times* a whole series of headaches. Initially both Smalley and the editors assumed he would make little effort to report the events of the war. Moberly Bell thought that he could employ a few war correspondents sufficiently competent to take care of the paper's needs in the traditional manner. Smalley urged an arrangement with the *New York Herald* whereby the *Times* would have access to the war reports of that paper. Neither scheme worked well. Moberly Bell was soon in despair over the accounts he received from the *Herald* reporters. "There seems such an insurmountable difference in the ideas of American and English journalists as to what constitutes news that I am getting quite hopeless of ever getting the N.Y. Herald people to understand it."[15] On his own the manager employed several correspondents from whom he received nothing worthwhile. E. F. Knight managed to lose his credentials and got locked up in a Cabanas prison. Another reporter failed to produce anything more than "trivial and stale" accounts from Tampa. Poultney Bigelow, a reporter Smalley recommended to the *Times,* submitted lengthy pieces that the *Times* editors rejected almost entirely.

Richard Harding Davis, another Moberly Bell "find," contributed comic relief without amusing anybody. The manager employed him at a good salary, assuming a willingness on Davis's part to become a member of the team in a way that differed greatly from Davis's idea of his proper place in the journalistic constellation. Davis maintained that he was employed to accompany the army at his own discretion, that he was engaged as "the Times correspondent, not as one of them," and that he would under no circumstances take orders from Smalley in New York

15. Moberly Bell to Smalley, 21 June 1898 [copy], PHS.

or allow the plans of other field correspondents to influence his own decisions. Moberly Bell thought all of this completely unreasonable and told Davis so in strong language. He had employed him with the expectation that Davis would do his best, placing the interests of the *Times* ahead of his personal feelings. In reply to a cable in which the correspondent declared, "Can accept orders from no one but yourself," the manager said, "Do you expect me to go over personally and give them? This letter will reach you by a postman—it is none the less mine. I trust you not to have any more of this." Davis resigned in a ridiculous display of childish anger:

You made the mistake of appealing to "my honour as a gentleman" to do my best for your paper. No one has had to do that since I was three years old and my nurse had to use such appeals to get me in a bath tub. And your calling upon me to remember my honor as a gentleman and journalist would have been insulting if it had not been so hypocritical and had it not shown that you had no idea whatever as to who was serving you, and who was not. . . . I return your letter which you must see in calmer moments is quite impossible. It is that of a cabinet minister to a consular agent. . . . I cannot of course accept any salary from the *Times* for the three weeks I served it. It gives me pleasure to make your paper a present of the two hundred and forty pounds, and so quit even.

Moberly Bell accepted the resignation and wrote Smalley that Harding Davis seems to have "gone off his head poor chap."[16]

In the end the *Times* gave Smalley the responsibility for compiling war digests in New York and they proved to be the best accounts the paper received. Smalley complained of overwork but managed to recall some of his old enthusiasm and get the job done. He relied largely on the reports of the *New York Herald* but applied a judgment based on long experience to separate fact from fiction. The *Times* used Reuter material and printed reports from Madrid and Manila as well as from New York. Smalley engaged in a long private battle over censorship with the American authorities, but the excellence of his summaries offset the sometimes tiresome distractions created by the

16. The Davis letter quoted at length is dated 2 June 1898, though Davis had resigned by cable in mid-May.

quarrel. The manager's frequent expressions of confidence and gratitude gave his New York correspondent a much-needed lift in spirits.

After living in England for nearly thirty years Smalley did not easily give up the social habits and tastes he had acquired. He found Washington society rigid with "far too much punctilio" though "agreeable enough if you make up your mind to conform." Unfortunately he was not always of a mind to conform. He had only been in New York a few months when he was suspended from the Metropolitan Club for six weeks for escorting a mixed group into club areas where ladies were not admitted. When called before a house committee to explain his conduct, he pleaded pressing business as an excuse for not appearing but was discovered asleep in the club library at the time of the meeting. One feels certain that Smalley enjoyed this occurrence, just as he obviously enjoyed the reappearance of the anecdote of his English days that labeled certain types of parties "Earl and Smalley" as a pun on "small and early." When the story was told to Smalley, he replied that "that would depend entirely on which Earl."

For the public, Smalley vigorously defended his Americanism, asserting time and again his love of America and admiration of Americans. When he found things he did not like, he often blamed them on European influences or charged them to recent un-Americanized immigrants. But he made little effort to conceal from his closer English friends that he counted England his spiritual home. He wrote the Duchess of Sutherland in a tone of pained resignation to the inevitable circumstances that kept him in exile, and he frequently told Moberly Bell how he felt. "My delight at the prospect of seeing England again is of the most unpatriotic kind—as the jingoes here consider patriotism," he wrote. . . . "If you knew how I longed for the other side and how I count the days before I sail you would consider me a hero and a martyr." The *Times* policy on vacations was extremely generous and Moberly Bell especially was very considerate. "Come home when you can," he wrote in the midst of the Spanish-American War when the correspondent's services were almost indispensable in New York. Despite illness, family troubles, and overwork Smalley refused on this occasion to return until there was a lull.

Vacations were virtually always more than a month, not counting the time taken in crossing the ocean, and sometimes were stretched into several months. If he was in good health, Smalley's spirits were high when he returned to England. In 1897 he asked the manager to insert a notice in the paper of his return, giving his Brown Hotel address. "It will bring joy to the bosoms of thousands of the bravest and fairest in the isle," he said. Customarily he divided his time between a stay in London and visits to the country homes of his old, aristocratic friends. The 1897 visit was marked by the London marriage of his daughter Eleanor Garnaut Smalley to George Gerald King Meares, widower and son of an army officer, who listed his profession on the marriage certificate as "Gentleman." Two of the official witnesses to the ceremony were Henry James and Ambassador John Hay.

In 1898 Smalley's personal affairs reached a nadir. For one thing, he broke with his family and thereafter lived separately. The separation with his wife was not a divorce; it was merely an agreement that the two should go their individual ways. The four unmarried Smalley children—all now grown—sided with their mother. This included Smalley's favorite daughter Evelyn who had often accompanied him on his European travels and to whom he paid high tribute for her aid in interviews and in other work. Mrs. Smalley told acquaintants that the decision was hers and that her close friends felt she was fully justified in taking the step. Smalley wrote Moberly Bell that he did not really know "why we part at all" but "I hate it." Joseph H. Choate, a prominent lawyer and Smalley friend who was soon to replace Hay as British ambassador, arranged the financial settlement as a personal favor rather than a professional service.

Smalley was convinced that his family difficulties were the main cause of his newly developing health troubles. "It was not the gout which brought on the separation but the separation which brought on the gout," he insisted. Before the end of the summer he was using crutches and had given up most of his work for employers other than the *Times*. The extra money from articles and from contributions to the *Herald* had increased his income by one-third and the loss came at a time when he sorely needed the funds. His house on Chester Place in London had not been leased after he left and was costing him £230 yearly plus repair bills. Smalley finally had to ask the *Times* for a quarterly advance in salary (£562 10s.) to permit him to make a cash settlement for his lease on the London house.

When the temperature reached 107° on 1 September 1898 in New York City, the ailing man gave up and returned to England for his vacation and a rest that extended until after the beginning of the new year. He felt unable to accept an invitation from Andrew White in Germany, but he spent some weeks during the winter at the palatial Riviera home of Sir Sydney Waterlow, a place visited by numerous prominent Englishmen including the Prince of Wales. He arrived back in New York in early February, by then able to resume a moderate work schedule.

12. "Ambassador of the Thunderer"

In the John Hay papers at the Library of Congress there is an undated copy of an invitation from Hay to Smalley that reads: "A man has just dropped out of our diplomatic dinner tonight. Will you come as Ambassador of the Thunderer? At 8." The title for a representative of the *Times* was not entirely original. President Abraham Lincoln greeted *Times* correspondent William Howard Russell as the ambassador of a great power when he came to the United States to report the Civil War. But it was a characteristic gesture by Hay, and it illustrates his knowledge of Smalley's susceptibilities and of his usefulness to an American secretary of state.

Hay, who became the American secretary of state on 17 August 1898 and remained in the office until his death on 1 July 1905, had a knowledge of the press unsurpassed by any other American secretary of state. His experience with the *New York Tribune* gave him the understanding of an insider. His service as U.S. ambassador in England immediately prior to entering the cabinet gave him a special and up-to-date acquaintance with the English press. Furthermore, he made efforts as secretary to remain au courant in journalistic matters. One of his frequent correspondents was A. Maurice Low, a devoted Anglo-American who worked in the United States for the *Boston Globe* and wrote at different times in England for the *London Chronicle* and *London Daily News*. At Hay's request, Low prepared in 1900 a careful analysis of the outstanding English journals, identifying their leader writers and depicting their attitudes toward the United States. When, a little later, Henry Watterson of the *Louis-ville Courier-Journal* wrote Hay to express amazement and concern over Henry Norman's unfriendly writings in the *London Chronicle,* Hay was able to inform him that Norman had no current connections with the *Chronicle* although he "has himself been turned against us by the action of our press and Congress."[1]

Another of Hay's English correspondents was St. Loe Strachey, editor of the *Spectator,* whom Hay characterized as "an unusually intelligent and fair-minded man—but capable of the grossest errors." On a visit to the United States in 1902 Strachey and his wife spent two days at the White House. The arrangements had probably been made by Hay since Strachey had not previously met President Roosevelt although he had corresponded with him and had written favorable articles about him.[2] Hay knew all of the leading *Times* people and Smalley sometimes suspected that Hay, while British ambassador, had kept a rein on him through private communications to the editors of the *Times.*

Hay and Smalley were friends of long standing and the good relationship held until the end with only an occasional ripple of disturbance. The secretary was generous with his time and in expressing his views to the correspondent. It was a subtle relationship, one that required understanding on the part of both men. Something of the secretary's indirect methods can be seen from his letter to Smalley pertaining to negotiations in the Alaska boundary dispute in 1899:

I need not tell you it is not customary to hold a government responsible for things said in officious [*sic*] and informal pourparlers. For that reason I cannot give out the conversation between Sir Julian [Pauncefote] and myself before his departure for England, nor the communication which passed between Mr. Choate, Sir Julian and Lord Salisbury in London. It is not proper for me to say that a suggestion came from the British Government for a scheme of arbitration, reserving only the settled towns of Dyea and Skagnay, which only failed because, at the last moment, the Canadians insisted as

1. Hay to Watterson, 28 December 1900, John Hay Papers, Library of Congress, Washington, D.C.
2. Hay to Roosevelt, 2 October 1901 [copy], ibid. See also Amy Strachey, *St. Loe Strachey: His Life and His Paper* (London, 1930), pp. 135, 138–48.

a preliminary to the arbitration that, whatever the result of it should be, they should have Pyramid Harbor. Yet this is precisely what took place.[3]

The information in Hay's letter was in no sense a scoop for Smalley. The points in it that he could use in print did not go beyond what was released by the State Department at approximately the same time to both Reuter and the Associated Press. The exclusive news Smalley received from Hay was rare and seldom of any great importance. The day had passed when an American secretary of state could afford to give any journalist exclusive news for immediate release or make him a sole mouthpiece. This did not prevent resentment on the part of Smalley's colleagues, some of whom suspected all Smalley utterances as coming from Hay. At least once the American ambassador in England cabled the secretary regarding the authenticity of a Smalley dispatch.

The situation was more advantageous than disadvantageous to the journalist, even though the secretary's friendship and frankness may have committed him to views he otherwise would not have taken. "Hay was here [New York] on Friday," he wrote a friend in November 1903 "and discoursed to me for an hour. . . . Having learned from him the full true confidential inside history of the whole matter, I know as a fact what I have all along believed and said [actually he had seemed a bit uncertain] viz—that we did not make the revolution [in Panama] nor abet it, but only when made prevented its being unmade. 'Strictly correct' throughout was the attitude of this government."[4]

In general, Smalley supported Hay's policies and Hay responded with appreciation. "Smalley and Maurice Low are standing by us like bricks," Hay wrote Henry White with reference to the Alaska boundary dispute.[5] But even on the boundary matter, Smalley could not be depended upon absolutely to follow the Hay line. A few months after Smalley had stood like

3. Hay to Smalley, 1 June 1899 [copy], Hay Papers.
4. Smalley to Mrs. Henry White, 30 November 1903, Henry White Papers, Library of Congress, Washington, D.C.
5. Hay to White, 29 May 1899 [copy], Hay Papers.

a brick, Hay wrote Henry Adams: "I spent a day in New York. I had a woeful three hours talk with S——, and never knew until the next day how he has been lambasting us all in the T——."[6] Now and then the correspondent's departure from a supporting role aroused the secretary's wrath, as in the case of Smalley's interpretation of U.S. policy with reference to a German move to embarrass the British during the Boer War. "I own I am amazed at Smalley," he wrote Henry Adams. "I found in the London Times of the 4th of October [1900] that he says our rejection of the first proposition was due to timidity, and our acceptance of the second to a desire to ingratiate ourselves with the Powers. I can't imagine where he gets these idiotic impressions unless by reading the yellow journals at the clubs."[7] Hay's anger did not last long. The bonds of friendship and the need for friendly journalists soon tempered the secretary's indignation.

By the turn of the century individual foreign correspondents in the United States had pretty well abandoned spot news to the press associations. Smalley's instructions from Moberly Bell were to leave routine news to Reuter save in crucial matters, and accordingly he was limited in his cable wordage. In 1899 he was told to limit his cables to 1,200 words per week "short of a new war or the death of the President," but the allowance was increased the following year to 6,240 words a month.[8] Under Melville E. Stone, the Associated Press, with an organization of nine men in Washington, became extremely aggressive. Representatives of individual papers complained that the Associated Press men not only demanded news but demanded a monopoly of official and semiofficial news, using threats of boycotts against chiefs of bureaus and department heads to back up their demands.

6. *Letters of John Hay and Extracts from His Diary* (printed but not published, 1908). In Henry Adams's copy in the Massachusetts Historical Society (Boston), Adams has filled in the blanks with "Smalley" and "Times."

7. Hay to Henry White, 16 October 1900 [copy], Hay Papers. Actually Hay misrepresented what Smalley had said and the comments were in the 5 October rather than the 4 October issue of the *Times*.

8. Smalley to Moberly Bell, 13 April 1901, Printing House Square, London (hereafter cited as PHS).

In reporting this turn of events to the *Times* Smalley said that Hay was strong enough to do as he pleased and could give him items on a personal basis, but that assistant secretaries and others who dispensed the bulk of the routine news were not able to act independently. Assistant Secretary of State Adee complained that "every hour some newspaper man—I beg his pardon, some journalist or special commissioner—brings me a mare's egg for inspection." Melville Stone did not hesitate to lecture the secretary on matters of policy. "[Stone] came to see me here," Hay wrote Smalley, "and for two hours dealt with me in a spirit of Christian candor, which was very amusing. He denounced not only everything that I have done in the last six years, but everything that anybody bearing a commission of this country has done."[9] In 1906 Stone complained to President Roosevelt that the American minister in Peking was giving information to the London *Times* correspondent in China to the disadvantage of the Associated Press and the United States. The president was sufficiently impressed to write the American diplomat asking that the Associated Press man should be given at least any news given to any other press representative.[10]

The major question in foreign affairs that concerned the *Times* correspondent during the Hay regime were the Hay–Pauncefote Treaty, the question of the Panama revolution and the relations of the United States to the new state of Panama, and the dispute between the United States with Great Britain and Canada over the Alaska boundary. There was nothing distinctive or distinguished in Smalley's dispatches on any of these. John Hay was himself essentially an Anglophile which made it possible for Smalley to support his policies and the cause of Anglo-American friendship without serious conflict. He took a more direct part in the Alaskan boundary matter than in the others. In February 1902 he went to Canada, spent a week at Government House at Ottawa, and had long talks with Sir Wilfrid Laurier, the Canadian prime minister, apparently con-

9. Hay to Smalley, 2 July 1904 [copy], Hay Papers.
10. Roosevelt to William Woodville Rockhill, 6 August 1906, in *The Letters of Theodore Roosevelt*, ed. Elting E. Morison, 8 vols. (Cambridge, Mass, 1951–54), 5:344.

veying to Laurier some of Hay's views that the secretary did not care to express formally. On his return, Smalley reported Laurier's statements to Hay and the president, and he believed that his report encouraged them to make fresh efforts toward a settlement.[11]

Smalley's defense of U.S. policy in the Panama crisis was more persuasive and more consistent after his briefing by Hay on the matter in November 1903. A month after the briefing the United States was accused by Senator Hoar of Massachusetts of meddling in the Panamanian revolution. Smalley replied to him in the *Times* to the effect that he could answer all of Hoar's questions that were pertinent and could assure him authoritatively that the United States neither made nor helped make the revolution.[12] Smalley's support of Hay's position in the Hay–Pauncefote Treaty negotiations brought action by Hay critics, some of whom tried to counteract Smalley's influence in England. Frederick W. Holls, for example, wrote a letter to the *Times* (published on 1 January 1901), and private letters to Valentine Chirol, Ambassador Choate, and L. J. Maxee, editor of the *National Review,* asserting that Smalley's intimacy with Hay had led him to a complete distortion of true American opinion on the treaty.[13]

Smalley never tired of stressing the friendly Anglo-American relations that had become so pronounced following the good will shown by Great Britain during the Spanish-American War. It was Smalley's account—actually the explanation of Sir Julian Pauncefote—that became the accepted version of British unwillingness to associate with the efforts of other European governments to put pressure on the United States for a settlement with Spain in 1898. A recent investigator has cast doubts about the validity of Smalley's interpretation of Pauncefote's actions,[14] but the Smalley version was reasonable for the evidence available to

11. Smalley to Moberly Bell, 11 February 1902, PHS. See also George W. Smalley, *Anglo-American Memories* (New York, 1911), pp. 260–76.

12. *Times* (London), 10 December 1903.

13. 21 January–15 February 1901, Frederick W. Holls Papers, Columbia University Library, New York, N.Y.

14. R. G. Neale, *Great Britain and United States Expansion, 1898–1900* (Lansing, Mich., 1966), pp. 18–22.

the correspondent. In 1900 Chirol became concerned over rumored activities in the German embassy at Washington designed to stir up the pro-Boer elements in the United States against the English. "I am afraid there is no longer any room to doubt the profound hostility and duplicity of Germany," he wrote Smalley. "She will not commit herself openly against us, but in every direction she is doing her best to obstruct and thwart us."[15] Smalley was entirely agreeable to a defense of the British against any possible German threat. He supported his friend Pauncefote strongly and had nothing but praise for his successor Sir Michael Herbert, but he was petulantly critical of German Ambassador Speck von Sternberg.

Scarcely less important than Smalley's relationships with Hay was his standing with Theodore Roosevelt who succeeded McKinley as president on the latter's assassination in September 1901. At the time of McKinley's death Smalley was in England on vacation. Moberly Bell was in the United States, however, on a visit that Smalley seems not to have known about until just before he sailed for England. The *Times* manager knew Hay rather well and knew also a number of American political and literary figures. He and Chirol were the most interested people connected with the *Times* management in American affairs and in all likelihood an incidental purpose of his visit was to check on his New York correspondent. He went to Buffalo during McKinley's last days and talked to Roosevelt. The results of the conversation are best revealed in a letter from Roosevelt to Smalley, dated Buffalo. 10 September 1901 [four days before McKinley's death]:

My dear Smalley:—
I have just come across Mr. Bell here where I have been called because of the dreadful affair about the President. We got [to] talking of you. I told him how very fond of you I was personally and my utter disagreement with your way of looking at the conditions of our American life, and especially the points of international policy upon which we touch England. He said to me that he wished I would speak to you personally, and I said that I should be only too glad, but that you considered me a jingo and did not trust, or in any way agree

15. Chirol to Smalley, 23 January 1900 [copy], Foreign Department Letterbook, no. 5, PHS.

with, my judgment in these matters. However, when next you come to this side, I should greatly like to have the chance to speak with you at length on these matters. I would like to have an opportunity to tell you why I feel as I do; why I believe that, with all your honesty and sincerity of purpose, you are in error as to the motives and wisdom of one school of our people in foreign affairs—the school to which I belong.

> *Most sincerely yours /s/*
> *Theodore Roosevelt*[16]

Roosevelt's gesture, under the circumstances, was surprisingly friendly and conciliatory. Smalley's reply, equally friendly, gave the impression that the writer was a judge in court, determined to consider the case solely on its merits.

My dear Mr. President—

Your letter of the 10th inst. has reached me here [Raith Kircaldy]. First of all, let me offer my personal congratulations on the great opportunity which opens before you. You know how much pleasure it gives me when you take a step onward or when Fortune, even in such melancholy and tragic circumstances, befriends you. Perhaps you don't know how high my hopes are, for your letter shows that you think I distrust your judgment in certain matters. It is true that I differed from you, and quite lately, but I never undertook to be infallible and since I have read what sayings of yours have been sent to us here, my hopes are the higher. I cannot but congratulate you on the moderation, loyalty, and statesmanlike good sense upon which you view your accession and enter upon your great office. As for questions of future policy, I may or may not be able to follow you—I hope I shall—but upon the spirit which animates you as shown in these declarations there cannot be two opinions. It is, if, I may say so, admirable.

I shall, of course, be delighted to come to Washington for the talk you suggest. I shall come with an open mind and, you will not doubt, with the heartiest wish to find myself mistaken in any opinion which divides us. I sail on Oct. 19 and will write you on reaching New York. Believe me, with many thanks for your kindly letter and your proposal,

> *Ever Very Sincerely Yours,*
> *George W. Smalley.*[17]

16. *Letters of Theodore Roosevelt*, 3:44. Smalley sent a copy of this letter to Moberly Bell.

17. Smalley to Roosevelt, 24 September 1901 [copy], PHS.

Shortly after his return to the United States Smalley had lunch with the president and two days afterward an hour's talk with him. As he reported the visit to Moberly Bell: "The President was very friendly and frank. Anything he said to you about our differences appears to have been related to the Canal and the Monroe Doctrine. Nothing could be more cordial than his reception and it was not wholly on personal grounds. He spoke to me of my work for you which he called 'the most distinguished that had been done by an American journalist' (adding 'I am a historian and I speak also for the historian's point of view'). He hoped I should come to see him often and discuss not only foreign but domestic affairs."[18]

Making use of his talks with the president, strengthened by two long sessions with Hay and one with Lodge, Smalley wrote a series of letters for the *Times* on the new president and the outlook for his administration.[19] The letters carried the correspondent's characteristic notes of caution and detachment, but these were in large measure offset by expressions of hope and praise. Smalley was delighted, of course, that Hay was to be kept on as secretary of state, but reminded his readers of Roosevelt's record of impulsiveness and the continued existence in the House and in the Senate of a minority capable of "great mischief." He became even more enthusiastic after the president's first message to Congress and commented: "In short, this most outspoken, convinced, inflexibly honest, uncompromising statesman has so handled a series of difficult questions of the first magnitude as to strengthen everybody's confidence in his prudence and ability."[20] A few days later he defended the president as a true friend of England and asserted that his view of the Monroe Doctrine was acceptable.

The delighted *Times* manager wrote a friend that both Roosevelt and Smalley were "behaving excellently." But in his exuberance he made a serious error in writing Smalley to praise him for his change of views. To Smalley it was the president who had changed, and he replied in some heat: "I have not, so far

18. Smalley to Moberly Bell, 18 November 1901, ibid.
19. *Times* (London), beginning 29 November 1901.
20. Ibid., 5 December 1901.

as I know, changed my views, though I do my best to conform to your wishes and instructions so far as I understand them; and I suppress the critical view so far as possible. . . . You were much impressed by what the President said to you about me in Buffalo. Yet what has he been doing ever since he became President but adjusting himself to that conservative view the want of which was my only reproach against him?"[21]

There was a good measure of truth in the correspondent's claim that Roosevelt, under the responsibility of high office, had toned down his public utterances and had softened his private statements to the journalists. At the same time Smalley's dispatches to the *Times* not only recognized these shifts but ignored points that he earlier would have seized and magnified. No longer was the label "jingo" applied to the president. In comparing him with Mark Hanna as a candidate for the Republican nomination, he said: "Mr. Roosevelt is known as a staunch advocate of friendly relations between England and the United States. He has given proof of that sincerity."[22] Even Roosevelt's pronouncements on trusts were taken in stride. Smalley admitted that Roosevelt had alienated banker J. P. Morgan and his trust policies but played up the enthusiastic support of the president in the West and South. These were the lines that the editors wanted Smalley to take and they did not let him forget it. As always there were some critics who were convinced that Smalley had sold his soul and moved into the president's camp because of flattery and the friendly attitude of Roosevelt's cohorts. Neither pressure from employers nor flattery was enough to budge Smalley unless he could be convinced he was right, but they may have helped to convince him.

In spite of the fact that the tiger seemed to have been tamed, at least temporarily, the *Times* editors were not fully satisfied. Moberly Bell could not get over the impression he received from Roosevelt and others on his visit in 1901 that Smalley did not really understand his fellow countrymen, and nagged him repeatedly on the point. "It is probably useless and worse to add anything about my Americanism, bad or good,"

21. Smalley to Moberley Bell, 7 February 1902, PHS.
22. *Times* (London), 31 December 1903.

Smalley wrote the manager. "You have an *idée fixe* on that subject, which I think is pure illusion."[23] The *Times* editors found other things to complain about. "Try to condense more and repeat less." Moberly Bell suggested that Smalley send more letters on literary and other nonpolitical subjects, then often failed to use them when they were sent. "You say I must not mind if literary (and other) letters should be 'Love's Labour Lost,' " Smalley wrote. "But I do mind. I can't like writing for the waste-paper basket. . . . It demoralises me. It is doubly difficult to do one's best when one is never sure whether it mayn't be thrown away. I shall lend you cheerfully whatever you wish sent, but I cannot be insensible to the ultimate fate of my letters."[24]

After 1900 the *Times* made greater use of writers who did special topics—American railways, for example—than it previously had and it made an arrangement with the *New York Times* for an exchange of copy. Smalley did not approve of the latter arrangement, especially when, in 1903, he was told to give his dispatches to the *New York Times* for transmission to London. The arrangement seems never to have worked well for either paper except during the Russo-Japanese War when the *New York Times* profited greatly by having access to the reports of the London *Times* correspondents.[25]

One can sympathize with Smalley in his efforts to meet the wishes of his editors. Their letters to their New York correspondent are often critical after the performance, and uncertain about future policy. The *Times* was in deep financial straits and its editors were troubled over Great Britain's position in world affairs. The abortive Anglo-German alliance negotiation, 1898–1901, the unfriendly attitude of most powers during the Boer War, the Anglo-Japanese alliance of 1902, and the Anglo-French entente of 1904 kept them in a whirl. They were sufficiently tradition-minded not to want to make obvious concessions to the United States, nor to abandon a faintly condescending tone to-

23. Smalley to Moberly Bell, 7 February 1902, PHS.
24. Ibid., 31 January 1902.
25. Meyer Berger, *The Story of the New York Times, 1851–1951* (New York, 1951), pp. 132–34, 161–62, 211–12; Elmer Davis, *History of the New York Times, 1851–1921* (New York, 1921), pp. 275–76.

ward her, but anxious at the same time to promote closer relations with the former North American colonies.

Next to Moberly Bell, foreign editor Valentine Chirol was more concerned about the United States than anyone else on the staff. He visited the United States in the spring of 1903 and again late in 1904. (Owner Arthur Walter visited America in 1902.) Chirol worked closely with the British Foreign Office and made his 1904 visit with the "warm approval" of Lord Lansdowne who had succeeded Salisbury as foreign secretary. Chirol reported to Lansdowne that Sir Mortimer Durand, who had become the British ambassador to the United States after the death of Sir Michael Herbert in October 1903, was not a successful representative and urged a more suitable appointment. But Chirol was frustrated in failing to get some assurances he had hoped to receive from Hay and the president, and concluded: "As usual I have returned from America rather depressed by the greatness and vitality of that huge and young nation with which it seems hopeless for us to compete in the long run on anything like equal terms."[26]

Chirol, unlike Moberly Bell, was never a close friend nor an admirer of Smalley. After both his 1903 and 1904 visits to North America, Chirol and the manager (doubtless influenced by Chirol) bombarded their New York correspondent with criticisms and suggestions as to how he might have done better in the past. Smalley was never at his best under fire. If anything, his performance worsened during these periods of editorial attack. He did not improve matters by relating in detail his continued good relations with Roosevelt and Hay, by forwarding some of Hay's letters to him on to Moberly Bell, and by straining to bring in other bits of evidence of the high esteem in which he was held by certain Americans.

One point that should have been a major one all along remained incidental until late 1904. Smalley was glued to New

26. Chirol to Hardinge, 4 December 1904, Sir Charles Hardinge Papers, Cambridge University Library. Other references to Chirol's 1904 visit to the United States are from Chirol letters to Hardinge, 15 November 1904, 5 January 1905, and 17 January 1905. See also Chirol to Hay, 3 December 1904, Hay Papers.

York City. His travels took him only as far west as Akron, Ohio (once in 1896), and as far south as Washington, D.C., although he did make several trips to Canada. His trips to Washington became less frequent and were usually brief. A number of his talks with the president and the secretary of state took place when they visited New York. In 1903 he changed residences in New York and took a new lease but failed to inform Moberly Bell. Both Hay and Roosevelt made important speeches in 1904 at the St. Louis Exhibition, which Smalley reported from New York. In the same year he did not go to Chicago to report the Republican National Convention in June, or to St. Louis to report the Democratic National Convention in July. His reporting of the Venezuelan crisis of 1902–3 started brilliantly and ended weakly as he tried to keep pace in New York with developments that centered in Washington. Sir Arthur Willert, who was one of Smalley's successors as the *Times* correspondent in the United States, felt that Smalley's insistence on living in New York constituted sufficient ground in itself for firing him.[27]

27. View expressed by Willert to the author.

13. Break with the Times

In late 1904 Chirol returned home from his visit to America determined that Smalley should transfer to Washington. Moberly Bell, who had urged Smalley to make the move earlier, now agreed to take vigorous action. On 30 December he wrote Smalley: "After much consideration we have come to the decision that the correspondent of the Times in the United States—whoever he is—must make Washington his headquarters and must live there entirely whenever either Congress is sitting or the President is in residence there. . . . As this is merely a confirmation of previous orders—which have been disregarded—we assume that you will be able to give effect to them at once."

Smalley argued the case, quoted Hay and others to the effect that the move was unnecessary, pleaded financial loss owing to a new lease he had taken in New York—all to no avail. Moberly Bell dismissed Hay's views with the unresponsive remark that "he is not now a journalist but a diplomatist and I am not surprised that he should not be warmly in favour of being surrounded by journalists." As for the New York lease he had no sympathy at all: "You must suffer the consequences of having renewed the lease without consulting us and ascertaining whether our views had changed."[1]

Smalley sold some of his books and other belongings, asked Hay to submit his name for membership in two Washington clubs, rented a suite of rooms and took up residence in the

1. Moberly Bell to Smalley, 28 January 1905 [copy], Manager's Letterbook, no. 39, Printing House Square, London (hereafter cited as PHS).

capital in February. His by-line now read "Our Washington Correspondent" instead of "Our New York Correspondent" and sometimes just "Our Correspondent." Through Whitelaw Reid he made personal arrangements with the *Tribune*'s bureau in Washington to obtain routine news. The few months he resided in Washington appear to have worked out well enough, but the time was not sufficiently long to make possible a judgment on the new arrangements. Hay, in failing health, was away much of the time and Smalley found him increasingly sensitive to any kind of opposition. The president, on the other hand, took everything as he "takes blows from Jefferies when they spar."[2]

The acceptance by the Russians and Japanese of the U.S. offer to serve as host country for negotiations looking toward the end of the Russo-Japanese War was a matter of major interest to Smalley and the *Times*. In Washington Smalley was disconcerted by how little he could find out about plans for the conference. "The President is usually a very outspoken personage," he wrote in June, but "for ten days he has been absolutely dumb. The State Department has not known what is going on. [Hay was away.] The Cabinet does not know—Taft excepted."[3] Even when he saw the president on 13 June, Smalley could learn nothing of special interest or importance. It was shortly agreed that he should return to England on 1 July for his vacation in order to be back in time to cover the Peace Conference at Portsmouth, New Hampshire.

The plans of the *Times* for covering the Peace Conference included not only reports from Smalley but also from Donald Mackenzie Wallace, formerly foreign editor and a one-time correspondent in Russia, and Dr. George E. Morrison, well-known *Times* foreign correspondent in the Far East. Moberly Bell, always inclined to be overly optimistic in anticipating harmonious relations between his representatives in the field, drew an idyllic picture of the arrangement: "The Times will therefore be represented by a conference in miniature—Morrison for Japan—Wallace for Russia—Smalley for the President umpire." He even hoped that the three could compose joint messages to be

2. Smalley to Moberly Bell, 17 March 1905, ibid.
3. Ibid., 12 June 1905.

headed "From Our Correspondents," but agreed to allow room for differences of opinion and the use of the labels "From Our Special Correspondent" (Wallace), "From Our Peking Correspondent" (Morrison), and "From Our Washington Correspondent" (Smalley).[4] Smalley was to serve as Chancellor of the office. Chirol went along with the plan but he was skeptical. "I shall be curious to see how this mixed team runs," he wrote his friend Charles Hardinge.[5]

Smalley and Wallace took passage for America on the *Kaiser Wilhelm der Grosse,* the ship that brought over Count Serge Witte and the other members of the Russian delegation to the Peace Conference. On board also were a number of journalists— Russian, French, English, and German—coming to cover the conference. Notable among them was Dr. E. J. Dillon, English journalist, Russian scholar, and friend of Count Witte's, who was to serve at the conference as the key adviser to the head of the Russian delegation on matters of publicity. Witte's famed policy of courting the press started before he left St. Petersburg when he granted an interview to a representative of the American Associated Press and continued on board the *Kaiser Wilhelm der Grosse* where Witte made it a point to meet and entertain journalists he did not know.

Smalley, but not Wallace, was impressed. He says in his memories that he had several conversations with the count on board ship and saw him almost daily during the Portsmouth Conference, but Witte does not mention Smalley in his own memoirs. The count was critical of Wallace, however, whom he considered, in spite of his supposed Russian leanings, a snob and a friend of the wrong people in Russia. (His Russian friends included Czar Nicholas II). Witte thought that Wallace was an undercover personal representative of King Edward VII and believed that Wallace was offended at the Peace Conference because he thought Witte had slighted him.[6] In a sense Witte

4. Moberly Bell to George Morrison, 21 July 1905 [copy], ibid., no. 40.
5. Chirol to Hardinge, 24 July 1905, Sir Charles Hardinge Papers, Cambridge University Library.
6. *The Memoirs of Count Witte,* ed. and trans. Abraham Yarmolinsky (London, 1921), pp. 137–39.

was right in his belief that Wallace was an agent of Edward VII. For some years Wallace had been indefatigable in keeping Edward informed on Russian affairs. Probably he had a similar mission at the Peace Conference—Edward's biographers do not say—but he did see the king the day before sailing and was entrusted with a personal message for President Roosevelt.[7] Even before the ship landed in New York on 2 August, Moberly Bell's pretty picture of Wallace's presenting the Russian view and Smalley's taking an impartial stand had been undermined.

The *Times*, in truth, did not want an impartial view of the negotiations—it merely wished to make a few gestures that would appear to present all sides of the case. Chirol, in particular, took this stand. In 1904 he wrote Hardinge that the policy of the *Times* in the Russo-Japanese conflict was based on the conviction that "it is impossible to run with the hare and hunt with the hounds," and that *Times* policy rested on the firm belief "that our interests and those of Russia are fundamentally antagonistic in these regions whilst those of Japan and ours are fundamentally identic." He added: "I believe that without boasting we [presumably the *Times*] can claim a considerable share in the Japanese Alliance and I want us to get the full benefit of it."[8] During the conference Moberly Bell, although pro-Japanese in his general attitude, was not as determined as Chirol to support Britain's ally on every point. His daughter has indicated that he thought there was considerable justice on the Russian side and much good sense in working to bring France's ally Russia and England's ally Japan together.[9]

Before the conference started, Smalley and Wallace visited President Roosevelt's summer home at Oyster Bay, where Smalley arranged an appointment for Wallace to meet the president and deliver his personal message from King Edward. On 7 August they arrived at Portsmouth, where Smalley had engaged rooms for the *Times* delegation. Morrison arrived shortly after. The

7. Sir Sidney Lee, *King Edward VII: A Biography*, 2 vols. (New York, 1927), 2:433–34; see also ibid., pp. 282n, 361, 390; Philip Mangus, *King Edward the Seventh* (London, 1964), p. 307.

8. Chirol to Hardinge, 14 June 1904, Hardinge Papers.

9. E. H. C. Moberly Bell, *The Life and Letters of C. F. Moberly Bell* (London, 1927), pp. 230–31.

Times tried a few composite accounts with the by-line "Our Special Correspondents" but the scheme was unworkable. The reports of the three men consistently represented different viewpoints. Wallace, pro-Russian according to Chirol, did not measure up to that prejudice by Witte's standards. His published reports were moderately pro-Japanese, pessimistic about a peace settlement owing to what he considered the unreasonable stand of Count Witte and the Russians. Morrison went further. He fervently hoped that the peace negotiations would fail and that war would continue. Both Smalley and Wallace thought him "bloodthirsty." Printing House Square found no complaints with Morrison's and Wallace's reports: Smalley was the culprit.

Smalley had long been considered somewhat too harsh in the rare statements he had made about Russian policy; in fact, Moberly Bell had once asked him to tone down his views. Smalley's indignation over the Dogger Bank incident of 1904, when Russian warships fired on British fishing vessels, was great. He disallowed the idea of a mistake and declared that the Russian naval officers must have been "bereft of their senses." A possible shift in Smalley's views was apparent in his first dispatch after the transatlantic trip with Witte, a highly laudatory description of Witte that the *Times* editors accepted without complaint. Throughout the conference Smalley's dispatches consisted for the most part of the views of the Russian delegation, openly attributing them to a spokesman he identified as "my Russian friend." His reports can scarcely be said to have advocated Russian policies—beyond applauding the Russian helpfulness to the press—at least as far as they were printed in the *Times*.

Morrison thought that Smalley had fallen for Count Witte's courtship of the press. When Morrison remonstrated with Smalley, the latter replied: "I am here to get news. I am not concerned with policy."[10] The Japanese pursued a very different press policy from that of the Russians. Baron Komura, head of the Japanese delegation, announced that he would give no interviews on the subject of the peace negotiations and the few

10. Cyril Pearl, *Morrison of Peking* (Sydney, Australia, 1967), p. 154.

journalists who talked to him at Portsmouth—these included Morrison—guarded the fact very carefully. Mr. Sato, secretary to Baron Komura, was designated to deal with the press but he gave out precious little information. Smalley declared that the 120 journalists attending the Peace Conference got nine-tenths of their news from the Russians. Morrison, on the other hand, wrote in vigorous defense of the Japanese policy of press aloofness and in criticism of Witte's "irregular complaints" to the press.

Chirol was even angrier than Morrison. On 22 August he wrote Ambassador Hardinge in Russia: "The way in which Smalley tumbled to Witte's gush was rather aggravating to me. Happily we had Morrison to redress the balance, and Wallace too whose messages considering his sympathies have been very judgmatic. But even the part of Smalley we published produced at first such an undesirable impression that we had to go agin the Russians in our leaders rather more vehemently that I had originally intended."[11] Chirol was especially upset that Smalley ignored a "service message" in which he was told explicitly that the line he was taking was wrong. Chirol said in the message that full publicity for Russian views was desired but that criticisms of the attitude of the Japanese delegates were not to be tolerated. "Remember Japan is our ally. Wallace can tell you special reasons why the policy of the paper must be governed not by dislike of Japanese reticence, but by fundamental justice of their claims and close ties uniting the two countries."[12]

Chirol's reference to the "special reasons" for the paper's attitude which could only be explained orally by Wallace is intriguing. Chirol, but not Wallace, was close to Foreign Secretary Lansdowne at this time but this fact alone, while suggestive, does not necessarily explain why the *Times* was following the official line. Chirol had no use for Wallace's good friend Edward VII—according to Morrison he called Edward an "unmitigated blackguard" in the presence of several newspaper editors. As

11. Chirol to Hardinge, 22 August 1905, Hardinge Papers.
12. Chirol did not keep a copy of this letter to Smalley but later (on 11 October 1905) reconstructed it from memory for Arthur Walter [copy], PHS.

already explained, Moberly Bell was only moderately pro-Japanese and Buckle was no longer as influential as he had once been. Although Arthur Walter, who owned one-third of the *Times* and more than one-half of its printing, served as a sort of final court of appeal in personnel squabbles, he rarely tried to dictate policy. Possibly Chirol was carrying the *Times* with him by sheer personal force, yet in little more than a year Moberly Bell was to attempt to replace Chirol with Morrison as foreign editor.[13]

One can only guess how much editing Chirol did of Smalley's dispatches from Portsmouth, but on 28 August a *Times* leader went to unprecedented extremes in its critical though somewhat indirect comment on one of its own correspondents. Smalley's dispatch of the day quoted his "Russian friend" who expressed the belief that Great Britain was secretly exerting pressure on her Japanese ally to make concessions. The *Times* leader asserted:

Our correspondent at Portsmouth has been furnished by his Russian informant with a series of visionary opinions as to the supposed views and policy of this country, which are so grotesque that, were it not for the immeasurable credulity and capacity for self-deceit exhibited by the Russians in other directions, we could not suppose they were sincerely held. . . . However much or little of them our correspondent's informant may believe, we imagine he was not uninfluenced in making them by the recollection that his interlocutor is an American and not an Englishman. No foreigner who knows us would make us the direct recipients of such confidences as these.

On another level, that of personal relations with his fellow *Times* correspondents, Smalley got into equally deep trouble at Portsmouth. Before leaving Portsmouth Morrison wrote his mother that he intended to recommend strongly that Smalley be removed from his post.[14] Encouraged by Chirol to register complaints, both Morrison and Wallace made charges against Smalley that seriously reflected on his judgment and even carried implications of dishonesty. One letter from Morrison summarizes most of the charges:

13. Pearl, *Morrison of Peking,* pp. 182–83.
14. Ibid., p. 158.

Smalley is the laughing stock of the place. He is friendly enough to me especially as I have occasion to swear at him rather forcibly but he is the most disagreeable crossgrained contradictorious [*sic*] sour old tuft hunter imaginable. He never lets Wallace see his messages. Just now 11:30 A.M. Wallace has come in to ask me to buy him a N.Y. *Times* so that he may read Smalley's dispatches of yesterday. Had I taken a strong pro-Russian view, Smalley would have done justice to the Japanese. . . . He has no ability in detecting deception. Witte simply has fooled him and my remonstrances have been useless. I have got him to tear up two dispatches (one actually on the Yellow Peril) and greatly modify several others but I am entirely dissatisfied with his work and think the sooner he goes into retirement the better.[15]

One other accusation of some importance was that Smalley refused to forward one or two of Wallace's dispatches and that he misrepresented the refusal to Chirol.

These are serious charges indeed and they are difficult to assess. Chirol made an issue of them and submitted the case to Arthur Walter for decision. Smalley was asked along with Wallace and Morrison to submit his version of the affair, but the author has not seen his account; he has seen only the Morrison letters to Chirol, the other letters presumably being kept by Mr. Walter with no copies deposited at Printing House Square. The highhandedness attributed to Smalley is believable though it does seem worse than anything else of the sort on his record; the accusation that he fell blindly for Witte's "gush" less so—unless Chirol did a lot of editing of his dispatches; the accusation that Smalley lied in reporting the circumstances is hard to believe. Whatever Smalley was, he was not a liar.

Predictably the decision went against Smalley. The case against him was strong, even if the evidence was stretched, and he was one against two, really one against three since Chirol must be counted as an active opponent, and the stature and influence of his accusers was in each instance as great or greater than his own. Wallace seems to have been only mildly stirred by the affair. Morrison in writing Chirol made a great show of his fondness for Wallace and how well they got on together. Actually, Morrison was a supreme egotist whose fondness for

15. Morrison to Chirol, 23 August 1905, PHS.

people was limited almost entirely to himself. He belittled Wallace's reports, laughed about his false uppers and lowers, and recalled that in spite of his very Scottish name, Wallace was a Jew. The tone of Moberly Bell's letters suggests that he was a reluctant convert to majority opinion. He was pleased with the coverage of the Peace Conference and wrote: "I think I have received more congratulations on the way we did the Peace Conference at Portsmouth than I have. on all the other things put together in ten years."[16] He had previously entertained no thought of retiring Smalley. Just before the Portsmouth Peace Conference he wrote Morrison urging him to consider an appointment as a roving correspondent for the Western Hemisphere, but there was to be no replacement of Smalley.

Smalley is 72 and the USA will in the future be one of our most important if not the most important post—but Smalley is young for 72 and the American Continent is large and more or less of homogenous interest. The man there should know—what Smalley does not— the whole of America—not only the USA—N—S—W—but also Canada and something of South America as well. Therefore I would suggest— if you are willing—that you take a hemisphere as your province—and that while Smalley lives you should travel in and study both S. America—Central America and the West of N. America.[17]

The task of delivering the blow to Smalley fell to the managing editor. In a letter dated 5 October 1905, he wrote:

Having placed before Mr. Walter the letters received from you, Wallace and Morrison while at Portsmouth, he instructs me to express to you his extreme annoyance at a state of things which he had carefully instructed you to avoid.

Considering who were your colleagues he thinks that the whole tone you adopted towards them was unworthy of you, prejudicial to the interests of the paper and such as entirely to destroy his confidence in your judgment.[18]

Walter offered to see Smalley in person if he thought he could "in any way remove this impression." Probably Smalley did see him because he returned to England for a brief period following

16. E. H. C. Moberly Bell, *Life and Letters of C. F. Moberly Bell*, p. 230.
17. Moberly Bell to Morrison, 21 July 1905 [copy], Manager's Letterbook, no. 40, PHS. Morrison replied at once that he was not interested.
18. Moberly Bell to Smalley, 5 October 1905 [copy], ibid., no. 41.

the Peace Conference, but he did not change Walter's views. Together Chirol and Morrison had convinced him that Smalley would no longer do as a *Times* man.

Further correspondence between Moberly Bell and Smalley concerned the correspondent's separation or end-of-service pay which was finally set by the *Times* at £2,500, a reasonably generous figure for the time and circumstances. Smalley was back in the United States by November and stayed on until the following June "to consult with friends about my future, which does not seem particularly clear, even in the light of their kindly interest." He added: "And I am myself rather dazed by what has befallen me."[19] Not long before he was fired he wrote the *Times* manager that he was reconciled to Washington and intended to "settle down" there for good. Presumably that was based on the assumption that he would continue as the representative of the *Times,* for he seems to have decided to return to England shortly after his release. This he did in June 1906, and remained in England for the last ten years of his life. In 1906 the *Times* made a large-scale reshuffling of its foreign correspondents, but it was some years later that the paper succeeded in getting a replacement for Smalley of more than ordinary ability.

19. Smalley to Moberly Bell, 21 November 1905, ibid.

14. Last Years

      Smalley spent his last years in the shadows, emerging briefly now and then with an article, a letter to the *Times*, or a book. The books consisted of the biography of a friend and two volumes of memoirs and selections from his writings. If he returned to the United States for visits, the writer has not discovered them. He is mentioned not infrequently as having been seen at one of the London clubs, or as a guest at one of the country homes where he had long been a welcome visitor. He watched the funeral ceremonies for King Edward from Lord Rothschild's balcony, "the best place in London," where he had witnessed the coronation ceremonies of the same king in 1903. Several times during this last decade of his life he changed his London address. Until his eyesight failed near the end his handwriting was firm and legible and, even then, his mind was keen and friends took turns reading to him.

      Beyond doubt Smalley had to live on a limited income. His separation pay from the *Times* would not have stretched far and his income from his publications could not have been great. He had sold many of his personal possessions, including most of his books, to meet the needs that had to be met before retirement. Throughout his life Smalley had been a knowledgeable but modest book collector. Some of his best letters to the *Tribune* dealt with book collections and book sales, one of the superior accounts being a description of the "Great Perkins Book Sale" in 1873. During his *Tribune* years he often purchased books for American friends. One of his ties with Senator Charles Sumner was a common interest in books. They had spent many happy hours together during Sumner's European visits searching in the bookshops of London and Paris. In 1887 Smalley sold about one-third of his library, "mostly the luxury items," for about $6,000 after the commission. When he moved from New York to Washington in 1905 he sold about three hundred items, mostly standard authors in fine bindings.[1] Among the personal belongings sold after his death were a few autographed copies of giftbooks, including a first edition of *Over the Teacups,* by Oliver Wendell Holmes, but not many volumes were left. The value of his estate on his death, including books, was less than $3,000.[2]

During his *Tribune* years in London Smalley published several volumes, contributed to collective works and anthologies, and was sometimes listed falsely as the author of another work. The false attribution was to *Society in London,* by a foreign resident (New York: Harper and Brothers, 1885) which was followed in 1904 by *Society in the New Reign,* by the author of *Society in London* (London: T. F. Unwin, 1904). No one attributed the second volume to Smalley; there is nothing in his correspondence to suggest that he was the composer of these works; besides, the style and tone are not his.[3]

In 1909 Smalley published a life of Sir Sydney Waterlow. It was his most curious and least satisfactory literary effort.[4] Waterlow rose from meager beginnings to be elected to Parliament several times, to be elected Lord Mayor of London, and to become a millionaire (Waterlow and Sons, printers) and philanthropist.

1. Anderson Auction Company, *Catalog,* no. 379 (1905), Library of Congress, Washington, D.C.

2. A statement in the records of wills for 1918, Somerset House, London, values the estate at less than £100. When his personal effects were sold in New York the proceeds came to slightly more than $2,800. Possibly there were debts to be paid after the sale.

3. Smalley's major publications for the early period are *London Letters and Some Others,* 2 vols. (London: Macmillan and Company, 1890), and *Studies of Men* (London: Macmillan and Company, 1895). Both of these publications have been mentioned earlier in the present work as have Smalley's contributions to *A Library of American Literature,* ed. Edmund C. Stedman and Allan Mackay Hutchinson, 11 vols. (New York, 1887–89). Also worthy of mention among his early publications is "Old Lamps for New," in *Among My Books,* ed. H. D. Trail (London, 1892).

4. George Smalley, *The Life of Sir Sydney H. Waterlow, Bart.* (London, 1909).

He gave Waterlow Park to the City of London and contributed to the support of numerous schools and good causes. He owned a fine home at Cannes on the Riviera where he entertained the great, including Smalley and the Prince of Wales. Waterlow died in 1906 and the biography may have been a commissioned job. In any case, it was a perfunctory exercise, published under the name of George Smalley without the middle initial W., and included none of the personal references that were so characteristic of Smalley's biographical descriptions. The pages were still uncut in the copy in the Bodleian Library at Oxford when examined by the writer a few years ago.

In 1911 Smalley published his *Anglo-American Memories,* the Chapters of which had run as weekly installments in the Sunday *New York Tribune.*[5] It is Smalley's best book. Most of the chapters dealt with people he had known, English and American, but Smalley had included semiautobiographical chapters on his early life, reflections on journalism, and a comparison of English and American methods of conducting diplomacy. Smalley described businessmen as well as men engaged in politics, journalists, artists, and actors; there were women in the book, too, mostly of the English aristocracy. A characteristic that at once strikes anyone familiar with the acidity of so many of Smalley's newspaper dispatches is the absence of rancor, the obvious effort to present the best side even of people toward whom he once felt no kindness. Not everyone was favorably impressed by the book. The review in the *Athenaeum* said: "Trivialities do not of course make up the whole of these 'Anglo-American Memories,' but there are too many of them. In the columns of a newspaper they may pass, but they are hardly worthy of book-form."[6] A more perceptive and appreciative reviewer noted:

There is, perhaps, no better living representative of what may be called the higher journalism than this veteran contributor to great newspapers in New York and London. Doubtless Mr Smalley has been able, when occasion demanded, to do the work of a journalist of a more ordinary kind—to collect news, tell it picturesquely, and dispatch

---

5. George W. Smalley, *Anglo-American Memories* (London: Duckworth & Co., 1911); also published in New York in 1911 by G. P. Putnam's Sons.
6. *Athenaeum,* 25 March 1911, p. 328.

it promptly. But his strong point has been elsewhere—in making himself *persona grata* to distinguished men and women, and in writing about them with frank appreciation. It is difficult to do this and yet to keep within the limits of what is permissible, and yet, to do Mr. Smalley justice, he has always been discreet, and has not stooped to the kind of gossip which—we have been painfully reminded of late —a large number of readers are much too fond. Thus his ephemeral writings have a certain permanent value. They record the impressions, or the recollections, of a skilled observer, generally in a way that can offend nobody.[7]

A year after the publication of his memories Smalley published a second volume of essays that he called *Anglo-American Memories: Second Series.*[8] The volume was less autobiographical than the first and only a part of it had appeared in the *New York Tribune.* On the whole it was less impressive than the original volume, though of some interest were his chapters on Theodore Roosevelt and Count Witte. None of Roosevelt's contemptuous remarks about Smalley—some of which he was bound to have known—was mentioned, but neither were Roosevelt's occasional favorable opinions. He dealt fairly enough with the ex-president and in a moderately laudatory spirit for most of his discussion. At the end, however, he returned to the skeptical tone of his one-time opinion of Roosevelt, ending on the harsh note that "the doctrines he preaches are the doctrines of Anarchy."[9] This was written in 1911 and in the following year Roosevelt and his friends thought Smalley the author of a letter to the *Times,* signed "An American Exile," that attacked Roosevelt bitterly for bolting the Republican party to run on a third-party ticket.[10] Smalley changed his mind later and spoke admiringly of Roosevelt.

He borders on the boastful in relating his presentation of the Russian viewpoint during the Portsmouth Peace Conference. Times had changed, of course, and Russia was now Britain's

7. *Times Literary Supplement,* 23 February 1911.
8. George W. Smalley, *Anglo-American Memories: Second Series* (London: Duckworth & Co., 1912). This second volume apparently was not published in the United States.
9. Ibid., p. 383.
10. *Letters of Theodore Roosevelt,* ed. Elting E. Morison, 8 vols. (Cambridge, Mass., 1951–54), 5:530n.

ally, or at least a loyal member of the Triple Entente composed of France, Russia, and Great Britain. Viewed from a later standpoint Smalley could feel that he had been wiser in 1905 than the *Times* editors who had fired him. In his 1912 account Smalley gave a number of details he had not given earlier regarding his relations with Count Witte. There is serious doubt whether Witte's open policy really converted American journalists to the support of Russia, but Smalley believed that it did. "He brought the American people back to their ancient friendship for Russia, and with them the President." And on Witte's larger role at the conference: "Out of the nettle of danger he had plucked the flower of safety. A novice in diplomacy, he overmatched a veteran. He came to Portsmouth an apprentice. He left it a master. In three weeks and in circumstances which would have tested the craft of a Metternich or the genius of a Bismarck, he did a service and won a renown which can never pass from the memory of men."[11]

The chapter on Olney and the Venezuelan crisis of 1896 is disappointing. He praises Olney—he had hoped that Olney would be appointed ambassador to Great Britain—but it is uninformative regarding the crisis in which he gave his most important performance in diplomacy. There is much that can be told some day, he says, but it is still too soon.

When Smalley died on 4 April 1916 the newspapers on both sides of the Atlantic paid him high tribute and proceeded to demonstrate with numerous errors of fact in their accounts of his life how poorly he was remembered. The dates of his service with the *Tribune* and the *Times* seem often to have been selected at random. His middle initial was well remembered as W, but "Washington" or "William" seemed as good as Washburn for the middle name. He was reported as "in the field" with the Germans in the Franco-Prussian War and as "attached to Bismarck's Headquarters." The *New York Tribune* was evidently so ashamed at the number of errors in its first obituary that it printed a second, fuller and more accurate. Almost all accounts emphasized that Smalley represented a past era in journalism.

11. Smalley, *Anglo-American Memories: Second Series,* p. 402.

In the American papers he was frequently called the greatest of American correspondents and there was a marked tendency in them to emphasize his literary talents and to focus on his earlier career. One English notice described his last days. It was written by Moreton Frewen, whose wife Clara was one of three New York Jerome sisters—another was Jennie, mother of Winston Churchill—who married prominent Englishmen. Frewen was an investor in American properties, a writer on the United States, and a sometime resident of the United States.

George Washington [*sic*] Smalley has been for now forty years a connecting link between England and the United States, and I think a few lines as to his last hours and where he stood amid this amazing wreckage of things will be welcomed by his friends on both sides. During his last few days the writer was a fairly constant visitor. He was evidently approaching the great crossing and this with regret. His faculties were quite unimpaired, his "unsatisfied curiosity" as to what is just over the bar was extraordinarily stimulated. Smalley's eyes had failed him, and it was left to his friends to construe for him the march of events which were clean outside all his wide studies and experiences. Smalley was always a Pope, his defect as an exponent of international matters was his unwillingness to transmit news! "What chiefly alarms me," Lincoln once said, "is not the Judgment Day but the day of no judgment." Smalley had for half a century been reviewing these frequent spasms of "no judgment," to which the American democracy is much more prone that ours. He was going out, he felt, at a moment when all the weaknesses of the American Constitution stood revealed. Thus he was greatly impressed and greatly depressed. The entire "Moral idea" for which the New York Tribune stood appeared to be doomed. I had known him very intimately for a quarter of a century. His critical facility and his uneasy political exactitudes made him, and particularly at Washington, more enemies than friends. That it should have been left to such a man to balance for "The Times" the relations of John Hay and the Senate! Looking back upon it, the position was high comedy. Yet no one knew the inner life there better, but his reluctance to report what shocked his sense of the fitness of things greatly reduced his value as a mere correspondent in times of crisis. To Lord Pauncefote he was invaluable at the time when Holleben, the German Ambassador, was quite openly laying the foundation at enormous cost of a reptile press and hyphenated vote. . . . The other day I was entertained to find that, albeit his preference was for Root, he had reconsidered his whole attitude as to Roosevelt, and he thought that the reunion of the

Republican party under one or the other was necessary if the United States were to survive.[12]

Smalley was survived by his wife and five children—Eleanor, Phillips, Evelyn, Ida, and Emerson. Mrs. Smalley died at her home in New York at the age of eighty-five on 4 February 1923. An appreciation of her by a close friend, Kate Douglas Wiggin, appeared in the *New York Times* on 12 February 1923. Mrs. Smalley spent her last years in retirement from social life, apparently in rather straitened financial circumstances and in delicate health, which prevented her—according to Mrs. Wiggin— from completing the reminiscences she had started earlier.[13] Daughter Evelyn received considerable recognition, including the Medal of Honor of the Federation of Women's Clubs in New York and the French Legion of Honor in 1923, for her work in the rehabilitation of France following World War I.

Shortly after moving to Washington in 1905 Smalley made his will leaving all of his property to two daughters, Ida Smalley of New York City and Eleanor Garnaut Meares, wife of Gerald Meares, then living in Seaford, Sussex, England. The will was registered in New York on 30 June 1905 and Ida was named as executrix. The sale to settle the estate was conducted by the Anderson Galleries in New York in March 1918. There were five letters to Smalley from J. McNeil Whistler, forty-three from James Russell Lowell, and one from William E. Gladstone. The considerable number of autographed photographs included those of Otto von Bismarck, Herbert von Bismarck, Giuseppe Garabaldi, Wendell Phillips, Henry Irving, Lord Rosebery, the Duke of Devonshire, Arthur F. Walter, Lord Wolseley, Lord Rothschild, and the Earl of Minto. The list of women with autographed pictures was also impressive: the Duchess of Sutherland, the Duchess of Marlborough, Lady Rothschild, Lady Curzon, Lady Minto, Lady Langtry, Ava Astor, Marie Bancroft, Mrs. Pat Campbell, Marie Lohr, and Emma Story. Among the per-

12. This item appeared first in the London *Spectator* and was then reprinted in the *New York Tribune,* 8 May 1916.
13. I was never able to locate this document nor any of the direct descendants of Smalley.

sonal items were tables, bowls, paintings, vases, engraved walking sticks, and seven razors, each engraved "GWS" and marked with a day of the week.[14] All of these items suggest something of the personality of George W. Smalley. Total proceeds amounted to $2,810.60.[15]

Unfortunately the writer began his study of Smalley too late to be able to talk to people who knew him. An exception was Wickham Steed, who was a *Times* correspondent in Vienna during most of Smalley's service with that paper. Steed did not know Smalley well, but he knew the circumstances of his employment and some of his problems with the *Times*. He did not like Smalley and recalled a dinner at the home of Moberly Bell in the late nineties at which Smalley had been inexcusably rude— or so Steed thought—to the *Times* manager. After all, Steed said, Smalley had been appointed and was kept in the service of the *Times* by Moberly Bell. After he had cited a number of Smalley weaknesses, and people who could not abide him, the writer asked why, then, had he been hired by the *Times* and kept on for ten years. Steed was thoughtful for a moment, then said: "Warts and all, Smalley was an excellent journalist."[16]

14. Anderson Galleries, *English Silver and Miscellaneous Art Objects to Close the Estate of the Late George W. Smalley and the Contents of the Apartment of Mr. James Lane Allen* (New York, 1918).
15. *New York Times*, 9 March 1918.
16. Interview with Wickham Steed, 27 October 1955.

Appendixes

Appendix A
The Battle of Antietam

Battle-Field of Sharpsburg,
Wednesday Evening, Sept. 17, 1862

Fierce and desperate battle between 200,000 men has raged since daylight, yet night closes on an uncertain field. It is the greatest fight since Waterloo—all over the field contested with an obstinacy equal even to Waterloo. If not wholly a victory tonight, I believe it is the prelude to a victory tomorrow. But what can be foretold of the future of a fight which from 5 in the morning till 7 at night the best troops of the continent have fought without decisive result?

I have no time for speculation—no time even to gather details of the battle—only time to state its broadest features—then mount and spur for New-York.

After the brilliant victory near Middletown, Gen. McClellan pushed forward his army rapidly, and reached Keedysville with three corps on Monday night. That march has already been described. On the day following the two armies faced each other idly, until night. Artillery was busy at intervals; once in the morning opening with spirit, and continuing for half an hour with vigor, till the Rebel battery, as usual, was silenced.

McClellan was on the hill where Benjamin's battery was stationed and found himself suddenly under a rather heavy fire. It was still uncertain whether the Rebels were retreating or re-enforcing—their batteries would remain in position in either case, and as they had withdrawn nearly all their troops from view, there was only the doubtful indication of columns of dust to the rear.

On the evening of Tuesday, Hooker was ordered to cross the Antietam Creek with his corps, and, feeling the left of the enemy, to be ready to attack next morning. During the day of apparent inactivity, McClellan had been maturing his plan of battle, of which Hooker's movement was one development.

The position on either side was peculiar. When Richardson advanced on Monday he found the enemy deployed and displayed in force on a cresent-shaped [*sic*] ridge, the outline of which followed more or less exactly the course of Antietam Creek. Their lines were then forming, and the revelation of force in front of the ground which they really intended to hold, was probably meant to delay our attack until their arrangements to receive it were complete.

During that day they kept their troops exposed and did not move them even to avoid the artillery fire, which must have been occasionally annoying. Next morning the lines and columns which had darkened cornfields and hill crests, had been withdrawn. Broken and wooded ground behind the sheltering hills concealed the Rebel masses. What from our front looked like only a narrow summit fringed with woods was a broad table-land of forest and ravine; cover for troops everywhere, nowhere easy access for an enemy. The smoothly sloping surface in front and the sweeping crescent of slowly mingling lines,was only a delusion. It was all a Rebel stronghold beyond.

Under the base of these hills runs the deep stream called Antietam Creek, fordable only at distant points. Three bridges cross it, one on the Hagerstown road, one on the Sharpsburg pike, one to the left in a deep recess of steeply falling hills. Hooker passed the first to reach the ford by which he crossed, and it was held by Pleasanton with a reserve of cavalry during the battle. The second was close under the Rebel center, and no way important to yesterday's fight. At the third, Burnside attacked and finally crossed. Between the first and third lay most of the battle lines. They stretched four miles from right to left.

Unaided attack in front was impossible. McClellan's forces lay behind low, disconnected ridges, in front of the Rebel summits, all or nearly all unwooded. They gave some cover for artillery, and guns were therefore massed on the center. The enemy had the Shepherdstown road and the Hagerstown and Williamsport road both open to him in rear for retreat. Along one or the other, if beaten, he must fly. This, among other reasons, determined, perhaps, the plan of battle which McClellan finally resolved on.

The plan was generally as follows: Hooker was to cross on the right, establish himself on the enemy's left if possible, flanking his position, and to open the fight. Sumner, Franklin, and Mansfield were to send their forces also to the right, co-operating with and sustaining Hooker's attack while advancing also nearer the center. The heavy work in the center was left mostly to the batteries, Porter massing his infantry supports in the hollows. On the left Burnside was to carry the bridge,

THE GREAT BATTLE OF SHARPSBURG

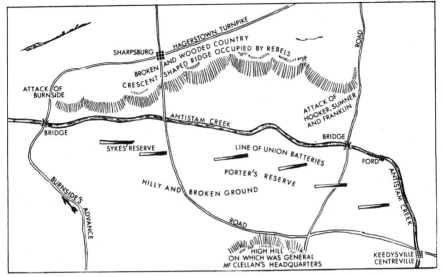

From the *New York Tribune*, 20 September 1862.

already referred to, advancing them by a road which enters the pike at Sharpsburg, turning at once the Rebel left flank and destroying his line of retreat. Porter and Sykes were held in reserve. It is obvious that the complete success of a plan contemplating widely divergent movements of separate corps, must largely depend on accurate timing, that the attacks should be simultaneous and not successive.

Hooker moved on Tuesday afternoon at four, crossing the creek at a ford above the bridge and well to the right, without opposition. Fronting south-west his line advanced not quite on the Rebel flank but overlapping and threatening it. Turning off from the road after passing the stream, he sent forward cavalry skirmishes straight into the woods and over the fields beyond. Rebel pickets withdrew slowly before them, firing scattering and harmless shots. Turning again to the left, the cavalry went down on the Rebel flank, coming suddenly close to a battery which met them with unexpected grape and cannister. It being the nature of cavalry to retire before batteries, this company loyally followed the law of its being, and came swiftly back without pursuit.

Artillery was sent to the front, infantry was rapidly deployed, and skirmishers went out in front and on either flank. The corps moved forward compactly, Hooker as usual reconnoitering in person. They came at last to an open grass-sown field inclosed on two sides with woods, protected on the right by a hill, and entered through a corn field in the rear. Skirmishers entering these woods were instantly met by Rebel shots, but held their ground, and as soon as supported advanced and cleared the timber. Beyond, on the left and in front, volleys of musketry opened heavily, and a battle seemed to have begun a little sooner than it was expected.

Gen. Hooker formed his lines with precision and without hesitation. Ricketts's Division went into the woods on the left in force. Meade, with the Pennsylvania Reserves, formed in the center. Doubleday was sent out on the right, planting his batteries on the hill, and opening at once on a Rebel battery that began to enfilade the central line. It was already dark, and the Rebel position could only be discovered by the flashes of their guns. They pushed forward boldly on the right, after losing ground on the other flank, but made no attempt to regain their first hold on the woods. The fight flashed, and glimmered, and faded, and finally went out in the dark.

Hooker had found out what he wanted to know. When the firing ceased the hostile lines lay close to each other—their pickets so near that six Rebels were captured during the night. It was inevitable that the fight should recommence at daylight. Neither side had suffered considerable loss; it was a skirmish, not a battle. "We are through for to-night, gentlemen," remarked the General, "but to-morrow we fight the battle that will decide the fate of the Republic."

Not long after the firing ceased, it sprang up again on the left. Gen. Hooker, who had taken up his headquarters in a barn, which had been nearly the focus of the Rebel artillery, was out at once. First came rapid and usually frequent picket shots, then several heavy volleys. The General listened a moment and smiled grimly. "We have no troops there. The Rebels are shooting each other. It is Fair Oaks over again." So everybody lay down again, but all the night through there were frequent alarms.

McClellan had been informed of the night's work, and of the certainties awaiting the dawn. Sumner was ordered to move his corps at once, and was expected to be on the ground at daylight. From the extent of the Rebel lines developed in the evening, it was plain that they had gathered their whole army behind the hights [*sic*] and were waiting for the shock.

The battle began with the dawn. Morning found both armies just as they had slept, almost close enough to look into each other's eyes. The left of Meade's reserves and the right of Ricketts's line became engaged at nearly the same moment, one with artillery, the other with infantry. A battery was almost immediately pushed forward beyond the central woods, over a plowed field, near the top of the slope where the corn-field began. On this open field, in the corn beyond, and in the woods which stretched forward into the broad fields, like a promontory into the ocean, were the hardest and deadliest struggles of the day.

For half an hour after the battle had grown to its full strength, the line of fire swayed neither way. Hooker's men were fully up to their work. They saw their General everywhere in front, never away from the fire, and all the troops believed in their commander, and fought with a will. Two-thirds of them were the same men who under McDowell had broken at Manassas.

The half hour passed, the Rebels began to give way a little, only a little, but at the first indication of a receding fire, Forward, was the word, and on went the line with a cheer and a rush. Back across the corn-field, leaving dead and wounded behind them, over the fence, and across the road, and then back again into the dark woods which closed around them, went the retreating Rebels.

Meade and his Pennsylvanians followed hard and fast—followed till they came within easy range of the woods, among which they saw their beaten enemy disappearing—followed still, with another cheer, and flung themselves against the cover.

But out of those gloomy woods came suddenly and heavily terrible volleys—volleys which smote, and bent, and broke in a moment that eager front, and hurled them swiftly back for half the distance they had won. Not swiftly, nor in panic, any further. Closing up their shattered lines, they came slowly away—a regiment where a brigade had been, hardly a brigade where a whole division had been victorious. They had met from the woods the first volleys of musketry from fresh troops—had met them and returned them till their line had yielded and gone down before the weight of fire, and till their ammunition was exhausted.

In ten minutes the fortune of the day seemed to have changed—it was the Rebels now who were advancing; pouring out of the woods in endless lines, sweeping through the corn-field from which their comrades had just fled. Hooker sent in his nearest brigade to meet them, but it could not do the work. He called for another. There was nothing close enough, unless he took it from his right. His right might be in danger if it was weakened, but his center was already threatened with annihilation. Not hesitating one moment, he sent to Doubleday: "Give me your best brigade instantly."

The best brigade came down the hill to the right on the run, went through the timber in front through a storm of shot and bursting shell and crashing limbs, over the open field beyond, and straight into the corn-field, passing as they went the fragments of three brigades shattered by the Rebel fire, and streaming to the rear. They passed by Hooker, whose eyes lighted as he saw these veteran troops led by a soldier whom he knew he could trust. "I think they will hold it," he said.

Gen. Hartstuff took his troops very steadily, but now that they were

under fire, not hurriedly, up the hill from which the corn-field begins
to descend, and formed them on the crest. Not a man who was not in
full view—not one who bent before the storm. Firing at first in volleys,
they fired them at will with wonderful rapidity and effect. The whole
line crowned the hill and stood out darkly against the sky, but lighted
and shrouded ever in flame and smoke. There were the 12th and 13th
Massachusetts and another regiment which I cannot remember—old
troops all of them.

There for half an hour they held the ridge unyielding in purpose,
exhaustless in courage. There were gaps in the line, but it nowhere
quailed. There General was wounded badly early in the fight, but they
fought on. Their supports did not come—they determined to win without them. They began to go down the hill and into the corn, they did
not stop to think that their ammunition was nearly gone, they were
there to win that field and they won it. The Rebel line for the second
time fled through the corn and into the woods. I cannot tell how few
of Hartstuff's brigade were left when the work was done, but it was
done. There was no more gallant, determined, heroic fighting in all
this desperate day. Gen. Hartstuff is very severely wounded, but I do
not believe he counts his success too dearly purchased.

The crisis of the fight at this point had arrived; Ricketts's division,
vainly endeavoring to advance, and exhausted by the effort, had fallen
back. Part of Mansfield's corps was ordered to their relief, but Mansfield's troops came back again, and their General was mortally wounded.
The left nevertheless was too extended to be turned, and too strong
to be broken. Ricketts sent word he could not advance, but could hold
his ground. Doubleday had kept his guns at work on the right, and had
finally silenced a Rebel battery that for half an hour had poured in a
galling enfilading fire along Hooker's central line.

There were woods in front of Doubleday's hill which the Rebels
held, but so long as those guns pointed that way they did not care to
attack. With his left then able to take care of itself, with his right im-
pregnable with two brigades of Mansfield still fresh and coming rapidly up, and with this center a second time victorious, Gen. Hooker determined to advance. Orders were sent to Crawford and Gordon—the
two Mansfield brigades—to move directly forward at once, the batteries in the center were ordered on, the whole line was called on, and
the General himself went forward.

To the right of the corn-field and beyond it was a point of woods.
Once carried and firmly held, it was the key of the position. Hooker
determined to take it. He rode out in front of his furthest troops on
a hill to examine the ground for a battery. At the top he dismounted
and went forward on foot, completed his reconnoissance, returned and
remounted. The musketry fire from the point of woods was all the
while extremely hot. As he put his foot in the stirrup a fresh volley of

rifle bullets came whizzing by. The tall soldierly figure of the General, the white horse which he rode, the elevated place where he was—all made him a most dangerously conspicuous mark. So he had been all day, riding often without a staff officer or an orderly near him—all sent off on urgent duty—visible everywhere on the field. The Rebel bullets had followed him all day, but they had not hit him, and he would not regard them. Remounting on this hill he had not ridden five steps when he was struck in the foot by a ball.

Three men were shot down at the same moment by his side. The air was alive with bullets. He kept on his horse for a few moments, though the wound was severe and excessively painful, and would not dismount till he had given his last order to advance. He was himself in the very front. Swaying unsteadily on his horse, he turned in his seat to look about him. "There is a regiment to the right. Order it forward! Crawford and Gordon are coming up. Tell them to carry these woods and hold them—and it is our fight!"

It was found that the bullet had passed completely through his foot. The surgeon who examined it on the spot could give no opinion whether bones were broken, but it was afterward ascertained that though grazed they were not fractured. Of course the severity of the wound made it impossible for him to keep the field which he believed already won, so far as it belonged to him to win it. It was nine o'clock. The fight had been furious since five. A large part of his command was broken, but with his right still untouched and with Crawford's and Gordon's brigades just up, above all, with the advance of the whole central line which the men had heard ordered with cheers, with a regiment already on the edge of the woods he wanted, he might well leave the field, thinking the battle was won—that *his* battle was won, for I am writing, of course, only about the attack on the Rebel left.

I see no reason why I should disguise my admiration of Gen. Hooker's bravery and soldierly ability. Remaining nearly all the morning on the right, I could not help seeing the sagacity and promptness of his maneuvers, how completely his troops were kept in hand, how devotedly they trusted to him, how keen was his insight into the battle; how every opportunity was seized and every reverse was checked and turned into another success. I say this the more unreservedly, because I have no personal relation whatever with him, never saw him till the day before the fight, and don't like his politics or opinions in general. But what are politics in such a battle?

Sumner arrived just as Hooker was leaving, and assumed command. Crawford and Gordon had gone into the woods, and were holding them stoutly against heavy odds. As I rode over toward the left, I met Sumner at the head of his column advancing rapidly through the timber, opposite the point where Crawford was fighting. The veteran General was riding alone in the forest far ahead of his leading brigade, his hat off, his gray hair and beard and mustache strangely contrasting with the fire in his eyes and his martial air, as he hurried on to where the bullets were thickest.

Sedgwick's division was in advance, moving forward to support Crawford and Gordon. Rebel re-enforcements were approaching also, and the struggle for the roads was again to be renewed. Sumner sent forward the two divisions, Richardson and French, on the left. Sedgwick moving in columns of divisions through the woods in rear, deployed and advanced in line over the corn-field. There was a broad interval between him and the nearest division, and he saw that if the Rebel line were complete his own division was in immediate danger of being flanked. But his orders were to advance, and those are the orders which a soldier—and Sedgwick is every inch a soldier—loves best to hear.

To extend his own front as far as possible, he ordered the 34th New York to move by the left flank. The maneuver was attempted under a fire of the greatest intensity, and the regiment broke. At the same moment the enemy, perceiving their advantage, came round on that flank. Crawford was obliged to give on the right, and his troops pouring in confusion through the ranks of Sedgwick's advance brigade, threw it into disorder and back on the second and third lines. The enemy advanced, their fire increasing.

Gen. Sedgwick was three times wounded, in the shoulder, leg and wrist, but he persisted in remaining on the field so long as there was a chance of saving it. His Adjt.-Gen., Major Sedgwick, barely rallying and trying to reform the troops, was shot through the body, the bullet lodging in his spine, and fell from his horse. Severe as the wound is is probably not mortal. Lieut. Howe, of Gen. Sedgwick's staff, endeavored vainly to rally the 34th New York. They were badly cut up and would not stand. Half their officers were killed or wounded, their colors shot to pieces, the Color-Sergeant killed, every one of the color-guard wounded. Only thirty-two were afterward got together.

The 15th Massachusetts went into action with 17 officers and nearly 600 men. Nine officers were killed or wounded, and some of the latter are prisoners. Capt. Simons, Capt. Saunders of the Sharpshooters, Lieut. Derby, and Lieut. Berry are killed. Capt. Bartlett and Capt. Jocelyn, Lieut. Sourr, Lieut. Gale, and Lieut. Bradley are wounded. One hundred and thirty-four men were the only remnant that would be collected of this splendid regiment.

Gen. Dana was wounded. Gen. Howard, who took command of the division after Gen. Sedgwick was disabled, exerted himself to restore order; but it could not be done there. Gen. Sumner ordered the line to be reformed under fire. The test was too severe for volunteer troops under such a fire. Sumner himself attempted to arrest the disorder, but to little purpose. Lieut.-Col. Revere and Capt. Audenried of his staff were wounded severely, but not dangerously. It was impossible to hold the position. Gen. Sumner withdrew the division to the rear, and once more the cornfield was abandoned to the enemy.

French sent word he could hold his ground. Richardson, while gallantly leading a regiment under a heavy fire, was severely wounded in the shoulder. Gen. Meagher was wounded at the head of his brigade. The loss in general officers was becoming frightful.

At 1 o'clock affairs on the right had a gloomy look. Hooker's troops were greatly exhausted, and their General was away from the field. Mansfield's were no better. Sumner's command had lost heavily, but two of his divisions were still comparatively fresh. Artillery was yet playing vigorously in front, through the ammunition of many of the batteries was entirely exhausted, and they had been compelled to retire.

Doubleday held the right inflexibly. Sumner's headquarters were now in the narrow field where, the night before, Hooker had begun the fight. All that had been gained in front had been lost! The enemy's batteries, which if advanced and served vigorously might have made sad work with the closely-massed troops were fortunately either partially disabled or short of ammunition. Sumner was confident that he could hold his own; but another advance was out of the question. The enemy on the other hand, seemed to be too much exhausted to attack.

At this crisis Franklin came up with fresh troops and formed to the left. Slocum, commanding one division of the corps, was sent forward along the slopes lying under the first ranges of Rebel hills, while Smith, commanding the other division, was ordered to retake the corn-fields and woods which all day had been so hotly contested. It was done in the handsomest style. His Maine and Vermont regiments and the rest went forward on the run, and, cheering as they went, swept like an avalanche through the corn-fields, fell upon the woods, cleared them in ten minutes, and held them. They were not again retaken.

The field and its ghastly harvest which the reaper had gathered in those fatal hours remained finally with us. Four times it had been lost and won. The dead are strewn so thickly that as you ride over it you cannot guide your horse's steps too carefully. Pale and bloody faces are everywhere upturned. They are sad and terrible, but there is nothing which makes one's heart beat so quickly as the imploring look of sorely wounded men who beckon wearily for help which you cannot stay to give.

Gen. Smith's attack was so sudden that his success was accomplished with no great loss. He had gained a point, however, which compelled him to expect every moment an attack, and to hold which, if the enemy brought up reserves, would take his best energies and best troops. But the long strife, the heavy losses, incessant fighting over the same ground repeatedly lost and won inch by inch, and more than all, perhaps, the fear of Burnside on the left and Porter in front, held the enemy in check. For two or three hours there was a lull even in the cannonade on the right which hitherto had been incessant. McClellan had been over on the field after Sumner's repulse, but had speedily returned to his headquarters. Sumner again sent word that he was able to hold his position, but could not advance with his own corps.

Meantime where was Burnside, and what was he doing? On the right where I had spent the day until two o'clock, little was known of the general fortunes of the field. We had heard Porter's guns in the center, but nothing from Burnside on the left. The distance was too great to distinguish the sound of his artillery from Porter's left. There was no immediate prospect of more fighting on the right, and I left the field which all day long had seen the most obstinate contest of the war, and rode over to McClellan's headquarters. The different battlefields were shut out from each other's view, but all partially visible from the central hill which General McClellan had occupied during the day. But I was more than ever impressed on returning with the completely deceitful appearance of the ground the Rebels had chosen when viewed from the front.

Hooker's and Sumner's struggle had been carried on over an uneven and wooded surface, their own line of battle extending in a semi-circle not less than a mile and a half. Perhaps a better notion of their position can be got by considering their right, center and left as three sides of a square. So long therefore as either wing was driven back, the center became exposed to a very dangerous enfilading fire, and the further the center was advanced the worse off it was, unless the lines on its side and rear were firmly held. This formation resulted originally from the efforts of the enemy to turn both flanks. Hooker, at the very outset, threw his column so far into the center of the Rebel lines that they were compelled to threaten him on the flank to secure their own center.

Nothing of all this was perceptible from the hills in front. Some directions of the Rebel lines had been disclosed by the smoke of their guns, but the whole interior formation of the country beyond the hills was completely concealed. When McClellan arranged his order of battle, it must have been upon information, or have been left to his corps and division commander to discover for themselves.

Up to 3 o'clock Burnside had made little progress. His attack on the bridge had been successful, but the delay had been so great that to the observer it appeared as if McClellan's plans must have been seriously disarranged. It is impossible not to suppose that the attacks on right and left were meant in a measure to correspond, for otherwise the enemy had only to repel Hooker on the one hand, then transfer his troops, and hurl them against Burnside.

Here was the difference between Smith and Burnside. The former did his work at once, and lost all his men at once—that is, all whom he lost at all; Burnside seems to have attacked cautiously in order to save his men, and sending successively insufficient forces against a position of strength, distributed his loss over a greater period of time, but yet lost none the less in the end.

Finally, at 4 o'clock, McClellan sent simultaneous orders to Burnside and Franklin; to the former to advance and carry the batteries in his front at all hazards and any cost; to the latter to carry the woods next in front of him to the right, which the Rebels still held. The order to Franklin, however, was practically countermanded, in consequence of a message from Gen. Sumner that if Franklin went on and was repulsed, his own corps was not yet sufficiently reorganized to be depended on as a reserve.

Franklin, thereupon, was directed to run no risk of losing his present position, and, instead of sending his infantry into the woods, contented himself with advancing his batteries over the breadth of the fields in front, supporting them with heavy columns of infantry, and attacking with energy the Rebel batteries immediately opposed to him. His movement was a success, so far as it went, the batteries maintaining their new ground, and sensibly affecting the steadiness of the Rebel fire. That being once accomplished, and all hazard of the right being again forced back having been dispelled, the movement of Burnside became at once the turning-point of success, and the fate of the day depended on him.

How extraordinary the situation was may be judged from a moment's consideration of the facts. It is understood that from the outset Burnside's attack was expected to be decisive, as it certainly must have been if things went well elsewhere, and if he succeeded in establishing himself on the Sharpsburg road in the Rebel rear.

Yet Hooker, and Sumner, and Franklin, and Mansfield were all sent to the right three miles away, while Porter seems to have done double duty with his single corps in front, both supporting the batteries and holding himself in reserve. With all this immense force on the right, but 16,000 men were given to Burnside for the decisive movement of the day.

Still more unfortunate in its results was the total failure of these separate attacks on the right and left to sustain, or in any manner cooperate with each other. Burnside hesitated for hours in front of the bridge which should have been carried at once by a *coup de main*. Meantime Hooker had been fighting for four hours with various fortune, but final success. Sumner had come up too late to join in the decisive attack which his earlier arrival would probably have converted into a complete success; and Franklin reached the scene only when Sumner had been repulsed. Probably before his arrival the Rebels had transferred a considerable number of troops to their right to meet the attack of Burnside, the direction of which was then suspected or developed.

Attacking first with one regiment, then with two, and delaying both for artillery, Burnside was not over the bridge before 2 o'clock—perhaps not till 3. He advanced slowly up the slopes in the front, his batteries in rear covering, to some extent, the movements of the infantry. A desperate fight was going on in a deep ravine on the right, the Rebel batteries were in full play and, apparently, very annoying and destructive, while heavy columns of Rebel troops were plainly visible, advancing as if careless of concealment, along the road and over the hills in the direction of Burnside's forces. It was at this point of time that McClellan sent him the order above given.

Burnside obeyed it most gallantly. Getting his troops well in hand, and sending a portion of his artillery to the front, he advanced them with rapidity and the most determined vigor, straight up the hill in front, on top of which the Rebels had maintained their most dangerous battery. The movement was in plain view of McClellan's position, and as Franklin, on the other side, sent his batteries into the field about the same time, the battle seemed to open in all directions with greater activity than ever.

The fight in the ravine was in full progress, the batteries which Porter supported were firing with new vigor, Franklin was blazing away on the right, and every hill-top, ridge and woods along the whole line was crested and vailed with white clouds of smoke. All day had been clear and bright since the early cloudy morning, and now this whole magnificient, unequaled scene shone with the splendor of an afternoon September sun. Four miles of battle, its glory all visible, its horrors all vailed, the fate of the Republic hanging on the hour—could any one be insensible of its grandeur.

There are two hills on the left of the road, the furthest the lowest. The Rebels have batteries on both. Burnside is ordered to carry the nearest to him, which is the furthest from the road. His guns opening first from this new position in front, soon entirely controlled and silenced the enemy's artillery. The infantry come on at once, moving rapidly and steadily up long dark lines, and broad, dark masses, being plainly visible without a glass as they moved over the green hill-side.

The next moment the road in which the Rebel battery was planted was canopied with clouds of dust swiftly descending into the valley. Underneath was a tumult of wagons, guns, horses, and men flying at speed down the road. Blue flashes of smoke burst now and then among them, a horse or a man or half dozen went down, and then the whirlwind swept on.

The hill was carried, but could it be held? The Rebel columns, before seen moving to the left, increased their pace. The guns, on the hill above, sent an angry tempest of shell down among Burnside's guns and men. He had formed his columns apparently in the near angles of two fields bordering the road—high ground about them everywhere except in rear.

In another moment a Rebel battle-line appears on the brow of the ridge above them, moves swiftly down in the most perfect order, and though met by incessant discharges of musketry, of which we plainly see the flashes, does not fire a gun. White spaces show where men are falling, but they close up instantly, and still the line advances. The brigades of Burnside are in heavy column; they will not give way before a bayonet charge in line. The Rebels think twice before they dash into these hostile masses.

There is a halt, the Rebel left gives way and scatters over the field, the rest stand fast and fire. More infantry comes up, Burnside is outnumbered; flanked, compelled to yield the hill he took so bravely. His position is no longer one of attack; he defends himself with unfaltering firmness, but he sends to McClellan for help. McClellan's glass for the last half hour has seldom been turned away from the left.

He sees clearly enough that Burnside is pressed—needs no messenger to tell him that. His face grows darker with anxious thought. Looking down into the valley where 15,000 troops are lying, he turns a half-questioning look on Fitz John Porter, who stands by his side, gravely scanning the field. They are Porter's troops below, are fresh and only impatient to share in this fight. But Porter slowly shakes his head, and one may believe that the same thought is passing through the minds of both generals: "They are the only reserves of the army; they cannot be spared."

McClellan remounts his horse, and with Porter and a dozen officers of his staff rides away to the left in Burnside's direction. Sykes meets them on the road—a good soldier, whose opinion is worth taking. The three Generals talk briefly together. It is easy to see that the moment has come when everything may turn on one order given or with-held, when the history of the battle is only to be written in thoughts and purposes and words of the General.

Burnside's messenger rides up. His message is, "I want troops and guns. If you do not send them I cannot hold my position for half an hour." McClellan's only answer for the moment is a glance at the western sky. Then he turns and speaks very slowly: "Tell Gen. Burnside that this is the battle of the war. He must hold his ground till dark at any cost. I will send him Miller's battery. I can do nothing more. I have no infantry." Then as the messenger was riding away he called him back. "Tell him if he *cannot* hold his ground, then the bridge, to the last man!—always the bridge!—If the bridge is lost, all is lost."

The sun is already down; not half-an-hour of daylight is left. Till Burnside's message came it had seemed plain to every one that the battle could not be finished to-day. None suspected how near was the peril of defeat, of sudden attack on exhausted forces—how vital to the safety of the army and the nation were those fifteen thousand troops of Fitz John Porter waiting in the hollow. But the Rebels halted instead of pushing on, their vindictive cannonade died away as the light faded.

Before it was quite dark the battle was over. Only a solitary gun of Burnside's thundered against the enemy, and presently this also ceased, and the field was still.

The peril came very near, but it has passed, and in spite of the peril, at the close the day was partly a success—not a victory, but an advantage had been gained. Hooker, Sumner, and Franklin held all the ground they had gained, and Burnside still held the bridge and his position beyond. Everything was favourable for a renewal of the fight in the morning. If the plan of the battle is sound, there is every reason why McClellan should win it. He may choose to postpone the battle to await his re-enforcements.

The Rebels may choose to retire while it is possible. Fatigue on both sides might delay the deciding battle, yet if the enemy means to fight at all, he cannot afford to delay. His re-enforcements may be coming, his losses are enormous. His troops have been massed in woods and hollows, where artillery has had its most terrific effect. Ours have been deployed and scattered. From infantry fire there is less difference.

It is hard to estimate losses on a field of such extent, but I think ours cannot be less than six thousand killed and wounded—it may be much greater. Prisoners have been taken from the enemy—I hear of a regiment captured entire, but I doubt it. All the prisoners whom I saw agree in saying that their whole army is there.

New York Tribune, 20 September 1862.

Appendix B
The Opening of Parliament

London, Feb. 5.—The credentials with which I set out this morning to see the Queen open Parliament were comprised within the limits of a sheet of engraved note paper. In so far as the printer's art can reproduce them they are:

ROYAL ARMS

February 5, 1880

OPENING OF PARLIAMENT
PALACE OF WESTMINISTER

Admit _____ Esquire

to the House of Lords this day.

FOREIGN GENTLEMEN'S GALLERY

Aveland,
D.C.G.

Not Transferable

FULL DRESS
PEERS ENTRANCE

FOR THE ADMISSION OF ONE GENTLEMAN

SIDE GALLERY.   LEFT.

Of the pageant outside I can say nothing. It was necessary to be in the House of Lords long before the procession started from Buckingham Palace. I found as I drove along Whitehall about noon that barricades had been stretched across just above the Horse Guards, the building through which the Queen and her escort were to debouch into the street. Early as it was, these defences were already garrisoned by mounted police and police on foot. The public had not been allowed to pass in carriages since half-past 11. I don't know how it may have been later, but at this hour the Guards were not very vigilant. They let you go by at the sight of a piece of white paper, not taking the trouble to scrutinize it. So I drove on through the barriers and between ranks of helmeted constables, of whom, altogether, some three thousand must have been on duty. From the Horse Guards to the Peer's entrance of Parliament Houses is a short quarter of a mile. At four intervals the police were formed, across the road and were turning back the unprivileged, but in every case I found the back of my card answered all the purposes for which the engraved front was designed. If a man had time and looked about him, or if, being unhappily only too familiar with the scene, he gave a moment to reflection, he would be aware that every inch of this ground is historical. Here have been enacted some of the most sorrowful deeds in English history. I don't think my driver goes a whit the slower for all that. He pulls up neither for the tragic past nor for the picturesque present, nor for the police until we have left St. Margaret's and Westminster Abbey on one hand, and find in front of us a string of carriages setting down at the gateway of the House of Lords.

Passing the Functionaries

At the door, more police. Once inside and along the endless corridors of this vast palace, you are in the hands of a more solemn type of functionary: or rather many types. They were, I suppose, doorkeepers and ushers, but I should not like to commit myself to any specific designation of any one of them. The majority were clad in black coats, with white ties, black breeches, and black stockings. About the waist of each hung a metal badge, which was sometimes of silver and sometimes of gold—on the surface. They proved a less confining race than the police. As I passed on, I was repeatedly asked to show my ticket, and on approaching the inner sanctuary a close examination of it took place; it was so early that no similar pass, apparently, had come under the notice of the gray-haired office-bearer who stood at the last doorway. "What's this?" he asked. I replied with humility that it was an order of admission to the House of Lords, proceeding from the office of the Lord Great Chamberlain, and signed by the Deputy Great Chamberlain. Satisfied on this point, the gray-haired one next scanned me sternly from head to foot. "You are not in full dress," said he. I answered that I believed my costume corresponded with the requirements of the Lord Chamberlain. "No," rejoined he, with increasing severity: "you are in evening dress. Full dress means court dress." I began to think. I was not only in peril of being shut out from the ceremony I had come to see, but perchance of being sent to the Tower of high treason. So I said, with as much polite decision of manner as I could muster: "I am an American. This dress is the dress I wear at the levées of the President of the United States. It is also the dress which the Minister of the United States wears at the Court of S. James." That settled the question; and I mounted the stairs and passed into the space known for the time being as the foreign gentlemen's gallery, without further ceremony. General Van Alen was already there. He had escaped the terrifying ordeal I had undergone, for he was arrayed in the full uniform of a General of the United States Army, and in the panoply of war had marched victoriously through all the legions of the enemy, and was comfortably established in the best corner of the gallery. He had been good enough to reserve the next best for me, and I sheltered myself beneath his plumes and thought as I have thought before, that the American uniform looked particularly well in a foreign land. I remarked, also, with satisfaction, that he wore a sword.

The Hall and Its Decorations

It is only quarter past twelve, and we have at least two hours to wait. But there is always something going on, and there is always the hall itself to look at. In the brightest sunlight that ever falls upon London it is but a gloomy room. Not a ray of white light enters it. The lofty Gothic windows are filled with painted glass; perhaps some of the worst painted glass ever seen. The walls and roof are panelled in oak of a deep color that would be admirable if it were due to age and not to the stainer. The flat groined ceiling—if groined be a permissible word as applied to a flat surface—is plentifully gilded, as are the throne, the balcony railings and bits of the woodwork here and there. Frescoes there are also, but gold leaf and frescoes alike have undergone the inevitable corrosion and tarnish of this climate, and they are at best a dull relief to the brown monotony they were meant to set off. In this dilemma the upholsterer has been called in, and this ingenious person has covered the floor with crude green and the benches with leather of a red that is neither cherry nor crimson, but the hue of curdled blood; the raw and ghastly tint in which Tintoretto has painted the wounds of his martyrs. What is tolerable on canvas in the half-hidden gashes of quivering flesh, is intolerable and utterly distressing when spread over bald surfaces of smooth and shining leather. There must be half an acre of it when the room is quite empty. To make the matter worse, the few peers scattered about the benches are robed in scarlet; the dais is spread with a fabric of Indian looms, a red beautiful in itself, but killed by the flaunting color to which it is opposed. By the time the British uniform of a scarlet more brilliant than the peers' robes has appeared upon the scene, the conflict of tints, that will not blend becomes distressing to the eye. The magenta hues of the windows and the nameless reds of the ladies' gowns add to the confusion, and it is not till a throng sufficient to hide the benches has assembled that anything like harmony of tone is diffused through the room. It is a partial compensation that the proportions of the hall are good. The decorations in wood will not, indeed, bear studying in detail. There is a perpetual repetition of the same *motif;* the same design recurring in every panel with wearisome monotony. The panels and crochets, the corbels, the mouldings, the treatment of shaft and mullion and rib, are marked by the same poverty of invention, the same incongruous application of Grecian theories to Gothic decoration. All the strength, the severe simplicity, the rigid adherence to a uniform model which suits the classic styles, are alien from every species of true Gothic, and betoken the feebleness of thought and want of individual freedom in the workman who has to deal with a style that becomes meaningless when it ceases to be various. The woodwork behind you as you sit in the gallery is carved into crosses, each cross of the same dimensions, and the limbs of each are inscribed with the legend: "God Save the Queen." To right and left as far as you can see this poor conceit is repeated. For aught I know it covers the whole side of the hall, and the other side, and the ends. Her Majesty would seem to be in a bad way if she needs so many invocations to preserve her from evil. For variety's sake you are inclined to add that blunt one from the prayer book: Grant her in health and wealth long to live.

Arrival of the Ladies

For the purpose of this ceremony the usual arrangements of the House have been disturbed. The veil in front of the throne has been withdrawn. The Peers' seats, all but the front row, are assigned to ladies: who, however, have to surrender a railed-off corner next to the throne to the diplomatists. The woolsack, in front of the throne—a broad sofa without back or arms—is left to the Princess of Wales and other Princesses. Two similar sofas in rear of this and at right angles to it are for the judges. The front bench below the diplomatic retreat is for the bishops. The ladies have the side galleries, except one corner devoted to foreign gentlemen, and the whole of the Stranger's Gallery, and the tribunes at either side of it. The press tribune is mercifully reserved for the press. As the seats in the side and end galleries were not reserved by name or number, holders of tickets for those places came early, and there was some competition for good places. On the floor, each seat was labelled with the name of the lady who was to occupy it, yet they, too, many of them, arrived in good season. In theory, each one of these privileged beings was the wife or daughter of a Peer. In practice, the Peer whose wife or daughter did not care to be present gave away the place to a female friend. The pressure for admission was very great: yet on the Ministerial side every seat was filled, but on the Opposition side there remained quite fifty vacant places. It may be that the Opposition Peeresses are too good Liberals to care to swell a triumph in which the Sovereign is made to appear as the ally of the Tory party.

The ushers who swarm about the doorway to the left of the throne meet each lady as she arrives. One of them inspects her card, examines the plan with which he is equipped, and solemnly conducts the high-born dame to her seat. You may have a look at them as they pass beneath the gallery. They are in full dress, or what passes for full, but as yet the fulness of it is hidden beneath a cloak. Nobody cares to sit for an hour or more in this cold hall with bare shoulders and arms. You remark that many of them seem to have been carefully drilled for this appearance. They advance with a measured step and collected air: their trains sweeping the floor three yards behind them. There have been disrespectful foreigners—some of them Americans, I fear—who said that the British female does not walk well. The disrespectful foreigner would have to reconsider his opinion had he been present on this occasion. Not all, but many of these brilliant creatures have a marked dignity of gait. It is, to be sure, rather more commonly dignified than graceful, but it is sometimes both. Lady Hood is an instance. She is one of the most beautiful women in England, and she walks up the aisle with an undulating ease of movement, a careless yet firm step, an indolent grace, and with it all a natural distinction of manner, which are more often found in the women of Southern Europe than here in this island of the North. On the opposite side sits Lady Musgrave, another beauty of an un-English type, to whom the diplomatists are paying court, and whose vivacity and rapidity of talk and gesture are such that she passes for French with those who don't recognize her. There are other beauties, but I saw none of those ornaments of society who are ill-naturedly called professional beauties, and I fear that it must be said that the average of good looks was not high. More pretty women are to be seen any morning during the season in Hyde Park than were gathered here on an occasion which ought to collect all the aristocratic loveliness of England. Ought to, perhaps, but certainly does not. The number of women here who can safely be said to be of the highest birth or of highest fashion is but limited. The majority of them have yielded their places to their sisters of less degree. A foreigner who has been told beforehand that he was to see the most splendid company in Europe would be disappointed. Neither in personal charms nor in splendor of adornment does this assembly deserve such a eulogy. There are not many fresh toilets, even when the cloaks come off. The

rule about court dress is but laxly observed. Many ladies seem to think
they have done enough in putting on the first low-necked gown that
came to hand. Some of them even wear those pretty morning caps
which a French lady puts on and off with her peignoir, and which only
a French lady's maid wears in the evening. There are diamonds, but I
have seen more of them at an evening party. For the better display of
such beauty and diamonds and costumes as there were, it would have
been better if the weather had been worse. The spectacle was given
from beginning to end by daylight; or, more accurately speaking, without gaslight. A dense fog without and no illumination within would
have added much to the effect.

The Diplomatic Corps

Presently arrives three Judges and twice as many Bishops; all robed.
The Judges are in scarlet and ermine and wear wigs. Now the judicial
wig is a sufficiently imposing headgear when the Judge is on the bench
and the spectator regards him from below. View from above, it bears
a close resemblance to a beehive. The Bishops are also in scarlet and
ermine, with some arrangement in black and white underneath. The
two Archbishops, he of Canterbury and his brother of York, are there;
and may pass as types—the former of the prelate on whose face compli-
ance is written, who owes preferment to his suppleness of soul and his
gifts as courtier; the latter of the prelate to whom intellectual ability
has brought promotion. They are both talking with the diplomatists:
of whom there are no two alike in dress or demeanor, as there are no
two who do not stand for alien races and represent nations or sovereigns of the widest divergence. Most splendid of them all is the
Persian Minister, a Prince and the envoy of a Prince. His dark face is
set off by a uniform resplendent with barbaric pearls and gold, with a
jeweled sword pendent from a coat whose brilliant green is only one of
a dozen colors that only an Oriental would dare wear together. So
subtly are they contrasted and complemented, that they no more quarrel with each other than the verdure of the trees quarrels with the
azure above or either of them with the sunlight. There are two men
who nobody recognizes; a tall soldier in plain blue and red, and another of less height, the front of whose long coat is a mass of silver
embroidery down to his knees, with a broad red sash across it from
shoulder to thigh. We are all agreed that one of them is the new Russian Ambassador, Prince Labanoff, but we don't know which. Count
Münster, standing three inches higher than any of his colleagues, is a
fit representation of that new German Empire which is a giant among
modern European States. Count Münster is as tall as Prince Bismarck;
but there the resemblance ends. In the first rows are the sailor Ambassador of France, Admiral Pothasn, the great Austrian noble, Count
Carolyi, the bluff old Dane, von Bülow, and the soldier diplomatist of

Italy, with his polished manner, Count Menabréa. John Chinaman waddles in under his priceless petticoats, with a petticoated secretary, yellow-faced like himself, and a sandy-whiskered Scotch interpreter in trousers, the well-known Mr. MacCarthy. But to whom do you suppose amid this assemblage as motley as it is magnificient, falls the post of honor, the front corner seat nearest the throne? To none other than the old Masurus Pacha, old but not venerable, the speaking representative of the unspeakable Turk, who, for 20 years or more, has been the Envoy of the Porte in London. He is as respectable personally, perhaps, as a Turkish Pacha can be, but it is appalling to think of the life the man has led so long as the representative of the most perfidious power in Europe. What must he not have on his conscience; or on what would be his conscience if he were not a Turk and a Pacha! Where would those jewels be if the bony holders came by their own; or if restoration were made to be plundered Christians of the Ottoman Empire?

But nobody puts such questions as these in this polite society. Polite society is more concerned to know who the diplomatist may be who, after all, is the most conspicuous figure in the throng—the one dressed like a gentleman, as I heard a lady remark innocently. He sits just behind Masurus, the gentleman remarked on earlier and he is the Chargé d'Affaires of the U.S., Mr. Hoppin. I asked him after the ceremony how he got past the doorkeepers. "O," he said, with a slight grimace, "I made the usual explanations." And I suppose it is true that the greatness of the American Republic is but imperfectly symbolized to the flunkey mind by the plain black dress and white tie which Mr. Seward prescribes to her Envoy and Minister Plenipotentiary. In the ranks of life where livery is not worn, our reputation does not appear to suffer. Mr. Hoppins' strong face and ample figure and dignity of manner are not a whit less remarkable from the simplicity of his apparel, nor is he the less cordially greeted by his bespangled companions.

The Peers Lounge In

Toward 2 o'clock the peers lounge in one by one. They are not easy to recognize in the queer scarlet dressing gowns they call their capes. The upper part of the gown has bars of white fur, edged with gold lace; the number of which increases, I believe, with the rank of the wearer. I don't know who looked most queerly in this disguise, whether Lord Houghton's kindly-cynical countenance or Lord Rosebery's handsome young face seemed to be more hardly treated. Lord Granville came as late as possible. The Duke of Bedford was one of the first, but the Duke, like many of his colleagues, postponed to the last the awful mement of robing. They wandered about the House in morning dress till shortly before the royalties were expected. In the end, less than 100 Peers took their seats. As their seats on this occasion would hardly hold more, the absentees could not be much blamed. Lord Salisbury we did not expect to see, for we knew he was ill at Hatsfield, though of what he is ill no two doctors seem to agree. But Lord Beaconsfield: where was he? It is for him that all this performance has been arranged: for him that the Queen quits her beloved Osborne and passes two nights in this hated London. Above all men, he delights in ceremonial pageant: in flashing gems and embroidered robes: in medieval parade and elaborate magnificience. Why is he absent? Nobody knows. We can only surmise that a sharper twinge of the gout has seized him. Neither now nor during the opening did he appear, but at 5 he was well enough to take his seat and make a feeble speech.

The Prince and Princess of Wales

At half past one the Prince and Princess of Wales were to leave Marlborough House. At quarter to 2 the Queen was to leave Buckingham Palace. As the hours drew on a hush gradually fell upon the House. The Peers stole silently to their places. The ushers had ceased to move to and fro. Mr. Justice Lopes who was lolling almost at full length, sat up. The Lord Chief Baron, who had slept upright at his side, opened his eyes. The murmur of talk died away. Even the diplomatists ceased their chatter, and Lady Musgraves' most devoted adorers spoke to her only with their eyes. Lorgnettes were put away in obedience to that unwritten but unbending law which enacts that they shall not be used to spy out the features of royalty. Cloaks began to fall off the fair shoulders they had covered, and just on the stroke of two, those outer garments disappeared as if at a signal mysteriously passed through the chamber. At the same instant, the whole audience rose.

Through the doorway on the left of the throne, the Prince and Princess of Wales were seen advancing. The Prince wore his Peer's robes (with more bars of rabbit skin than anybody else), and underneath what appeared to be a Field Marshal's uniform, with a plumed hat in his hand. His stout figure looked stouter than ever, and if I were prepared to flee the country forever, I should almost say that he might have passed for some city dignitary. His good-natured face gets no enhancement of dignity from this travesty, but his ease of manner and his bearing dispel that dreadful suggestion of the adlerman. Next him walks the Princess, radiant in her still youthful loveliness, sparkling with diamonds, perfectly dressed, perfect in every movement. So deliberate is the pace that you have ample time to note how admirably the lady has been bred for the part she has to play: how complete in her composure: how clear and untroubled! is the glance of her eyes: how brilliant the smile: what an utter absence there is in the face of anything like self-consciousness: how natural is her expression and easily her glance takes in the whole assembly: how quietly she accepts the silent homage of her future subjects: being all the while if one dare say so, perhaps just conscious of the administration offered to the woman. The prince conducts her to the woolsack, greets her with a scarcely perceptible bow as she takes her seat and establishes himself comfortably in the chair to the right of the throne. With these two, entered a dozen others of the royal family and their kin; the Princess Frederica of Hanover, the Duchess of Connaught, the Duke of Teck, and I know not who else. They passed almost unregarded.

The Queen Appears

Once the Heir-Apparent and the Princess have taken their seats, we were permitted to resume ours, and again we waited. The silence grew deeper than ever: broken only by the frou-frou of robes and the coughing that had broken out when the cloaks were dropped. Not an audible word was spoken. Ten minutes passed. Then again as if at a signal, though no signal is seen nor heard, the multitude rises to its feet. The herald and pursuivants in strange tabards of fantastic device and color are entering. Rouge Dragon and Rouge Croix, Portucullis and Bluemantle head the procession. The middle ages are walking in. The feudal systen is here in person, and all you have read of tournaments and court pageants is masquerading before you. To mention anybody out of his order, or not to mention him at all is, I fear, a sort of petty treason; but, on the other hand, a knowledge of precedence and heraldic mysteries and official titles is a requisition of a lifetime. I can only jumble together such as I happened to know and have heard of and the best of these great people did not all know their business. They had to bow to the prince on the left as they entered, to the Princess on the right, to the Duke of Edinburgh, to the Duke of Connaught, to the Duke of Cambridge and I know not who else. Long before they had completed these obeisances, the heads of some of them began to swim, and royalty was cheated of some of its due genuflexions. The greater people are behind. Equerries in waiting, the Controller of Her Majesty's Household, Norroy King of Arms, Clarencoux King of Arms, the Gentleman Usher of the Black Rod, then, the Earl Marshal of England, the Duke of Norfolk, the Lord High Chancellor, and then the Queen. Before Her Majesty was borne the Cap of Maintenance, whatever that may be and the Sword of State, which the Duke of Richmond and Gordon held aloft, but slanting. The Duke of Northumberland carried the crown: and then followed Prince Leopold and Princess Beatrice, the Duchess of Wellington, who is the Mistress of the Robes, and Lady Southampton, who is first Lady of the Bedchamber. With them, came the Lord Steward and the Master of the Horse, with Field Marshall the Lord Strathuairn as Gold Stick in Waiting. These and many other great personages streamed in, so far as one could see, in no particular order but each in shining raiment or uniform of blazing scarlet and gold, and grouped themselves about the throne.

Her Majesty on the Throne

Her Majesty acknowledges the grave greetings of her lieges by scarcely more than a glance of the eye. The head bent slightly perhaps, but I am not sure. She too, walks slowly; there is no vulgar hurry about any part of this business. As she rounds the corner of the dais, her face is turned full toward our gallery. It is the business of courtiers to say that the Queen looks always well. For my part, I thought she had grown gray since last I saw her, and that the lines at the temples and about the mouth were cut deeper than ever. It can never have been more than a comely face, and there is nothing, strictly speaking, in its contour, or nothing in the figure, which can be called beautiful or noble. What strikes you nevertheless, was the air of authority and the air of stern sincerity which sits upon this royal brow, and marks the least gesture of the Queen. The sadness of the face is profoundly touching; the dignity with which the burden—the all but intolerable burden—of her life is borne, appeals to your respect. She is here, they say, to mark once more her sympathy with the First Minister of the Crown and with the party which, under his guidance, has been leading this country so strange a dance these three years past. But politics are forgotten in such a presence; and any criticism one has to offer is put decently aside so long as the woman and the Queen is here.

When she had seated herself upon the royal robes spread over the throne—which she might have worn, one would think,—there is again a pause, almost solemn and there is time to observe the gown which the Majesty of England has on. The Majesty and the Beauty of England are face to face; for the Princess sits nearly opposite; and as the Princess is perhaps the best dressed woman in the room, so is the Queen almost the worst. Her gown is of velvet, with broad longitudinal streaks of miniver or ermine running down the skirt and horizontal trimmings to match about the body. But we need not stop to look at it; the Koh-i-noor glows in her corsage, and a miniature crown of diamonds shines above the stony head. The Princess Beatrice, in blue velvet, stands by her mother's side, with traces of the womanly attractiveness which belongs to her sister Louise now reigning over the hearts of our Canadian friends. There was some maneuvering of the footstools and arrangement of trains, and the Queen's veil had to be extricated from the netted work of the throne. Then the Queen said: "Pray be seated," and once more came silence and a pause.

The Commons Storm the Hall

For once, the silence was rudely broken. A messenger had gone to summon the Commons, and soon there came a sound as of the rushing of a mighty wind, and then appeared the Speaker with his Chaplain and Sergeant-at-Arms; the three borne forward quite irresistibly by the crowd behind, and vainly striving to preserve an air of repose. They walked as if that mighty wind were thrusting them on—you have seen men in that attitude of being helped forward faster than they liked. Behind them waved the multitude. They poured in upon this decorous audience room as if they would take it by storm. But there is a barrier beyond which they cannot pass. They rage against it, but it holds firm. In fact, today as always, Her Majesty's faithful Commons are only admitted into a pen at the further end of the room, holding perhaps a third of their number, all standing. They and the members of the Fourth Estate in the gallery above are the only persons who venture into the presence of the sovereign in morning dress.

The Queen's Speech

When the storm had subsided and stillness had come again, the Lord Chancellor turned to the Queen, knelt and offered her a roll of paper, which she put aside. Obedient to her gesture, he rose and unrolled it and it proved to be Her Majesty's speech, which he read slowly and clearly. When it had been read, the Queen, with only a moment's delay, rose and walked out. The ceremony was over. Parliament had been opened by the Queen in person. The throng broke up. As we passed out, I met a member of Parliament of much distinction, who remarked: "It's a comfort to think what a jolly smash we shall make some day of this Japanese mummery."

New York Tribune, 22 February 1880.

Appendix C
Louis Blanc

If ever a man lived free from stain, it was he who had just died. All his life long the fierce light of passionate political, and still more passionate social, controversies beat upon him. He made innumerable enemies; he was the object of innumerable calumnies. Not one of his enemies hated the *man*, not one of the calumnies touched his private worth. He plunged into every conflict of his time. From the first he made himself felt as a formidable antagonist. He attacked with fearlessness the classes and creeds which were then, and still are, the most powerful in modern life. His criticisms went to the root of the existing social organisation, which he strove to dissolve and reconstruct. His theories were destructive to the idea of property as at present held, and to the processes by which property is accumulated. For forty years he was a foe to every government and form of government which maintained its power in France. Even after 1870, which saw a Government republican in form rise on the runs of the Empire, Louis Blanc preserved his attitude of reserve and distrust. It was a Republic, but it was not his Republic. And again, after the Constitution had been voted which baptized the new *régime* and gave it the sanction of the coveted name Republican, it was not socialistic and therefore not to his mind. So late as the autumn of 1877, after the decisive overthrow of the royalist conspiracy which went by the name of the Seize Mai Ministry, with the Duc de Broglie at its head, I heard Louis Blanc say, "Yes, thank God for the defeat of that intrigue, but it is only the beginning of the end." And not long after: "Wait till we get a real Republic; then you'll see what we shall do." The Extreme Left, the group to which he has always belonged in the Chamber and of which he was president, is a minority, and necessarily a minority. It has practically been in opposition to every Republican Ministry, which has not prevented it from saving many of those Ministries at critical moments from disaster. Louis Blanc allowed himself in most cases to vote with his colleagues, but if the vote involving upholding a policy or a measure which he thought unsound, the utmost pressure had to be used to secure his adhesion. If he had followed his inclinations he would have let any Ministry go to pieces sooner than swerve a hair's breadth from his loyalty to the most abstract principle. The doctrine of Opportunism was distasteful to him, yet he lent a substantial support to M. Gambetta, with whom he had, at any rate, among other points of sympathy, a hearty detestation of clericalism.

Thus he had against him from the beginning to the end, Government, Society, the Church. He was hated and feared. His pen was never idle; his books, his letters, his newspaper articles, were read from one end of France to the other. His voice, while it was allowed to be heard in his own country, had an echo from every quarter. He was never forgotten and could never be despised. All possible means were used to discredit and crush him. But none of his enemies was quite stupid enough to suppose that any disparagement of Louis Blanc's private character would find credit with the people.

But that merely spotless purity is, after all, negative. He had much more than that. He had the most positive private virtues. He was not only unselfish, he was generous in a rare degree. He was devoted to something more than an idea. He became the benefactor of those whose place in the world and share of the world's possessions was less than in his view it ought to be. He never thought it enough to plead their cause; to devote his life to their advancement. Always a poor man, he gave lavishly. I do not think he always gave wisely. Nobody who knocked at his door was ever sent empty away.

He gave on a much greater scale than this, and with prodigal recklessness of his own interests. A story of his financial experience with his *History of the French Revolution* will show to what lengths he allowed his sympathies with the supposed troubles of others to carry him. He made a contract with a publisher for 300,000 francs, out of which a certain sum was to be paid him yearly; the balance on conclusion of the work. After some years the publisher came to him with a pitiful story of depression in business, lessening sales of the early volumes, and loss of all profit; in short, he declared that the price first offered was greater than the publication would support, and besought Louis Blanc to forgo 100,000 out of the 300,000 francs. A cooler piece of impudence would perhaps be found with difficulty in the annals of the publishing trade. Legal claim this man of business had none; of morality the less said the better. But it was precisely the sort of appeal which Louis Blanc could not resist; an appeal (no matter how unfounded) once to his sympathies and his sense of justice. He assented, and with a stroke of his pen made M. Pagnerre, then a rich man, a free gift of the 100,000 francs. I believe I am right in saying that Louis Blanc had not at that moment a dollar in the world except what he was earning from day to day. Emboldened by his success the man of business presently made another attempt, repeating the old story, and finally inducing his victim to abandon another large sum to him—either another 100,000 francs or 50,000. And so it happened that when Louis Blanc had finished his great work, to which he devoted eighteen of the best years of his life, he was not a penny the richer for it. He had parted with his property in the book, and he had received during the writing of it just enough to keep body and soul together.

Charles Sumner used to say that the first volume of this History was one of those profoundly philosophical studies which mark an epoch in literature and in the development of human intelligence. Nobody had traced the causes of the Revolution to their deeper sources, or with such wide knowledge of men, events, books, and the movement of thought. Of the later volumes, the other eleven, it is to be said that they contain a fuller narrative of events than any other single history then written. But, like every other French history of that period, it is a pamphlet. Louis Blanc, by some strange caprice of Fate, became the apologist of Robespierre, and his History is Robespierrist throughout. He does full justice to no one else, and he does far more than justice to the man who, in his eulogist's conception, was the incarnation of the revolutionary spirit. Starting with a preconception of this sort, he has written a misleading book. He does not so much defend the worst acts of Robespierre—for example, the Orange Commission, the Loi du 22 prairial, the murders of Danton and the Dantonists—as colour them, and too often deny Robespierre's responsibility for them or culpability for them. The book must be read, therefore, with constant reference to the writer's prepossessions and with unfailing caution on the part of the student. But it must be read.

So must many other books of his, and among them the three collections of his *Letters on England.* These cover a large portion of the time he spent here in exile. They deal for the most part—as the conditions of French journalism, which is, in its best mood, really more serious than almost any other, permitted them to deal—with subjects of more than ephemeral interest. He made a study of England; knew its history, social organisation, and current daily life, both political and personal, as few foreigners have known it. His letters are composed with the care he gave to everything he wrote—never slovenly, or hurried, or superficial, or gossiping. There are, on the whole, perhaps no ten volumes about England more instructive, nor many more readable.

I first met Louis Blanc soon after I came to live in London, and the friendship which grew up between us lasted without a break till his death. His life in London was the life of a student. He passed the day among his books in the quiet little house in Upper Montagu Place, or in the British Museum. It was the Museum that he wrote his *History of the French Revolution;* and there alone, he used to say, could the Revolution be fully studied. Beginning with the collection made by John Wilson Croker, and sold by him when he found himself forestalled by Alison in his project of a history of that period, the Museum has since bought pretty much everything it could lay hands on. It has a mass of rare pamphlets and contemporary literature not to be found in the National Library at Paris. It has not, of course, the archives which repose in the various departments of State, and the want of acquaintance with them is evident in Louis Blanc's work. I suppose he might have returned to Paris if he had wished, but nothing would induce him to set foot on French soil so long as it lay under the yoke of Napoleon the Third. It was the Republic of '48 which had driven him from France but it was the Bonapartist Empire for which he reserved all his resentment. He pardoned the injustice done to himself; the outrage upon his beloved France he would pardon never.

That will serve as well as anything for the keynote to his public character, or to one rare and attractive side of his character. He was the most disinterested of men. His great fame has been won by a life filled with sacrifices, one after the other, of almost everything that brings fame to a man. It is not that he was careless of honour and reputation or ever affected a superiority to applause. He valued it, coveted it, hungered for it, and sacrificed it all the same. Praise pleased him as it pleases a child, as it pleases most simple natures. But with a passion for popularity he was for ever doing, and consciously doing, the most unpopular acts. By birth he belonged to the upper middle class, and his life was given to strengthening the hands of a class below his own, intensely hostile to it, whose idea of rising is to pull down whatever is above it. The bent of his mind was naturally toward culture. Nobody could have made more admirable contributions to purely elegant literature; nobody was more academic, more capable of the last refinements and polish which are the results of a leisure devoted to making the most of one's natural gifts. But from his first article in a newspaper to the last page of his History he made himself the servant of an idea. He was fond of society, of salons, of conversation, of art, and he turned away from them all to preach a gospel which in the hands of less scrupulous practitioners would surely put an end to them all.

His socialism—for I may as well say the inevitable word about it at once—was very far-reaching in theory, yet with him I always thought it less theoretic than sympathetic. In his stringent analysis of the existing social structure he found faults enough, and not in the structure only but in the whole scheme and idea which were the foundation of it. He had drunk deep at the half-poisoned fountain of Rousseau. He thought for himself, boldly, clearly, with singular power of logic, with endless critical ingenuity, and his socialism, as I said above, was essentially of a destructive kind. He would not have destroyed a fly himself;

he invariably refused to apply on any great scale the subversive principles he announced in his books. He never foresaw and hardly ever admitted the consequences which others drew from them, and the results to which his so-called disciples would have made them contribute. What in truth underlay these utopian speculations was not so much a reasoned conviction as a passionate pity. He could not witness the misery of the poorer classes without longing to relieve it. His books on social questions were a cry of distress. When his heart was touched his head became its instrument. No doubt he had argued himself into the belief that the organisation of society was radically faulty and radically unjust. He described himself as hungering for justice, and it was a true description. But a passion for all the gentler virtues lay just as deep in his being. Charity, mercy, infinite compassion and affection for whoever was weaker or poorer or less gifted than himself, were the constant motives of his acts and thoughts.

His books, whether historical or political or socialistic, are all one long panegyric on the people. An American reader is liable to forget that the word people does not mean in his mouth what it means with us—the whole people. These paeans are sung in honour of a class, and that the lowest class of all. Louis Blanc's faith in the people was not in the true sense a democratic faith. He was not for the rule of a majority. The people meant with him in theory the whole sum of the population of France excluding the nobility, the aristocracy, the clergy (albeit springing mostly from the soil), the professions, the whole middle class in whose hands are the wealth and the property accumulated by successful industry. The artisan and the peasant were the people. They were a majority, it is true, but there never has been a moment since '93 when the peasantry was revolutionary in the social sense. It was the artisan, and above all the artisan of Paris, to whom Luis Blanc looked as the arbiter of the destinies of France. Paris was to give law to the rest of the country, and the Paris working men to give law to Paris. He was for the rule of the section which had accepted his doctrines. But when the people of Paris appeared in the streets in 1848 and invited him to govern the country, he shrank back appalled from the task; and he was appalled with reason. Of the particular charges brought against him, and on which he was expelled from France, he was not guilty. But he was certainly a danger to any Government of which he was not the head, and the choice lay between his dictatorship and his exile. Such is the irony of fate. Louis Blanc believed in a Republic without a head, and because he would not govern his mere presence made a Republic impossible.

Those who have once met Louis Blanc in society or at his own house will not forget the charm of his manner. To those who have been fortunate enough to meet him often, the memory of it will remain as among the best life has had to offer. It may be said in one sense that his manner never varied. He had the same kindly and polished greeting for visitors of every rank. It was never cold. To his friends it was affectionate, whether you had seen him yesterday or not for many months. His eye was as beautiful as a woman's, with that luminous depth which betokens a profoundly sympathetic nature. He was something more than sympathetic; he was a man to be loved. His conversation was varied, imaginative, abounding in reminiscence and anecdote, every now and then lighting up the remotest depths of a subject with flashes of penetrating intelligence. He was in earnest, but never heavy; serious, but free from gloom; the life of a dinner-table and a delightful companion in private. From everything like pretence or affection he was absolutely free. It was too much his custom to take sombre views of affairs, especially the affairs of his own country, for which he had a love that knew no bounds. But of the men who were mismanaging France he had little to say that was hard, nothing that was uncharitable; while of his personal enemies he hardly ever spoke with severity. He had to bear during the last eighteen months of his life acute and unremitting torment. It never disturbed the serenity of his temper nor checked his interest in public matters. To the last he was at work for others. I saw him in September; sadly altered in face, but then as ever the same simple, genuine, heroic nature that for so many years I had admired, and that I now think I never admired enough.

A word only about his funeral, which I went to Paris to attend, not to describe. The people were true to their true friend. Every effort was made by the Reds to prevent a popular demonstration. Of late years Louis Blanc, like almost every sane and honest Radical, had been hated by the insane and unscrupulous factions which seeks again to set up the Commune in blood and fire. The political brigands who have usurped a name once respected made a good many people believe that they had Paris—the Paris of the Faubourgs—behind them. It was one service which Louis Blanc did in his death to expose this imposture. The Paris which had over and over again given him its suffrages had not forsaken him to follow the blind guides who proclaim themselves its new leaders. All the efforts to keep people at home failed. The streets were thronged from the Rue de Rivoli to Père la Chaise. The feeling of grief among the spectators was unmistakable and profound. The presence of Ministers and senators and deputies, the many associations and deputations who came from all parts of France, the crowns of *immortelles*, the wreaths of white and violet which covered his coffin and hearse, the military guard, the officiall conduct of the ceremony by the Government of the Republic—all these were marks of deserved honour, and a late

Appendix D

Queen Victoria's Golden Jubilee

London, June 21.—A ceremony without fault or flaw, wanting in no element of dignity or circumstances of pomp. Such is the summary of this great day from beginning to end. The pageant is over, the Jubilee is over, the Queen has gone to the Abbey and returned to her Palace, and not one mishap or mistake has marred the royal progress or royal return. I speak of what I have seen and heard and of that only. I have seen the ceremony in the Abbey. I have seen the return procession from what I think is the best point, a house at Hyde Park Corner. Take both together, take the day as a whole, take the Abbey and the streets, the procession inside and the procession outside, and I think on the whole I have nowhere at any time witnessed a spectacle so splendid and impressive.

I do not mean that if the Queen had opened a hospital or laid a corner stone the mere splendor of escort or glitter of trappings would have been more remarkable than many others. But this is an occasion which appeals to the imagination as well as to the eye; to historic sense not less than to visible effect. Something, no doubt, might have been added. The Queen would immensely have gratified her subjects had she worn the crown and royal robes. Another battalion or two of Foot Guards or Life Guards would not have been amiss had not precedent, that musty mother of mischief, prevented. But what this vast multitude in the streets saw was ample to call forth admiration, as the mere presence of the Queen was adequate to provoke every possible demonstration of loyalty.

London was astir at daylight, waking gratefully to a blaze of sunshine, and had descended into the streets long before its usual hour of breakfast. The police took no lesson from yesterday, when the populace·on foot and the classes in carriages blocked every inch of the route along which the procession was to pass to-day. They adhered to the letter of their orders, which tolerated traffic till half past 8 this morning, though hours before London was not only awake, but in motion toward the Abbey. Open at 9, closed at 10, was the order of those who had the ordering of the matter.

Meaning to be early, I drove into Piccadilly at Hyde Park Corner at half past 7. It was already a hopeless block. I had a police pass which gave me an absolute right of way wherever it was physically possible for a carriage to move. It was for a long time perfectly useless. A line of vehicles was allowed to come westward, while vehicles going eastward were in five ranks and either at a standstill or moving now and then forward at foot pace.

Decorations in Piccadilly

To cut a long story, it took me an hour and a quarter to get from Apsley House to St. Jame's-st., not over half a mile. The delay mattered nothing. There was time enough, and Piccadilly was itself a spectacle. Nowhere were decorations so abundant, so costly, so effective or so original. Lord Rothschild's home was worthy of his name. Apsley House did not disgrace the memory of Wellington. Baroness Burdett-Coutts's mansion was as rich as its benevolent owner. Devonshire House had enlivened its gloomy courtyard and its wall, fronting for a hundred yards on the street, with a gayly decorated stand, and covered its terraces with flowers. Sir Algernon Borthwicks' house was the most charming of all. Here Byron once lived and to-day it looked like the home of a poet as well as one of the most successful journalists of his time. From pavement to roof, the front of this house was hung with garlands and bouquets of flowers. Lavish expense and good taste had gone hand in hand. So had they elsewhere. If the delicate fancy of the French were lacking, the loyal Briton set to make up by abundance for every deficiency of taste. No house that did not array itself in cloth of many colors; many that were rich with velvet, with cloth of gold, with oriental fabrics, with pendant baskets of roses, with flags of all nations. Arches of triumphs line many a street. Loyal mottoes and salutations were written in broad letters of gold wherever you went. At the bottom of St. Jame's-st. rose tall, solid columns on either side in white and gold. Waterloo Palace was a forest of fanciful structures that filled but did not darken its broad spaces.

The Queen, in one word, drove all the way from Constitution Hill to Westminster through one long avenue of lovely color. Far more lovely to her, no doubt, was the loyalty which expressed itself in cheers from the immense multitude who came abroad to welcome her. To enter the Abbey out of these gay streets and hurrying crowds was like entering another world. Certainly it was a shock to be shown along passages and staircases freshly built of deal; to see men wearing hats far inside this sacred fabric. But once inside all sense of sacrilege vanished. Too much has been said about the desecration of the Abbey. I never cared to see it in its scaffolded state. Possibly today it looked amphitheatrical, with tiers upon tiers of crimson seats rising from mosaic pavement to the chancellory and against the east window, almost to the groined roof itself, but if I have joined in any protests against what has been done in the Abbey, I retract them. What has been done was well done. The architect of this great church certainly never foresaw that it would be used for a Jubilee celebration. No building could be worse adapted for spectacular purposes, yet nothing could be more clever than the way in which the difficulties have been overcome. Not everybody saw well, but everybody saw something. The long hours during which we waited were not dull hours; there was ever something to study, ever something fresh to see. Moving about was impossible, once in your seat you kept it, whether you were peer or journalist. Journalists were, let me say, treated at least as well as peers and saw as much or more. If anybody had cause to complain among the great ones of the earth it was the diplomats. Their gallery looked into the south transept and to witness the procession they had to look round a huge pier at the angle of the transept and the choir. The Colonials, mostly in scarlet, fared better. The peers were not in their robes, but they and all the officials were either in uniform or court dress; so that wherever the eye turned, there was a bewildering variety of color.

Just before 10 o'clock, when I reached my place, the Abbey looked already almost full. The doors were far from closing at 10, as announced. There were arrivals till past 11. The diplomatists, peers, Members of Parliament and Lord Salisbury came late. The Lord Chancellor, with the mace duly borne before him, was already in his seat. Peeresses once threatened with exclusion were as numerous as peers and far more ornamental. Two at least could carry their memories back to fifty years ago. The Dowager Lady Stanley, of Alderley, was there present by the Queen's invitation. The Duchess of Cleveland, Lord Rosebery's mother, had been one of the Queen's bridesmaids and one of the bearers of her train at the coronation in 1837. Both were in the Abbey today. Ministers and ex-Ministers were numerous. Gladstone, I was told, was in his seat, but I saw him not. Sir William Vernon Harcourt I saw resplendent in green and gold, and William Henry Smith, the Right Hon. H. C. E. Childers and a score of others. I looked in vain for those men of letters and science to whom this reign owed so much distinction. Robert Browning I know, was not asked, nor Matthew Arnold, nor Professor Huxley. Sir George Otto Trevelyan was refused an invitation. The only man of first rank in literature I really saw was Mr. Leckey, the historian. Crowds of unknown and unknowable persons were visible. Friends of officials, 600 of Dean Bradley's to begin with, were in the two best galleries in the building, rising in rear of the sacrarium.

Only a Few Americans in the Abbey

The Americans present were few. The American Minister, of course, was there, and Mrs. Phelps and Mr. and Mrs. Henry White.

Mr. Blaine was invited and so was ex-Minister Lowell, but both preferred to see the procession outside. Gen. Lawton, the American Minister to Austria, was in the Abbey. Senator McPherson was invited, but not Senator Hale, who had not thought it worthwhile to call at the United States Legation.
Minor royalties began to arrive at half past 10. Minor officials of the royal household met them at the screen and gravely led them to their appointed seats. The vacant choir stall filled slowly. Up and down the vacant aisle in the center restless beings in blue and gold, more gold than blue, paced incessantly. The first real sensation was the coming of the Oriental princes. Never when seen separately had they appeared such dazzling creatures as now, when in a group and clad in such embroideries as the Western world had seldom gazed on and bedecked in jewels that would more than ransome all the European kings now on English soil. There are princes of such lineage and such antiquity as put to blush the most ancient of Europe, yet they are not thought worthy of a place by the side of such a mushroom monarch as he of the Belgians. They are all conducted to the choir stall and there sit meekly ranged against the wall at the back. Other royalties arrive, but are not now to be catalogued.
The real Kings and Queens make us wait for them—the Kings of Saxony, of Denmark, of the Hellenes, of the Belgians, all, indeed of those known as Her Majesty's royal guests, who form that separate procession which leaves the palace in advance. They are due at a quarter of twelve; they arrive at a quarter past. They march serenely up the aisle amid what seems to be cold civility, but with every outward form of reverence. Not one is allowed on the dais; all pass either into the choir stall or take a chair in the railed space before the altar.
Noon came but no Queen. As her guests, who had but just settled into their places, had left Buckingham Palace half an hour before her, she could not be expected before half past 12. So the murmur of talk and light laughter went on again all over the building.

The Coming of the Queen

It was twenty-five minutes to one o'clock when, after one false signal which brought the spectators to their feet, came a blast from the Queen's state trumpeter which told of her arrival at the west door of the Abbey. The white band of choristers in the galleries on either side of the choir rustled up and the whole vast audience rose with them and remained standing. Only the Kings and Queens in sacrarium remained seated, not caring to rise till the Queen was actually visible. Then came a pause and the minutes glided by. The vice chamberlains and other gold laced officers of the royal household group themselves at the entrance to their choir. Then they stood suddenly apart and the head of the royal procession showed itself, the ecclesiastics first. A dozen canons, minor and major, formed a guard of honor to the Lord Bishop of London, the Lord Archbishop of York, the Dean of Westminster and the Lord Archbishop of Canterbury. These episcopal and archepiscopal dignitaries were in gorgeous robes of dark velvet and gold strangely fashioned and monastic. More strange were the heralds in tabards, who came after. Then followed a long array of great officials, then hereditary princes, hereditary grand dukes, Serene Highnesses, Imperial Highnesses and Royal Highnesses. Whispers of admiration greeted the tall, well-set figure brilliantly uniformed in white, of the Crown Prince of Germany. These personages walked three abreast, the last of the trios being the Duke of Connaught, the Prince of Wales and the Duke of Edinburgh. Then came, preceded by the Lord Steward and Lord Chamberlain walking bravely backward, the Queen. Alone of all that glittering procession, Her Majesty was plainly dressed in a gown of black and gray in broad stripes, a bonnet that looked like another crown of gray hairs, and the blue ribbon of the Garter from left to right across her broad shoulders. She moved, as ever, with dignity as beautiful as it is marvellous in a woman of such physique, her face gravely radiant, her eyes turned right and left as with her unequalled demeanor she acknowledged salutations addressed to her from either side. The bishops, great officers, hereditary dukes and princes all passed to the right or left of the dais, where stood the coronation chair, over which the coronation robes had been thrown, and passed on to the sacrarium, or entered the dais at the side. The Queen alone kept on, unswerving to the right or left, and reached the broad steps left untrodden by all but the royal foot, which she mounted slowly with some help from the Lord Steward and the Lord Chamberlain, and so arrived near the throne. There she stood a moment before seating herself and with one sweeping movement of head and body signified her royal recognition of the homage the wonderful company offered her. That was the most brilliant moment of all—kings, queens, peers of England, commons of England, her youngest loveliness and her oldest nobility, ambassadors, ministers, princes, princesses and sovereigns doing honor in person or by deputy to this sovereign of England. All were standing, all heads were bent, the music was still echoing through the arches and cheers were still faintly heard from the street. It was the supreme hour of her life, and the spectacle one on the like of which no living soul has looked before.

The sunlight streamed in upon the Queen and the people, and the gray walls and dim arches of the Abbey were all glowing with myriad hues—with scarlet and gold, delicate tints of silks and more delicate bloom on the wearer's cheeks. Jewels flashed and swarthy Oriental faces for once lighted up. When the Queen sank into her gilt chair, this multitude remained standing, as if under a spell until she had twice signed for them to be seated.

A Service of Thanksgiving

Of the service which followed I can only say it was a service of thanksgiving, in which prayers and musical praise had each its due part. The picturesque figure of the Archbishop of Canterbury framed itself against the altar. His Grace's head was literally set in a halo of gold, like a medieval saint, for he happened to stand precisely in front of the large gold dish which rested edgewise on the sacred shelf. The religious resources of the Church of England were all invoked to declare on the Queen's behalf her gratitude for the fifty years of her honored, beneficent and admirable reign. The Dean of Westminster had his due share, perhaps the organist and choristers more than their share.

When the last note had died away there came the most touching scene of all. The Queen's sons, daughters and other kin by blood or marriage, who were grouped about her on the dais, came up, one by one, to her. The Prince of Wales came first, bowed low and kissed his mother's hand. She, as he rose, kissed him on both cheeks. Prince after prince performed his affectionate homage, each receiving the Queen's salute in return, though on one cheek only. The princesses followed, one by one, curtseying to the ground. The Crown Princess of Germany came first, then the Princess of Wales, then Princess Christian and Princess Beatrice, who impulsively kissed her mother's hand a second time, as she rose from her lowly obeisance. It was such a glimpse of domestic love as the world rarely gets into royal circles.

The Return to the Palace

This charming little episode over, the procession was reformed. The Queen moved slowly down the aisle of lofty arches and bending heads and so vanished from our sight beneath the screen which divides the choir from the outer nave. Then came the question. Was it possible to get away from the Abbey and reach Hyde Park Corner in time to see the return of the procession? With good fortune and much kindly official help the question answered itself, Yes; so that long before the first horseman appeared I was on a balcony which gave a superb view of Piccadilly and the green park in all the freshness of an English June. The great arch on Constitution Hill, just opposite the house, was crowded with human beings. All the spaces which the police did not keep clear for the procession was solid humanity. St. George's Hospital was one great display of balconies filled with men and women. There must have been 50,000 people in sight. The sun beat down fiercely on all these heads. Never all day has there been a cloud in the sky any more than a cloud on the Jubilee. Good humor has been universal. I have spent hours in the streets besides those in the Abbey and elsewhere, and heard never an angry word. All these scores of thousands of people had waited patiently on foot for hours and waited patiently still. They gaze up with what I think most admirable temper at these comfortable balconies. It is well past 2 o'clock when a mounted police-man brings promise of the recoming of the Queen. A troop of the First Life Guards comes not far behind him. I have left myself neither space nor time for describing in detail the cortege which now passed before us. Yet it was a thing as memorable in its way as the ceremony in the Abbey. The calvary, if not numerous, for she will allow herself only a field officer's escort, is perfection. The long lines of mounted headquarter's staff is more gorgeous still. The royal carriages conveying the royal suite seems to be the most magnificent of equipages till the Queen's own carriage appears. But before the Queen herself comes the feature of the features of this procession, the mounted princes, who form Her Majesty's real escort. Again, as in the Abbey procession, her three sons are next to her; the Prince of Wales rides in the middle, the Duke of Edinburgh on the right, and the Duke of Connaught on the left. They bestride horses which are only surpassed by the Duke of Portland's black hunter, who has just gone before and in whom connoisseurs delight. One irrever-ent critic declares that the Duke of Edinburgh rides like the sailor he is, but he does not. The bronzed face of the Duke of Connaught is kindly greeted by the crowd, but the Prince of Wales gets most of the cheers. So did he, say my friends, when he rode by the first time.

Cheers in Volleys for the Queen

But the Queen is nigh. There is no mistaking those eight cream-colored horses, whose cream color is almost invisible beneath their trappings. Each horse is led, the coaches all gold and blazonry, the harness is heavy with gold, crimson tassels are hanging heavy from the horses' necks, and the flunkeys are armored in gold lace. The whole turnout is splendid beyond compare to uncritical eyes. The critic de-clares that the cream-colored horses will not keep step and pronounces them brutes, but no criticism matters. The Queen is inside the marvell-ous chariot, the Crown Princess of Germany and the Princess of Wales being on the front seat and now for the first time today I hear the thundering cheers of the street. All these people have seen her and cheered her before, but they cheer with steady British perserverance as if having begun they meant never to leave off. The Queen's face is shining with delight as I never saw it before. She looks ten years younger and happier than a month since, when the West End and the East End together turned out to greet her. Cheers follow cheers in volleys and all hats are off. There are cheers even from those balconies where fashion sits in all her cold loveliness and bored indifference. The Queen looks up to the balconies as she passes, recognizes on all of them friends, bows straight at them, passes on and away and round the broad curve which takes her to the arch, enveloped and encom-passed with this marvellous music of the human voice in multitudinous

Appendix E

Theodore Roosevelt
as President of the United States

The two or three days I spent with Governor Roosevelt at Albany left me with the impression that his masterful good intentions would lead him far. We all know that they did, though whether we have even yet measured the whole distance may be a question. For the considered judgment of the community embodied in statutes he seemed to have less respect than for his own individual opinion. He had, I thought, less reverence for law than most Americans have: or once had. Those who have studied his seven years' Presidency will judge whether the impression derived from his Governorship was right or wrong.

It was my business during five of those years to follow him step by step and to compose a daily history of his administration for *The Times*. I saw him often. Sometimes he sent for me. Sometimes I asked for an audience. He talked, as a rule, freely; not always for publication. He meant to hold the balance even as between all journalists and all the papers they represented. I rather imagine that if ever by inadvertence he did not, he was sharply reminded ot it. If—it can only have been seldom—*The Times* published a piece of news exclusively, he or Mr. Loeb, his secretary, would be asked why favour should be shown to an English paper, or to me. I do not think it ever was shown intentionally. The President knew, of course, that any such news would be re-cabled to America and he had no wish to rouse needless jealousies. Whatever kindly feeling he might have for me his instinctive preference would be for an American rather than for an English journal.

His Americanism was a prevailing, continuous, overmastering passion. He was American all the time; and perhaps *quand même*. Whether England then came next, *longo intervallo*, after America, I should doubt. During the Boer War his sympathies appeared to be with the Boers. Dutch blood flowed in his veins, not a drop of English, as he himself often said. He took pains to be civil, and something more than civil, to the Irish enemies of England. There came a change, but he does not seem to have been one of those Americans who in 1898 were convinced by England's resistance to European intervention in behalf of Spain that England was really our friend and not the enemy held up to execration in America's schoolbooks and in Senator Lodge's biographies. Possibly it was not till Mr. Hay's farseeing diplomacy brought the United States into the circle of world-powers that President Roosevelt perceived clearly why co-operation between England and the United States was for the interest of both; and for ours not less than hers.

Next after Mr. Hay, it was perhaps Lord Pauncefote whose influence on the President led him gently to an attitude of benevolence toward the Mother Country. He accepted Lord Pauncefote as a type. The British Ambassador had a directness of method and a transparent honest sincerity in all his dealings which profoundly impressed the President. He knew that when Lord Pauncefote said a thing it was so, and that in all Anglo-American issues the Ambassador's voice was the voice of England. Therefore it was that the German cabal in 1902 against Lord Pauncefote left the President cold; or rather, to speak more truly, impelled him to reject the Berlin story and to make it the occasion for a noble tribute to Lord Pauncefote and a complete public recognition of his friendship for America. He expressed it to me. It was not asked for, and it was almost the only occasion on which the President allowed himself to be quoted at first hand. "You may say I said it, but not that I said it to you."

With all due reserve in great matters and with strict precaution President Roosevelt, like Governor Roosevelt before him, was ever ready to take the Press into his confidence when he could. The Press owed him much, and he owed much to the Press. He made use of the Press; a most skilful and legitimate use; and not of the Press only. He said to me once: "You think I am impulsive and perhaps I am. But I will tell you one thing. Never yet have I entered upon any great policy till I was satisfied I had behind me a great body of public opinion."

Some of this evidence of public opinion he must have derived from the Press, and from representatives of the Press. He could, and did, put questions as well as answer them. He held that a journalist who knew his business must know what was thought and said in his own constituency. From some other and not less useful sources of information he deliberately cut himself off. He set the business world against him; and the big men of finance in New York and elsewhere had no reason for giving him help or expert counsel except where some great public interest was concerned. In the year of the crisis and shortly before the climax of it, I was for six weeks in and about New York. I met a great many people, some of them among the most important in the world of finance and business. Neither from any one of them nor from any other human being did I at that time hear one good word said for the President. He had alienated the business world. He was hated. They thought him a menace to peace and prosperity. Yet somehow or other the President knew what was going on in those upper regions. I should think no President was ever better served; and surely no President was ever more adroit in tapping the sources of opinion. He had his own standard of values. At one critical moment he said: "I have means of knowing that the thirteen Bishops of the Methodist Episcopal Church are with me. That being so, I don't care who is against me."

He liked to declare himself in that large way, but of course he did care very much who was against him. What he meant was that the thirteen Bishops were representative; that they did not divorce religion from politics; that their authority over their millions of co-religionists was great, and that they spoke for these millions as well as for themselves.

That sense of "fun" which came out in the Police Commissioner was not always repressed in the President. As I sat with him in his private room we saw through the open door into the Cabinet chamber two men enter.

"Do you know these men?"

"No."

"They are men in whom America is just now much interested; Reynolds and his colleague whom I sent to Chicago to inquire into the stockyards and slaughterhouses. Part of their report, enough for my purpose, has been sent to Congress and no doubt you have read it. The rest is too awful to publish. You would like to see it, wouldn't you?"

"Yes."

"You never will."

Often enough the surprise in which he delighted came in a different way. During a crisis which affected England as well as the United States he sent for me and began: "I am going to talk to you in confidence; not a word for print. I think it desirable that you should know privately what the view of the Government is and what, in certain contingencies, I intend to do."

His statement lasted for twenty minutes. He talked with that lucidity and force which came to him when he dealt with great affairs. Now and then I asked a question which he answered without reserve. When he had finished I said: "I, of course, understand that what you have told me is not to be repeated. But may I say that from a talk I have had with a high official authority I draw such and such conclusions?"

The lips parted over the white teeth, the eyes gleamed behind the glasses, and the President answered: "That is why I sent for you."

I was to take the responsibility and not he. It was my business to take it, and I did. If my conclusions had been challenged I had all the evidence to support them and could have used none of it. But that is one of the risks which a journalist has to accept. In fact, there was no challenge from any quarter worth noticing, and *The Times* dispatch had, I think, the effect the President meant it to have.

One other detached and I hope illustrative anecdote.

When I came back from Ottawa with Sir Wilfrid Laurier's authority to repeat to Mr. Hay and the President what he had said to me about Alaska, I brought with me a long memorandum which both the Secretary of State and the President read. It contained the substance of several conversations and a statement of what I believed Sir Wilfrid ready to do. I have always thought that if the President had then had a free hand, he would have been disposed to avail himself of this knowledge of what was in Sir Wilfrid's mind, as a basis for negotiations. But there stood the Senate, in its most implacable mood, and neither Mr. Hay nor the President thought the moment propitious for approaching that august body with any fresh proposals. I was given to understand that, much as the Canadian Prime Minister's desire to close the controversy was appreciated, no step could then be taken. During a long audience I pressed it as much as I thought permissible, and finally said to the President that I was still unwilling to take No for an answer. I felt that he was as unwilling to give it as I was to take it. He answered: "Well, you are coming here this evening and I will consider the whole question meantime. Stay on after the others are gone and we will have a final talk."

Mrs. Roosevelt had a reception after the dinner and it was past midnight before her guests departed. Then Mr. Roosevelt and I tramped up and down the long passage between the East Room and the Conservatory till half-past one. At the end the President said: "I am very sorry but it must be No."

"Then I can only say good night. I oughtn't to have kept you so late."

"Late? You think I am going to bed? I have a hundred and sixty pension bills to read before I turn in."

"Why not veto them all unread?"

"That's easy for you to say but did you ever hear of the Grand Army of the Republic?"

Upon which we parted. Politics had to come in. They often had. They were never very far from the President's mind. An old and loyal friend of his said to me: "No man's sense of public duty is higher than the President's but he is the 'slickest' politician of them all. He can give points to Platt or anybody else. And yet he somehow manages to put duty first and politics afterward."

An appreciation which I hope Mr. Roosevelt will himself appreciate.

Anglo–American Memories: Second Series (London, 1912), pp. 346–52.

Index

ald correspondent in London, 80
Houssaye, Arsène, Paris correspondent of *New York Tribune*, 71–72
Howard, General O. O., 182
Hozier, Sir Henry, 59
Hughes, Thomas, member of Parliament and correspondent for *New York Tribune*, 5, 33, 34, 36, 42, 43, 46; referee for Oxford-Harvard boat race, 55
Huntingdon, Henry, 72
Huxley, Thomas W., 43

I

Illustrated London News: on the Oxford-Harvard boat race (1869), 53, 54, 56
Independance Belge, 34
Irish: influence in U.S., 89, 105, 107
Irish Question, 7; Smalley's anti-Irish writing, 88, 103; *New York Tribune's* attitude, 89, 106
Iron Chancellor. *See* Bismarck, Prince Otto von
Irving, Sir Henry, 95, 99, 100, 173

J

Jackson, General Stonewall, 21
James, Henry, 135, 142; admiration of Smalley, 3; *New York Tribune* Paris correspondent (1875–76), 72
Jameson Raid, 120
Japanese news policies at Portsmouth, N.H., 161–62
Jeffries, James J., 158
Jingoes, 133–34, 137, 153
Johnson, Reverdy, 6, 48–49
Journalism: how Smalley entered, 12; English press, 73; foreign correspondent's freedom, 81; need to protect news sources, 104; contrasting views of a correspondent's position, Donald Nicolson vs. G. W. Smalley, 104–10; English and American interests compared 113–14

K

Kaiser Wilhelm der Grosse, 159
Keedysville, 175

Kinglake, A. W.: admires Smalley, 6, 78; *Invasion of the Crimea* reviewed, 37
Komura, Baron, head of Japanese delegation at Portsmouth Peace Conference, 161–62
Kruger, President Paul, 120

L

Labouchere, Henry du Pré, 62
Langtry, Lady, 99, 173
Lansdowne, Lord, 155, 162
Laurier, Sir Wilfrid, 148–49, 218
Lincoln, Abraham, 22, 144
Lincoln, Robert Todd, U.S. minister to Great Britain, 102
Lodge, Senator Henry Cabot: on the influence of Smalley's English dispatches, 116, 117
Lohr, Marie, 173
London *Daily News*. See *Daily News* (London)
London Letters, 96
London Society, 56
Loring, Edward Greeley, 14
Louisville Courier-Journal, 145
Low, A. Maurice, 144–45
Lowell, James Russell, U.S. minister to Great Britain, 6, 210; gives a party on Washington's birthday, 80; friend of the Smalleys, 85, 101–2, 173
Lucy, Sir Henry, 7; substitutes as *New York Tribune* writer for Smalley, 89, 104

M

McCarthy, Justin, 33, 34; writes for *New York Tribune*, 88–89
McClellan, General George B., 24–25; commands Union forces at Antietam, 175; his plan of battle, 184; orders to his generals, 185, 186, 187
McCulloch, Hugh, 43
Mackenzie, Sir Morell, 99
McKinley, President William: tariff record, 131; campaign of 1896, 132; cabinet appointments, 133; "music hall" statement, 135; Cuban crisis, 138; death, 150–51